About This Book

"*DIAL 911 MARINES*  ten *book containing enlightening . . .* ger *puller feels in a modern, hos*

Colo. . . . phonso B. Diggs, USMC,
Commanding Officer, 3ʳᵈ Tank Battalion

"*This is not just a book about military history. This is a book about life. Wonderful read!*"
Alan Johnstone, Software Engineer

"*Great book! Required reading for all young people in service, officers and enlisted. Learn more than you saw on CNN.*"
Colonel Bob Reid, USAF (retired)

"*DIAL 911 MARINES comprises the perfect balance of wit and solemnity. A vivid account.*"
Thomas Neal and Heidi Ellinghausen McGowan, Educators, Historians, Book Critics

"*An adventure well told, well researched, beautifully written. The story is important because it is presented from the mud, in this case sand, at Marine level; war never changes there.*"
Colonel J. Barrie Williams, USA (retired)

"*Thanks for your clear and hard-hitting insights.*"
Colonel David Hackworth, USA (retired)

"*A detailed first hand account of modern desert warfare at the end of the 20ᵗʰ century.*"
David Ziblatt, Professor of Political Science

Hoist the Colors!
27 February 1991

The Executive Officer's tank, C-52, at her limit of advance on the night of G-plus 3. To this day, the Eagle, Globe and Anchor Flag flying from one of the main antennas is one of Captain Chris Freitus' prized possessions, oil-smoke stains and all. This photograph in original color is used as the cover for *Dial 911 Marines.*

Photo by C. Freitus

Dial 911 Marines

Adventures of a Tank Company

in

Desert Shield and Desert Storm

by
Joe Freitus

as told by
Chris Freitus,
Company Executive Officer

New American Publishing Company

Dial 911 Marines
Adventures of a Tank Company
in
Desert Shield and Desert Storm
by Joe Freitus

as told by

Chris Freitus, Company Executive Officer

Published by: **New American Publishing Company**
3033 Waltham Way
McCarran, Nevada U.S.A.

Publisher's Cataloging-in-Publication
(Provided by Quality Books, Inc.)

Freitus, Joe
  Dial 911 Marines : adventures of a tank Company in
Desert Shield and Desert Storm / Joe Freitus with Chris
Freitus.
  p. cm.
  Includes bibliographical references and index.
  LCCN 2002100787
  ISBN 0-9713324-2-8

  1. Persian Gulf War, 1991--Tank Warfare. 2. Persian
Gulf War, 1991--United States. 3. Operation Desert
Shield, 1990-1991. 4. United States. Marine Corps--
History--Persian Gulf War, 1991. 5. Freitus, Chris.
6. Persian Gulf War, 1991--Personal narratives, American,
I. Freitus, Chris. II. Title.

DS79.74.A75F74 2002   956.7044'242
              QBI02-200216

Printed in the United States of America
by **Patterson Printing Company**, Benton Harbor, Michigan

Contents

A Special Flag

The day after the cease fire is announced at the end of Desert Storm, the mail was brought up. In the mail was this letter and paper mache flag from my niece's kindergarten class. Hali, I still have the flag. Thank you.

Photo by C. Freitus

List of Illustrations

C-52
Executive Officer's Tank, right side

The M60A1 Rise-Passive Main Battle Tank (Medium) is the tank that brought Lieutenant Chris Freitus and crew through the Persian Gulf War.

Photo by C. Freitus

THIS BOOK IS DEDICATED TO
THE 3rd TANK BATTALION,
Task Force Ripper,
1st MARINE DIVISION,
AND ALL MARINES WHO FOUGHT IN
OPERATIONS DESERT SHIELD
AND DESERT STORM,
1990 - 1991.

Five Star Room with View

Typical living conditions for a tank crewman include luxurious bed,
excellent laundry facilities, and mile upon mile of ocean front view
minus the ocean.

Photo by C. Freitus

Acknowledgements

Impossible is the task of a writer who attempts to work in a vacuum and write about actual history. This task was greatly reduced by a number of wonderful folks, especially members of the United States Marine Corps.

I decided to utilize the document, "U.S. Marines in the Persian Gulf, 1990-1991, With the 1st Marine Division in Desert Shield and Desert Storm," by Lieutenant Colonel Charles H. Cureton, USMCR, as a means of introducing segments of the book. Using the actual history of the 1st Marine Division, as it stood up against the Iraqi forces, allows me to depict the situation from the written historical view. Oral histories rarely concur with the written version; each partner in the action views the same situation somewhat differently.

Thank you:

Colonel Alphonso B. "Buster" Diggs, Commander, 3rd Tank Battalion, for reading this text, for valuable comments and for your foreword to this book.

Frederick J. Graboske, Head of the Archives, Marine Corps Historical Center, Washington, D.C. and his staff for untiring efforts on our behalf.

Captain R.J. Hallet, Public Affairs Office, Quantico, Virginia for your time and patience.

To all Marines who have read and commented on the manuscript as a work in progress.

First Shirt

1st Sergeant Al Martinez, wearing the helmet, pays a visit to the crew of C-52. The 1st Sergeant joined Charlie Company in Saudi Arabia after 1st Sergeant Steven Jensen left to assume the duties of Sergeant Major of the 3rd Tank Battalion.

Photo by W. Florence

Preface

Those who have served in the military realize that it has its own language, vocabulary and style of saying something, anything. There is a very distinctive sound to military speak, one might say a flavor. Difficult as it is, we have tried to capture that sound within these pages.

To accomplish this task, the many hours of oral interviews have been tampered with only where need be. This allows us to maintain the flavor and sound of a combat Marine.

History records that whenever the United States cannot resolve an international, political situation through the usual channels of diplomacy, the call has gone forth, "Send in the Marines!" This need has become a part of the history and lore of the United States Marine Corps.

Keeping a mighty fleet at sea has proven to the world that the United States declares its right to keep international sea-lanes open to all world travel and commerce. On these ships we maintain detachments of Fleet Marines, ready to move on shore and fight at a moment's notice. They rescue citizens from riots, terrorists, civil wars, marauding armies, defend our far flung embassies, rescue hostages, provide medical care and cleanup services during and after major natural disasters, and be ready within 24 hours to pack up and go off to fight a war in some distant land. Such was the case in the Persian Gulf, 1990.

In recent years the RDF (Rapid Deployment Force) has become a catchword to describe the use of troops in responding to a national or out-of-country emergency. The term is one that aptly describes the United States Marine Corps and its mission. If you need us, just *DIAL 911 MARINES!*

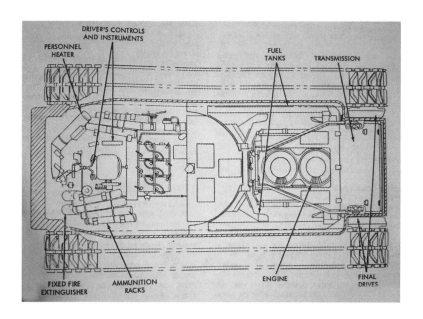

Top Schematic View of the M60A1

This is the top perspective, schematic representation, taken from the print in the Technical Manual on the M60A1 tank.

Courtesy of the Pioneer Museum, El Centro, California

Foreword

I think it is human nature to be a little apprehensive about doing something for the first time. Taking your first step, sneaking your first kiss, or making your first attempt at public speaking produced perhaps sweaty palms and butterflies in your stomach. You can magnify these feelings at least tenfold when you think about knowingly going into a life or death situation. This was the fate of all the Marines in Charlie Company, 3rd Tank Battalion, Task Force Ripper, 1st Marine Division, I MEF (Marine Expeditionary Force) from 1 August 1990 until 17 March 1991.

Men have been experiencing first-time combat since they began to compete for the same resources. When Roman Legions went off to conquer what was then the known world, there were numerous first-time legionnaires in each campaign. When the shot heard round the world was first heard in Lexington, Massachusetts, almost all of the men on the colonial side were first-time fighters. When the 1st Marine Division landed at Guadalcanal on 7 August 1942, very few officers or men had tasted combat. When Charlie Company, 3rd Tank Battalion, led Task Force Ripper's assault in Kuwait, only a few men had ever given or received a shot in anger.

"Where one sits determines what one sees" applies to combat. *Dial 911 Marines,* an exceptionally well-written book containing enlightening specifics, shows what the trigger puller feels in a modern, hostile situation. He sees the enemy before him and that is what I expected him to see and focus on. He sees day-to-day survival in his framed world and hopes somebody else, somebody higher up, is planning for his tomorrow that he prays he will see. His world is almost limited to what he can see or touch.

Charlie Company was fortunate to be where they were when the conflict first began in early September. The Corps' most ready brigade resides at Twentynine Palms, California. 7th Marine Expeditionary Brigade continually trained for and practiced immediate deployment. The ground combat element of the brigade consisted of 7th Marine Regiment with three infantry battalions: 3rd Battalion, 11th Marines, a direct support artillery battalion; 5th Battalion, 11th Marines, a general support artillery battalion; 3rd Tanks and Company D, 3rd Assault Amphibian Battalion. Charlie Company, 3rd tank Battalion, was as well trained as any peacetime unit can be trained. Personnel had been in key billets both in and above Charlie Company for months. This was no throw together unit as had occurred at the initiation of previous wars.

Arriving in theater early meant you were never bored. The tedium and frustration experienced by other units in the rear was not shared by this forward tank company. You knew from time of landing that if anything happened, you, your tanks and your men were the first real line of defense. Although the infantry would dig in at each phase of our advance north, we tankers knew, if the Iraqis were even somewhat intelligent, that a dug in, determined infantryman is tough to root out. You must go around his prepared position. The Germans, who invented such warfare, did it twice in WWII. They accomplished this feat first at the outset of hostilities by outflanking the famed Maginot Line. The second instance was against the allied forces during the Battle of The Bulge. Dug-in infantrymen can be outflanked easily and left to wither on the vine. Only 1st and 3rd

Tank Battalions had the capability of countering such a movement. At the initiation of hostilities and for the next two months, two Marine tank battalions faced two mechanized and one armored Iraqi division poised in Kuwait. If they came south, it would be a fight, but a brief one. Charlie Company would compose 1/8th of this mobile striking power. It wasn't until the 193rd Mechanized Infantry Brigade, of the 24th Mechanized Infantry Division landed, that this commander got a good night's sleep.

Captain Freitus had a good seat to both view and participate in this conflict. Charlie Company was both aptly lead and staffed. They became the base of 3rd Tanks upon the cross attachment with Alpha Company, First Battalion, 7th Marines. I had traded for like companies with my brother commander of infantry. He needed his own armor. I needed infantry to accomplish any close-in missions. Although Company "A" 1/7 was a godsend, they were Infantry in assault amphibian vehicles. The AAV is no Bradley. Against armor, it has no chance. Company "D", 1st Tracked Vehicle Battalion, came from Okinawa and was an unknown to us. Company "B" was both 3rd Tanks and a regimental reserve. Charlie Company was the battalion's rock.

I certainly have a slightly different view of the war than Captain Freitus. My tactic was if you let the "Jedis", the company commanders, fight and you only coordinate their efforts while giving them the means to take the battle to the enemy, they will prevail. The captains in 3rd Tank Battalion were probably the best group in the division. You can have great captains and a weak battalion commander and his staff and still prevail. It does not work the other way around. Bad captains equal a bad unit. Fortunately, as you will read in this work, you will see that Charlie Company had both superb officers and competent tankers and were always a track width ahead of our advisory.

The trouble with fighting on the modern battlefield is there is just too much information. Information comes in from ground reports, aircraft, national reconnaissance assets, predictions from government agencies, you name it. Yes, some of the information was not passed to me so I could focus on the challenging task of fighting a tank battalion. Likewise, right or wrong, some information was not passed down from my headquarters so Charlie Company could focus on their task at hand, fighting a tank company. With the information Charlie Company did have, and some innovative tactics, they did accomplish what I MEF needed them to accomplish even if they were often in the dark.

The leadership of the I MEF knew, before the ground war started what our goals and objectives were for hostilities to terminate. Some Smart Guy and a retired Marine Lieutenant General told us in a briefing long before we officially received our mission. Our goal was not to kill Saddam or occupy Iraq. The overall goal was to eliminate or severely cripple Saddam's ability to wage war on his neighbors while driving his forces from Kuwait in the process. I MEF had the job of fixing enemy forces in place by conducting a deliberate supporting attack into the teeth of the Iraqi defenses. Our supporting attack would hold forces in Kuwait while Tenth Corps enveloped from the west and destroyed those fixed forces. Charlie Company, being the lead of the supporting attack, was the focus of a dilemma for Task Force Ripper.

If we attacked too rapidly, the forces we were supposed to fix would retreat and not be there to envelope. If we did not attack with all the gusto we could muster, attrition at and between the two obstacle belts could be all that was predicted. Our goal was to make the Iraqi ground forces feel the same as his air forces felt after the second day of the air war, i.e., if you oppose us, it is not if but how quickly you will die. Maximum and overwhelming combat power at the decisive point is the objective of the offense.

With great captains, an excellent task force organization

and mutual respect for all, we were able to turn a supporting attack into a rout. This was great for us because our causalities were minimal. It was poor for the overall theater objective because Saddam quickly saw that his forces were going to be annihilated and withdrew a large majority of his Republican Guard forces back into Iraq. It was beyond the coalition forces objective to penetrate deep into Iraq and seek them out. Thus, you still have people second-guessing our goals, but we do have all of Charlie Company to talk about the experience.

This country could not have picked a worse place to fight a war. It is almost half way around the world from either coast so lines of communications were stretched thin, and the area had little infrastructure.What was good for the Corps was that it was next to the sea and had great seaports. This conflict would have been significantly more difficult, if you can imagine that, if our forces had had to fight even 200 miles inland. For the Marine Corps, distances in excess of 100 kilometers from a seaport become most challenging.

You will read about tank movement on several occasions. It is true that tanks are made to be driven, but great distances are hard on the tracks. Track wear for us, having been there since September, was becoming an item of real concern. The Marine Corps had no tank transporters in theater. Most of our movements were driving, with only occasional assistance from Saudi or British HETs (Heavy Equipment Transporters). This was a real thrill to me because in my twenty two years, I had only seen tanks hauled on commercial nine axles in the states. Without weight restrictions per axle, you can get a lot of tank on a short truck. Moving great distances inland is a problem that any force must temper. If you want to be able to move inland, with a mechanized force, it takes trucks; trucks to haul fuel, trucks to haul tanks, trucks to haul in repair parts and trucks to haul food.

Captain Freitus mentions, and the author writes about,

being hungry in this work. Feeding Charlie and the other companies soon became my highest priority. I could see the men gradually losing weight. Oh, we had plenty of food in the form of MREs (Meals Ready to Eat). After three months in theater, they were no longer appetizing. The average consumption of MREs in the First Marine Division was one per day; just enough to survive on. Cooking hot meals was not the only problem. Charlie Company, being way up on the tip of the spear, was at the limits of truck reach. Meals were cooked at a central mess hall and then trucked to us in the field. At first it was one per day, then two per day and then back to one per day when we moved to our final assembly area. The troops would come up to the vat cans and look to see if it was brown on rice or green on rice. Any hot meal beat a MRE but often the men would just look and leave. Thank goodness for the US Postal Service and friends, parents, school children, organizations and just everyday Americans back home. I even looked forward to my weekly care package.

A former father-in-law, who fought in WWII, had told me about how they had to forcibly go back to the docks and get supplies they needed at the front. They were freezing to death in Belgium while the rear echelon personnel had the best of clothing. I too experienced the same thing. I wanted fruit for the men at least every other day. MREs and the stuff on rice would be a lot more palatable and nutritious if we had a fruit supplement. Oranges and apples are not tough to ship and will keep. We could not seem to make this happen. Then while I was back at our direct support unit checking on some tank engines that we badly needed, I went in to see a friend of mine. I walked into his "office" and there on his table was a bowl of fruit. Some things never change.

I do hope every reader can forget about the end of this book before he or she begins reading. Like reading a book about the Revolutionary War or WWII, we all know the final outcome.

Try to think how the men in Charlie Company felt at Al Jubayl pier, Cement Ridge, the Triangle, and finally, in our attack position, not knowing the end of this book. Try and imagine how Captain Freitus felt knowing he could have been a fatality had he not made the correct decisions. Try and forget that Saddam's army was more rhetoric than combat power. I personally was preparing for up to fifty percent casualties with my executive officer finishing the mission. Remember, it was almost everyone in Charlie Company's first time. There were more than just sweaty palms in this company.

Colonel Alphonso B. Diggs
Commanding Officer
3rd Tank Battalion
United States Marine Corps

Many Manly Men

Members of the Headquarters Platoon staging a moment in history. Back row *l-r*: Corporal Cory Farmer, Corporal John Dilling, Sergeant Jeff Welsh, Gunnery Sergeant Rich Cronin, Lieutenant Chris Freitus. Front row *l-r*: Sergeant Norton, Lance Corporal Ryan Hoover, Corporal Alister Millwood, Lance Corporal Wesley King.

Photo by unknown member of Charlie Company

Prologue

Writing this makes me realize how difficult it is to relate oral histories, to sort out what is real and what is unreal and to separate fact from fiction.

Serving as a Marine Lieutenant assigned as Executive Officer of Charlie Company, 3rd Tank Battalion during the Persian Gulf War, then later serving as a Marine Captain assigned as instructor of armor and basic infantry tactics at TBS (The Basic School), Quantico, Virginia has given me something of a perspective. Exactly what that perspective is will remain difficult to identify as it remains a work in progress. While an instructor I was able to review the history from a military standpoint of what happened in the early days of the invasion of Kuwait by the Iraq Armed Forces.

Let me start with the beginning of Saddam's war.

In the hot, predawn desert darkness of a Thursday in August 1990, Iraqi troops slashed across the border into the city of Kuwait. The Iraqis utilized some 100,000 soldiers, 300 tanks and assorted mechanized equipment to mount the invasion calculated to overwhelm the small military force maintained by Kuwait.

Kuwait had three small brigades, basically just ground units. These three brigades were deployed close to Kuwait City, one to the north, one to the south and the last to the west near the Al-Burqan oil fields. The Royal Brigade, the so-called palace

guard, the ones that presented themselves for all the Emir's
parades and dog-and-pony shows, were stationed at an army
base south of the capital. All three units had some modern anti-
tank weapons but not sufficient to stop Iraq's armored columns.

Saddam's divisions included eight elite divisions from his
famed Republican Guard, the so-called Palace Guard. Three of
those divisions were the famed Tawakalan plus two armored
divisions, the Hammurabi and the Medina. The battle plan was
simple, as all plans should be, and direct. One division was to
race in along the coastal road and seize the city of Kuwait. A
second would then seize the inland oil fields of Al-Burqan, Al-
Wafra, Al-Manageesh and finally the Al-Magwa. The third
division was to secure the all-important Kuwait/Saudi border,
especially along the coastal road that linked the two countries.

For all the sophisticated electronic warning systems
employed by the Kuwaiti it was a simple aerostat, balloon-borne
radar, floating above Kuwait that first warned the Kuwait military
of the assault by the Iraqi military. It detected large formations
and numbers of military vehicles speeding along the multi-lane
highway from Iraq in the north to Kuwait in the south. For the
Emir it was sufficient warning to allow him, his family and others
to escape to nearby Saudi Arabia. With very slim advance
warning the Kuwaiti soldiers had little opportunity to organize
any kind of a cohesive resistance. Iraqi armored and mechanized
infantry units, accompanied by assault helicopters from the Gulf,
charged ahead along the highway. Kuwaiti soldiers were forced
to fight, where it was possible to fight at all, in small combat
units against much larger Iraqi units.

Although the Kuwait army was able to conduct organized
resistance for up to a week or so those that could eventually
escaped to Saudi Arabia. Those that stayed behind, either by
choice or because they were cut off from any escape, became
the nucleus of the Kuwait underground resistance movement.
This small but effective resistance kept the Coalition Forces

supplied with much needed intelligence about what was happening during the occupation of Kuwait. With their excellent military leadership the resistance units were very effective. There was a constant search for them by the Iraqi military police and when caught they were usually tortured to death.

Little known is the Kuwait Air Force, with its A-4s. It kept operating even after the Iraqis had destroyed their two major airbases, one at Al-Jaber and one at the Kuwait International Airport. At Al-Jaber, a nearby road that serviced the air base was utilized to keep the planes flying. Ammunition and fuel was replenished to keep the aircraft in the air but, after three days, the fuel and ammunition finally ran out. At that point the small but effective Air Force flew off to seek sanctuary in Saudi Arabia, thus saving their planes to fight another day, a fact we should all be thankful for.

The small Kuwait Navy managed to escape with two of its fast attack gunboats. As they ran down the coast they fired on visible targets such as tanks and personnel carriers. The Iraqis seized the remaining gunboats and eventually carted them off to Iraqi waters.

With the Kuwait government and the Emir effectively escaping out of country, it was impossible for Saddam to claim victory with his invasion. The very reasoning used by Saddam to time his invasion was also why most of the officials of the Kuwait government were out of the country; it was the time of the hot months.

Kuwait is located at the very edge of a large desert and despite the fact it borders the Persian Gulf, it is extremely hot during the summer months. When temperatures reach 110-120 degrees Fahrenheit, it is hot! Therefore, to escape the dreaded summer heat, many of the Kuwaitis, government officials included, simply traveled abroad and vacationed where it was cooler. This action greatly reduced the number of officials that normally would be in the country.

It is assumed that Saddam's timing was based on three logical advantages: first, the summer season brought little rain; therefore, dry soils would allow him easily to push his armored and mechanized forces into Kuwait. Second, it came at a time when the temperatures were summer high, making constant combat especially difficult. If he chose to utilize gas warfare, as he had against the Kurds, it would be next to impossible for the Kuwait Army to wear protective clothing in such intense heat. They would literally cook within the MOPP (Mission Oriented Protective Posture) suits. Third with a number of Kuwaiti officials known to be out of the country relaxing somewhere abroad on holiday, it would make it difficult to organize an effective resistance to the Iraqi troops. It is unfortunate that with the massing of the large numbers of the Iraq Army on the Kuwait border the CIA folks apparently did not put all Saddam's advantages together. Or if they did put it together there seemed no apparent, appropriate response.

Iraqi planners, however, understood the military situation very well and planned accordingly. They knew that the larger Iraq Army easily could overwhelm their small neighbor. Kuwait is primarily a large seaport surrounded by very little land; it is smaller than the state of New Jersey. The country is surrounded on two sides by Iraq, to the south by Saudi Arabia and to the east by the Persian Gulf. There are no mountains or other such natural barriers except for a wide wadi, the Wadi Al-Batin, that runs north and south along the Kuwait/Iraq border. The wadi is dry during the summer months and often fills with water during the winter rains thus forming a temporary, natural barrier.

Two paved, main roads reach as far as Kuwait City. The inland track, which crosses the Saudi/Kuwait border, links eastern Saudi Arabia with Kuwait City. The coastal road, a multi-lane highway links Kuwait City with Kafji in Saudi Arabia to the south. In the north it crosses the border into Iraq. By sending a mechanized division of troops to the south Saddam effectively blocked an invasion route north into Kuwait City by a possible Saudi force.

In Kuwait City the crack troops of the Republican Guard were taken out of the line and replaced with poorly trained, less seasoned troops. Stories filtered out of Kuwait City reporting the rape of women and young girls, the systematic torture by the Iraqi military and secret police, looting of every thing that could be removed, as well as eating all the animals in the city zoo.

In the months of June and July, despite the angry protestations and posturing by the Iraqi, no one fully expected Saddam to actually invade Kuwait. No one in the International Community thought Saddam Hussein to be the thug he was despite his behavior during the Iran/Iraq War. State Department officials refused to believe that Iraq would actually cross the border and invade Kuwait. The result was not only relaxation of intelligence surveillance but also the misinterpretation of intelligence data. The State Department's unwillingness to accept the massive Iraqi troop buildup as anything more than a bluff is a typical example of how the Intelligence Community was misreading Saddam's intentions. Indeed, there were those in the military that completely understood that Saddam possessed the capability of driving his forces into Kuwait then into Saudi Arabia. Their understanding as usual, went unheeded, actually discarded. The question remains, why did not Saddam continue on into Saudi Land?

Of course the immediate response from the world community was to vehemently protest the invasion of Kuwait by Iraq with strong words. The United Nations warned Iraq to withdraw its forces or pay the consequences, but at the same time it totally lacked any standing military force to reinforce the warning. However, it must be noted that after a period of ten days to two weeks, Saddam began to withdraw his vaunted armored divisions. The world breathed a collected sigh of relief.

With no show of force by Saudi Arabia, why did not Saddam continue on into Kafji and then swing into the heart of Saudi Arabia? From Kafji he could have continued south and overrun the small Emirate States. Doing so would have given Saddam considerable control of the world oil market. He could have dismembered OPEC single-handedly.

Instead of following through with this strategy, he was withdrawing from Kuwait, and most visible were his tanks and mechanized vehicles. Was Saddam really playing the good guy for the International Community, a little theater, or was there another reason?

Careful examination by some observers noted that Saddam's tanks, as displayed on TV, were in terrible shape. These tanks, already in terrible condition from the past war, were loaded on tank transporters and hauled ignominiously off to Iraq for badly needed repairs and maintenance. The much vaunted logistics trains were insufficient to maintain and supply any further offensive maneuvering. The maintenance groups were simply unable to provide the necessary logistical servicing of broken down vehicles in the harsh conditions of the desert, and so back to Iraq. Ammunition, fuel and food stocks were next to impossible to deliver to maintain a fast moving mechanized army. This was a fact learned early on by the Germans during WWII.

The Iraqi army had really fought a set piece battle, a stalemate type of war with Iran. They had little skill at maintaining a fast moving desert action like that fought during WWII in North Africa.

Saddam would have to remove his troops and vehicles badly in need of repair to Iraq and replace them with fresh troops and tanks. With a limited transport system, this was next to impossible. Add to that the fact that the drive south into Saudi Arabia lost momentum when the Republican Guard paused to loot Kuwait City, shades of Genghis Kahn. The pause provided the small Kuwait army with the time to organize a suitable resistance, thereby causing the Iraq army to take the time to subdue the remnants of the Kuwait army. Whatever Saddam's plans demanded, he had lost the momentum and had to give up the drive into Saudi Arabia and the other Emirate States.

Despite United Nations pressure and threats, Saddam decided that the enormous loss of face would be too humiliating, especially after the war with Iran. A move such as this would ultimately weaken his hold on the Iraqi people and force him from power. Knowing the tricks of gutter power, Saddam decided to reinforce his army already in Kuwait and wait.

The United Nations had a solution to Saddam's invasion of Kuwait. The various western nations and Arab states could form a coalition to deter any rogue nation such as Iraq. This resolution was sought by President Bush and immediately passed by members of the United Nations. All that remained after the embargo was put in place was to select a coalition military leader. General H. Norman Schwarzkopf was selected to command CENTCOM (Central Command).

The immediate build up of a coalition force brought the various combat units to the Gulf. Several countries hurriedly sent combat and supply ships to reinforce the embargo. The United States sent the 2,300 troops of the 82nd Airborne Ready Brigade to provide a defense against invading Iraqi troops. These troopers were lightly armed, without their airborne tanks and artillery. Once the airborne unit was in place, CENTCOM looked about its inventory of troops and battle gear to see what was available on such a short notice. The call went out to the Marines at Twentynine Palms, California, home of the 7th Marine Expeditionary Brigade.

The 7th MEB, as it is known, was the only mobile ground force capable of sustained combat. Their equipment was already loaded on pre-positioned ships in the Pacific at Guam and in the Indian Ocean, at Diego Garcia. These MPS (Maritime Pre-positioned Ships) were pre-loaded with food, ammunition, water, weapons and most important, the Marine's tank, the M60A1. There were many at CENTCOM that believed the M60A1 was a lightweight compared to the Army's M1A1.

Up to this point the MPS ships were extremely controversial with the branches of the service that wanted that money for their own reasons and within the Marine Corps itself. The cost of maintaining ships at pre-deployed positions can be outrageous. It is similar to maintaining a double set of equipment with the possibility that one set may never get used. The Marines, especially those at Twentynine Palms, the 7th MEB (Marine Expeditionary Brigade) had extensive training in the utilization and understanding of pre-positioned equipment. The Marines were able to stand up their two battle brigades upon twenty-four hour notification.

The airlift of the 7th MEB commenced on August 12, 1990 and placed Marines on the ground at the Al Jubayl Airport on August 14th. The MPS supply ships sailed from the Islands of Diego Garcia on August 8th, arriving at the seaport of Al Jubayl August 15th.

It soon became a strange organizational dance, bringing in the MPS ships and joining the unloading crews. After considerable jostling and negotiations, the ships were docked and the unloading began. The 7th MEB quickly tackled the task of bringing their equipment on line to combat readiness. Simultaneously the 3rd Marine Air Wing deployed to the Gulf, nearly 85 percent of the air strength of the Marine Corps, in support of the 7th and 1st MEBs.

With the 7th MEB already in the Gulf and the 1st MEB on its way from Hawaii, Amphibious Group 2, which included three helicopter carriers, transported the 4th MEB from Camp Lejeune to the Gulf. The 4th MEB remained as an amphibious force throughout the war. It was soon reinforced by the 13th MEU (Marine Expeditionary Unit), from the Philippines. The 4th and

5th MEBs and the 13th MEU orchestrated a number of practice landings which became highly publicized, especially on the evening news, CNN.

Meanwhile, the Iraqi military must have watched the rapid buildup of the Coalition Forces with considerable trepidation. The response was to fortify the border between occupied Kuwait and Saudi Arabia. The Republican Guard was withdrawn to rest, replenish, and above all repair their broken down equipment; they were replaced by regular army units. Fearing a sudden counterattack by the Marines Saddam set about constructing a series of obstacle belts. These consisted of a large earthen berm, followed by open trenches that could be filled with highly flammable gasoline, belts of razor sharp barbed wire and extensive fields of different types of land mines. It has since been determined that the Iraqi engineers set in place nearly three million anti-personal mines and anti-tank mines. Entrenched well behind these obstacles were infantry arrayed in fighting positions.

Breaching these obstacles the military intelligence communities estimated 10,000-15,000 deaths and considerable wounded. By the time the 7th MEB moved up to the Kuwait/Saudi border, it is reported the Iraqi force in place in Kuwait consisted approximately of 360,000 men, 2,800 tanks (the number that were actually serviceable remains in question), 1,800 personnel carriers and 1,450 assorted artillery pieces.

The 7th MEB arrived at Al Jubayl on August 14, 1990 and were in place near the Saudi/Kuwait border, August 20th, ready for combat. A few days later the 1st MEB married up with the 7th, forming the I MEF (Marine Expeditionary Force). Beginning with August 25th, the I MEF consisted of 15,248 Marines, 425 artillery pieces, 124 aircraft and 123 of the all-important M60A1 tanks. Shortly after standing up at the border, the I MEF was joined by the British 7th Armored Brigade, the famed Desert Rats of WWII. Statisticians note that the I MEF constituted one half of all ground forces in Saudi Arabia, late

August, early September.

The most significant ground action, prior to the main offensive, occurred at the Saudi border town of Kafji. Saddam's forces were unable to maintain any presence of regular air reconnaissance or any other type of intelligence gathering. The Iraqis launched a blind ground attack on January 29th.

A large unit of the Iraqi 5th Mechanized, attacked across the border. However, they were detected before they crossed the border as they formed up north of the border in Kuwait. The JSTARS radar-equipped aircraft recognized the assemblage and so notified CENTCOM. Attacking in three separate columns, one Iraqi brigade ran along the border, behind the obstacle berm on the Kuwait side. It ran into the light armored infantry of the 1st Marine Division. Eight LAVs (Light Armored Vehicles), which were never designed to do battle with Russian made tanks, met the Iraqis head on and with the use of their night vision sights destroyed the Iraqi tanks. This was the battle wherein an Air Force A-10 destroyed a Marine LAV with a Maverick missile, the friendly fire tragedy.

The second Iraqi brigade crossed the border and ran directly into the 2nd Marine Division. Once again it was the LAVs that fought it out with the heavier armed Iraqi tanks. The TOW (Tube launched, Optically tracked, Wire guided) missile equipped LAVs decimated the Iraqi armor. This encounter reinforced the practice the Marines had rehearsed with the TOW missile system. It worked well as a tank killer, thanks to some very competent crews.

The third Iraqi brigade attacked Kafji itself, which was held by Saudi, Qataris and the Marines in support. The Iraq 15th Mechanized Regiment struck the town and collided with a Qatari tank unit. Equipped with the French made AMX-30s, the Qatari unit was wiped out. The Iraqi infantry entered Kafji and moved from house to house.

The various troop units that held Kafji were initially

confused for when the Iraqi tanks approached the town their main guns were facing aft, the traditional signal of surrender. The accompanying infantry had their hands raised in the air. As soon as the Saudis emerged from their entrenchments, the Iraqis reversed their turrets and commenced firing. While the surviving Saudi troops fled, a Marine Recon team remained inside the town, on a rooftop, without being discovered. Quick thinking of the leading NCO alerted the Marine artillery and quickly called in supporting fire. Timed with overhead coalition planes, this allowed the Iraqi troops to think they were being hit by air cover. The slaughter was incredible.

After three days of hard fighting and terrifying air strikes, the Saudis counter attacked and some four hundred Iraqi troops gladly surrendered. Saddam claimed a tremendous victory and celebrated throughout Iraq.

When the Marines stood up at the Saudi/Kuwait border, facing approximately 360,000 Iraqis with 5,800 tanks, the Marines of the I MEF consisted of approximately 15,000 men with 123 tanks. The odds were great and the hope of victory shimmered in the desert heat, but the Marines, true to their tradition, stood up to the Iraqis within 24 hours notice and in six days were ready for combat.

Lieutenant Christopher J. Freitus
Executive Officer
Charlie Company, 3rd Tank Battalion
United States Marine Corps

C-52 and Crew

The crew of C-52 during early Operation Desert Shield. *L-r*: Corporal
Cliff Scott (Gunner), Lance Corporal Billie Florence (Driver), Lance
Corporal George Reedy (Loader) and Lieutenant Chris Freitus
(Company Executive Officer, Platoon Commander, Tank
Commander).

Photo by A. Martinez

Introduction

Twelve kilometers southwest of the Kuwait/Saudi triangle, Task Force Ripper slowly uncoiled itself like a deadly Egyptian cobra, and in absolute darkness began heading North.

Leading the Marine task force into Kuwait was the 3rd Tank Battalion, 7th Marines.

It had been a grueling six-month stay in the hot, unrelenting Saudi desert, waiting for the Iraqi Juggernaut to cross the Kuwait border and strike deep into the heart of Saudi Arabia, but every Marine was resolved that if the Iraqis struck, they would have to go through the Marines of the 1st Division.

At 0700, 24 February 1991, Charlie Company, 3rd Tank Battalion, passed through the first of the obstacles on the way to liberate Kuwait. Engineers cleared lanes through which Marines could travel; heavy weapon platoons in HMMWVs (Humvees) provided firepower; Cobra helicopter gunships hovered at the ready.

Like that Egyptian snake, Ripper positioned itself to strike the awaiting Iraqi forces. Obstacles cleared, the Marines refueled and re-armed then headed north to take the Al-Jaber Military Airfield. Infantry Marines then took the airfield.

Ripper Marines, with their armored vehicles silhouetted against the burning oil wells of the Al Burqan oil fields, paused for the night to consolidate. They awaited an expected, and ferocious, Iraqi counter attack.

With the morning of 26 February Marines pressed on to capture the Kuwait International Airport. They left in their wake a desert littered with hundreds of destroyed Soviet made tanks, BMPs (Personnel Carriers), and assorted anti-tank weapons. They also had a capture in excess of 9,000 prisoners.

Impressive as the numbers were, it was the professionalism of the Marines, their spirit, confidence, élan and willingness to sustain themselves through the ordeal of war and isolation in the Saudi Arabian desert that captures the imagination.

Chapter 1
Deployment of the 1st Marine Division

The movement of the 1st Marine Division to Saudi Arabia began with the deployment of 7th MEB (the 7th Marine Expeditionary Brigade) and MPS 2 (Maritime Prepositioning Squadron 2). The successful initial deployment of Marine forces hinged on the combination of personnel airlift, aircraft ferry, and depot ships embodied in the MPS concept. On 8 August 1990, President Bush responded to Iraq's invasion of Kuwait and Saudi Arabia's subsequent request for American support by directing the deployment of United States forces to Southwest Asia. The desert-trained 7th MEB immediately went on the alert and on 7 August the brigade commander, Major General John L. Hopkins, requested operational control of contingency force units from the 1st Marine Division, he got these units the following day. On 10 August the United States Commander in Chief Central Command (USCINCCENT), General H. Norman Schwarzkopf directed General Hopkins to begin deploying the brigade, two days later, after a period of intense effort readying personnel, weapons, and equipment, the brigade began its movement to the port of Al Jubayl, Saudi Arabia. The mission General Schwarzkopf gave the 7th MEB was to prepare to protect critical oil and port facilities and delay any advancing Iraqi force as far north as possible. First to depart were 143 Marines of the SLRP (Surveillance, Liaison and Reconnaissance Part).

A group of off load preparation personnel departed shortly afterwards with the mission to join MPS 2 before it sailed and prepare the equipment for use upon arrival at Al Jubayl. MPS 2, stationed at the island of Diego Garcia in the Indian Ocean, immediately set sail. The squadron departed so quickly that it left before the 7ᵗʰ MEB's off load preparation personnel arrived. This set the stage for a sequence of delays getting M60A1 tanks, LVT-P7AI and LVT-C7AI assault amphibian vehicles, HMMWVs, trucks and 155mm MI 98 guns into the field, in addition, because of the initial belief that the brigade might be going into a "non-permissive" environment. The port of Jubayl was within 12 hours of the border of Kuwait and might soon be under direct enemy attack. General Hopkins decided to stage the combat units before the service support units arrived. This put too few service support personnel at the port, which complicated the process of preparing and issuing equipment. Nevertheless, by 17 August 1990, General Hopkins reported all of the 1ˢᵗ Battalion, 5ᵗʰ Marines, at Jubayl, and he expected elements of the 1ˢᵗ Battalion, 7ᵗʰ Marines: the 3ʳᵈ Tank Battalion: the 3ʳᵈ Assault Amphibian Battalion; the 1ˢᵗ Combat Engineer Battalion; and the Headquarters of the 7ᵗʰ Marine Regiment, referred to as RCT 7 (Regimental Combat Team 7) in the 7ᵗʰ MEB messages within the following 24 hours.

General Hopkins fully expected to have his maneuver battalions issued equipment and deployed to the field by 20 August, that proved impossible because of delays arising from the shortage of service personnel and from a reluctance on the part of the Saudi to allow Marines to leave the immediate area of the port facility. With more units arriving every day, General Hopkins faced the Brigade's first crisis. By 20 August, Hopkins had 9,307 Marines at the port, with most confined to four warehouses located on the pier, where they faced overcrowding, unsanitary conditions, temperatures above 120 degrees Fahrenheit. The shock of unremitting heat proved bad in itself, but it was the unexpectedly awful living conditions that caused immediate concern. Marines discovered that the warehouses lacked facilities for washing and the few available toilets broke down. Efforts to augment the non-functioning warehouse toilets with portable toilet facilities quickly failed due to overcrowding and inefficient contractors.

Morale among Marines at the port plummeted and unit commanders grew desperate to get to the field. Major Michael F. Applegate of the 3rd Assault Amphibian Battalion later said of this period, "The time we spent in those warehouses was the worst experience of my life. At least in the desert you can move around and you have the evening breezes."

When I reported to the Marines at Twentynine Palms, California, in September 1988, it was as 3rd Platoon Commander, Charlie Company, 3rd Tank Battalion, 7th MEB (Marine Expeditionary Brigade). Through all the training that followed we never actually thought of going to war, but then again, does any Marine?

The Brigade intelligence groups' OPCON (Operational Contingency) plans for the Mediterranean and Middle East were for Saudi Arabia invading Yemen, Iraq invading Iran, Iran invading Iraq, Jordan invading Iraq, and so on. Utilizing pre-positioned ships and equipment, how would Marines respond to all this? Where would we off-load, set up our gear and await further orders? Despite all the intensive planning that we were involved in, I do not believe that anyone ever believed we would ever haul out of Twentynine Palms and really become involved.

During 1990 the tankers practiced strategic fly-outs, that is Lieutenant Colonel "Buster" Diggs had the Battalion practice what is called a strategic mobilization exercise. This meant the various companies prepared their equipment they would have to take in case of a rapid call up. The troops of Charlie Company underwent several inspections to see that they had all the proper gear required, both personal and company. During the month of July, we went to the field and conducted an exercise to measure the battalion's preparedness. Remember, Twentynine Palms is Southern California desert, hot and dry, so if we were to be called to the Middle East we not only would be equipped properly, but we would also be acclimated. This was supposed to be a two-week operation, but 2nd August rolled around and while we were in the field Iraq invaded Kuwait. Perhaps the 3rd Battalion commander had been informed, but we certainly knew nothing of the event.

Gradually, while we were still in the field, news of the Iraqi invasion drifted through the heat and sand to us. Then word came for the Company Commanders, the Battalion XO and Commander to report to HQ. We knew that something was happening and the real possibility of a call up was becoming a reality.

Then the word came for us to prepare to embark, settle our personal affairs and get our gear ready to go. There was a rush on the PX for the usual small, personal items: soap, toothbrushes, toothpaste, underwear, socks, pencils, paper and writing materials. Meetings of staff personnel to relearn the various plans for deployment were conducted. When the Company Commander was absent, I, now the Company XO, would fill in for him. It was at these meetings that I began to realize just how serious the situation was. This was no longer a bluff; this was a serious deployment.

We started the routine of crating equipment that we would need to supplement the pre-positioned equipment. This was the drill we had practiced during the spring and here we were doing it for real. All went smoothly and the off-load preparation parties were quickly sent to Saudi. They would prepare and de-mothball the equipment on the pre-positioned ship, so that when we arrived, little would have to be done for the main body of Marines when they arrived on station. Every thing would be pre-staged, as we had trained.

During the 7th, 8th and 9th of August, my wife and I started making phone calls to inform family that there was a good possibility we were actually heading to the Gulf and war. The night of the 9th rolled around and it became a reality that we were heading into a shooting war. We were informed to form up the Battalion and get ready to board buses to deploy to the Long Beach Naval Air Station, California. As usual, the way these things work, we were placed on a restricted standby. On the morning of the 10th the word was we were leaving that night. The Company Commander dismissed the troops and basically told them to get their family affairs in order. The staff checked to see that everyone had their shots updated, all the required paperwork completed, and everyone was given a gamma-globulin shot. You know where, of course.

When everything was complete, as best we could, I went home, got something to eat, showered and spent the rest of the day with my wife and young son. When it was time, I placed my gear in the car and we went to where the Company was forming up.

As I looked at Charlie Company, I realized that here was the reality we had prepared for, so much time spent in rehearsing for a war we thought would never happen. It seemed so unreal, or perhaps I should say, surreal. Men were arriving with their gear and standing around speaking softly to their wives or sweethearts, to each other, trying to make these precious moments tangible, tangible enough to last a war. It seemed to me that it was something that had happened for centuries, men and women saying goodbye to each other, each hoping to meet the other again. It was my turn to be a part of that same ritual. I could now share the emotion my grandfather felt when he left his wife for the war in Europe and my father leaving for the war at sea in Korea. Now it was my turn. Some things never change!

There was no longer any question of our going. I looked

around and all I could see was a sea of Marines dressed in their new desert camies (camoflaged uniform for the desert). We knew at the time of issue that this was for real, no longer a drill. We said our goodbyes, tearful as they were, and as the Company XO, I sent my wife away, trying to set the example for the rest of the men. I went to Captain Ed Dunlap, Charlie Company Commander. He was saying goodbye to his wife. She looked over at me with that look that said, "Bring him back to me."

Later the buses arrived. We stowed our gear and began quietly loading. Watching the men board, their quiet professionalism, I was suddenly reminded of a comment made by the television personality, Geraldo. If memory serves correctly, he said something to the effect that the Marines were an anachronism, an out-dated force, no longer needed in today's society, outmoded and should therefore be abolished, done away with, eliminated! Yes sir, the Marines certainly had become obsolete, old fashioned, and no longer necessary, that is why we were now boarding buses so that we could go off and fight an obsolete war. Right on Geraldo!

With all our gear on board we drove the distance from the Stumps, our affectionate term for Twentynine Palms, to the Long Beach Naval Air Station. Arrived at a hanger, and welcomed by fellow Marines, we noticed the heavily armed security. Here we were, all armed with weapons, the grunts with their M-16s and the tankers with their 9mm handguns.

Ammunition was issued to all hands, shipping manifests checked and rechecked, again and again, making certain everything we needed was in place. There were no stores where we were going. If we did not have it with us when we arrived in Saudi, we would have to make do without. This was a routine Marines have been doing for a good many years.

It was dark when the first American Airlines plane pulled up to the hanger. At first light we called the roll and marched out to the aircraft. It seemed strange that here we were boarding a commercial airliner and armed to the hilt. The fact that we were so heavily armed startled the flight crew and made them very uncomfortable. All they needed was to have some crazy Marine start shooting up the plane! Talk about stress.

The boarding went quickly, quietly and smoothly. When the plane was loaded, it taxied from the hanger to the airstrip. We knew we were underway.

From the Long Beach Naval Air Station we flew to Bangor, Maine, where we stayed for a brief period. The flight then took us to Brussels, Belgium and from there directly to Dhahran, Saudi Arabia and the big sand box. Of course we ate deluxe meals enroute, chicken a la king, breakfast, noon and evening meals. Great stuff!

The flight crew, once over the fact that we were armed and going off to war with weapons neatly stowed, was just great and I am certain we all appreciated each member. Whenever we landed, we were not allowed to deplane and so it was a long, long 36-hour flight.

I think Geraldo would have enjoyed the fact that we were going to the land of the black veils, and the in-flight movie was "Pretty Woman" starring the gorgeous Julia Roberts. She was clothed in a mini skirt with boots up to her thighs and we were traveling to a place where this would never be allowed or seen. Believe me, we took it all in!

After what seemed like forever, we finally landed in Dhahran. The aircraft taxied near a hanger and the crew opened the doors. The first sensation was the overwhelming heat. It was a wall of moist, hot air, with a temperature of 104-106 degrees at 0200 in the morning. This was a tad warmer than Twentynine Palms, with a humidity factor of about 80-90 percent.

Other than heat, the first sensation I had of the Middle East was the smell. My father had often said that the Middle East smelled different from the rest of the world. Boy was he ever right! The smell was different from anything I knew. The smell, humidity and wall of heat quickly permeated the entire plane. Welcome to Saudi Arabia and the start of what I considered to be phase two in this operation.

We deplaned and formed up the Company and then did as Marines have done for 220 plus years, we waited and we waited; no one arrived to greet us or give us direction. All around us airmen and airborne troopers were running about, paying absolutely no attention to the company of Marines quietly doing their waiting thing.

I asked Captain Ed Dunlap, Company Commander, what was happening.

"Don't know at the moment," he answered.

Off to one side stood a gentleman, dressed in pressed long sleeve desert camo shirt, blue jeans and a baseball cap. Captain Ed went over and tapped the man on the shoulder, asked, "Excuse me, sir, do you know what is going on here?" Who turned around with a nice smile on his face, none other than Dan Rather. He looked at Captain Ed and said, "You 're their Captain?"

"Yes sir," Ed replied.

"Well," Rather nodded, "I don't know what is going on, but we should go and find out."

After getting over my initial shock of realizing we were in the presence of the great Dan Rather, I watched as he and Ed walked away.

Finally, we were shown where to set down and made all the usual preparations to spend the rest of the night, such as it was, and get some sleep. Sleep had been next to impossible on an airliner filled with excited, young warriors setting off to war for the first time. Here was a chance to get a few short hours of sleep.

We had spent considerable time in the California Mojave Desert, but it was unlike the Saudi desert with its temperatures always in the low 100s along with a humidity of near 90 percent. It also made sleep near impossible. By early morning the temperature had cooled somewhere close to 95 or so, making it possible to catch a few hours of sleep, if one was able. Upon waking we found the good night desert moisture had worked its magic and corroded just about everything that was metal.

After chow we called the role and then waited again, doing what Marines do best, grumbling, muttering and waiting. Eventually some buses pulled up. Understand that these were not the standard, drab, plain, Navy-gray buses we had all come to know and love. No, these were the wildest buses we had ever seen! Colored orange and white, these tandem buses appeared to be two buses married together with a pivotal hitch. They were about as long as the typical tractor-trailer. Both units were double-deckers and so we were able to get all of Charlie Company and others loaded into the two buses. Once loaded, off we went and I mean off we went! To this day I am uncertain of exactly how we got there all in one piece, which in itself seemed a miracle. I am not sure just how fast that bus setup could go and what lane we were in half the time, but that crazy driver did manage to get us there. Where was there? There was the port city of Al Jabayl.

We drove from the airport at Dhahran to the eastern coast of Saudi Arabia and the port city of Al Jubayl in what I consider must have been record time. This very modern port served primarily as a container ship facility, which would eventually fit very nicely into our off-loading plans for the MPS ships. It was enormous and not quite what we expected given our western view of what the Middle East was supposed to look like.

The wild buses finally pulled up to a docking area and came to a screeching halt alongside an enormous transport ship. Surrounding the facility was an equally sizable warehouse complex. Wherever one looked you would see the Marine security detail, which made us feel somewhat safer and right at home.

Everyone off-loaded. The staff and junior officers as well as the NCOs were rushed into a large warehouse. Each Company was assigned a space. A space! Looking about one could see nothing but emptiness, but it was all *our* space.

"Where are the tanks?" everyone asked, looking about the facilities. The answer given: "The ships have not off-loaded as yet." Well, so much for the MPS program and having our equipment waiting for us so that we could drive directly to the battle scene and engage in combat with the enemy. The watchword of the day, knowing the Iraqis were only a few klicks away, "You'll just have to wait." So, we sat around and waited, mumbled and grumbled, as warriors are prone to do when made to sit on their hands.

Finally our tanks and other equipments were off-loaded and our crews quickly got to work. Remember the Iraqi war machine was encamped in our back yard, so to speak, which kept the pucker factor reasonably high. The mechanics, with the leadership of Gunnery Sergeant Cronin and Sergeant Welch, began putting our tanks in working order.

The work on the tanks was not what we expected. The removal of cosmoline, mothball material, the usual draining of fluids, and unpacking was expected. The equipment however, came off with SL3 incomplete. The SL3 is the kit of accessories used to keep the equipment operational, including the optics, tools, fluids, everything needed to make a tank work properly, especially in a combat situation. Sergeant Welsh and his force of mechanics improvised. Needed material was scrounged from anything that was handy. Despite the stress of working with incomplete equipment, we realized we had to hurry and setup; the Iraqi were too close for comfort.

With all this sweat and sore muscles add the heat factor and the work almost became unbearable. We stayed about 8-10 days at the warehouse working on the tanks, all the while feeling extremely vulnerable. It became a tiring routine of work on the equipment, return to the warehouse to eat and sleep, more work, eat and sleep, always with an increasing pucker factor. Saddam had to know we were there, struggling to ready our equipment. The question became, how much longer would he wait before smashing across the border and taking a stab at us? After all, we were the only armored force between him and the capital of Saudi Arabia.

During our work stint we soon made contact with many of the locals who worked there and lived nearby. Dealing with the locals could get you into some serious trouble. There is the story of a poor Marine Captain in his HUMVEE, who told his driver to pull over to the side of the road and stop. He then got out of the vehicle, took some pictures of a Saudi woman and her two female children, all dressed in the usual traditional black garb. Along came the famed Saudi Military Police who immediately clubbed him about the head and ears, dragged him into their vehicle and took him away. It seems they did not release him until after the war was over and then it was some time thereafter. Taking pictures of another man's wife and children is a major offense. We were totally unprepared for how to handle this type of incident, even how to relate to the civilians, so we learned to stay away from them altogether. These situations only added to our stress levels.

The off-loading effort soon established the routine of work, eat and sleep. With the Iraqis at the border no Marine needed to be told to work. There were some interesting moments to relieve the stress.

One day a very large Russian cargo ship docked near us. It just sat there, no cargo unloaded or loaded, just sat there for days. It was humorous to note the splendid array of communications antennae on board. We all knew what they were up to, keeping a vigilant eye on us.

Marines being Marines entertainment was not too far

away. Watching the female crewmembers sunning themselves on deck certainly made the time pass, breaking up the routine.

For me the highlight of the unloading was a package from home. Not just any package, but one with my mother's famed Congo Squares, a kind of blond brownie. I cut the squares into smaller sections and shared with my fellow marines. It was a very good moment and lifted everyone's spirits, especially as we were not receiving regular mail. Thanks, Mom!

Before we could move into the desert and take up our positions to defend all of Saudi, many problems had to be resolved with the Saudi folks. The fact that the Saudis really did not want us there made any resolution more difficult. Water quickly became a problem. Where were we to obtain the all-necessary water in the desert? Back at Twentynine Palms we of course solved that problem easily, but here we were in someone else's back yard. While at the warehouse complex we could obtain all the water we needed from the MPS ships. We dared not drink the local stuff for fear of losing men to dysentery.

The answer was to use bottled water. But where were we to find bottled water? Well, we were told by the Saudis that it could easily be bought from Prince so and so; he held the local concession for bottled water. Special arrangements had to be made for bottled water. There we were, ready for fighting to protect them, and they wanted arrangements and discussions of price!

All types of special arrangements had to be worked out with a local Prince. I was not involved. When it came time to make a move to the desert, some one had to ask the inevitable question, "Where does one have a healthy bowel movement in the sand box?" The answer seems rather obvious to someone not aware of the social and religious mores of the Middle Easterner.

"But, you may not go into the desert and use our sands for that purpose. That sand is Holy land and you are infidels!"

All one had to do was spend a moment or two and look into the desert where there were a bazillion or two animals running about the giant litter box; goats, sheep, camels, dogs and the local folks excreting copious amounts of fecal matter all over Holy land!

"But they are not infidels, like you. They are Allah's creatures, but you are infidels and therefore cannot do that in Holy land! It is Allah's will."

Okay, now what? Do we pack up and head for home?

"Ah, you infidels can use a plastic bag, tie it up and have it picked up for disposal." I suppose that Prince what's-his-name had the concession on plastic bags. Can you imagine using a plastic bag in 110 degrees heat, piling it somewhere and waiting while the sun and heat worked on it? Give us a break!

"Well then, we will construct out houses for you to defecate in. But that needs further negotiations, because Prince so-and-so owns the plywood concession, and these out-houses will have to be constructed out of plywood."

Then, of course, sand bags needed to be filled to augment protection for the armor. This is a very old Marine Corps tradition, you know, protect your equipment so it will work when you need it

"No, no, no... that is impossible!"

"Come again?"

"Infidels may not put the Holy Land into sandbags!"

"Seems odd. Then where do we get the sand?"

We were in one of the world's largest beaches with no water and we cannot dig up the sand to fill sandbags!

"Ah, Allah be praised, you can buy all the sand you need from Prince so-and-so; he has the sand concession for this part of Saudi."

Hard as it is to believe, with a war on, this sort of thing went on day after day, until most problems were solved and we made ready to move to the desert to await the Iraqis.

Everyday in the distance we could hear the locals and their prayers being broadcast over a loudspeaker system, and believe me it was loud. All of this seamed unreal to most of us. After all, we generally go inside a church to pray; here they spread a prayer rug on the sand and go down on their knees no matter where they are. It took some getting used to that routine. Some five times a day they face Mecca and pray.

As usual, we spent what available time there was doing the ongoing maintenance and set up required on tanks. In the California desert there were many tricks we had leaned to defeat the ever-encroaching fingers of the corrosive effects of the fine wind blown desert sand. One trick was to keep the fine sand from penetrating the inside workings of the tank; we did not want that stuff in the optics and such!

One day, while working at the maintenance program, who pops around the tank, none other than Mr. Dan Rather! This is the second time we have seen big Dan. It was an awesome time to be a Marine! This was just great. He waved to us and asked, "Hey, you guys want to be on TV?" "Are you kidding? Marines that don't want to be on TV? Of course we do!"

He started walking toward us with his film crew, when around the corner pops Mr. Marine, Warrant Officer so-and-so, with his starched camies creased in all the correct places, clean flack jacket, helmet, looking for all the world like he has not been outside of an air conditioned room for five minutes. We, of course, by this time were greasy, smelling like camels, just plain nasty, as one Marine once described, "Raggedy Marines".

The sterling clean Warrant Officer placed his clean hand over the lens of the minicam and clearly stated: "No, I'm afraid we cannot have this. These men do not project the image the Marine Corps wishes the public to see. There will be no pictures, thank you so very much."

Of course what resulted was a very heated discussion

between Dan Rather and the Marine Corps image himself, as to what Dan Rather could and could not film. Rather finally snorted something like, "We'll see about this," and off they went. Of course we did not make our TV debut because we did not project the image the Marine Corps wished to project. Oh well, off to the war.

Word finally came down to us peons that General Hopkins's job was complete and Major General James K. "Mike" Myatt had been named to lead the 1st Division into battle. General Boomer would become the I MEF Commander with the 1st Division as the main ground element. He brought a wealth of experience from his time as a Colonel with the Fleet Marine Force in the Atlantic. That sat well with us; Marines do not like to be led from a desk.

With all this we were assigned the mission as part of RCT 7 (Regimental Combat Team 7). We were given the glorious name of Task Force Ripper! Sounds like something one could sink their teeth into, no pun intended.

In spite of everything, most problems were quickly worked through, including the lack of equipment. We hunkered down to await orders, another thing that Marines are good at. Finally word came through for us to make the move to the desert and stand up to the Iraqis.

Camel, The Horse Designed by Committee

Camels were a source of constant amusement and entertainment for us. They tried to consume our camouflage and plastic spoons.

Photo by C. Freitus

Chapter 2
Conscientious Objectors

I give no historical preamble to this short chapter, especially because officially it did not happen. Also this is perhaps the part of my story that Marines will not be very happy with. I must back-track a little to that point where we were poised for war.

Very early in our deployment to the Persian Gulf two of our folks decided that they did not want to be in a shooting war and decided to become conscientious objectors.

Men have taken this course through all wars fought by our country, therefore it isnot really news. It is important to the reader to remember that like all the branches of the armed forces, these days it is composed of all volunteers. No Marine is drafted. You put up your hand knowingly and you do so freely. When deployed to the Gulf everyone in Charlie Company was a volunteer. We had all signed our name on the dotted line of the paperwork, volunteering our lives, in exchange for payment from our country for X number of years.

It was deemed necessary to call up the Marines because our mission fit the required parameters of the action in the Gulf. This was something we had trained long and hard for. Because Marines are the 911 Service, they are expected on station earlier than other types of troops, we were there early on. It was an uncertain time for everyone arriving as no one knew just how long Saddam would wait before making an attempt into Saudi Arabia.

During the deployment, I noted the quiet calm confidence of the young Marines in my unit and others in the area. There was no uncertainty as to why we were in the Gulf, what was expected of us and what our mission was. That quiet confidence comes from the training that Marines have experienced for many years.

Here we were in the warehouses, 120 degrees, unloading and fitting out the tanks. Early in the war we were using only two or three warehouses. Later, all were utilized. We were only two or three days in country.

In the Marine Corps every individual is important, a member of a team effort.

This episode began with, "Sir. "I want to shoot myself! I do not want to do this. I am a conscientious objector."

Whoa! Time out! This is not one of Hemingway's great novels on war. This is not WWII. This is not Viet Nam where you may have been drafted. You voluntarily signed your name on a piece of paper committing yourself to the Marines and country. Now you want to state that you are a conscientious objector? Functioning as a member of a team, This episode came as a very big surprise and a real let down, to be honest. Up to this point these two men had been excellent Marines. So, when we all arrived in country it was a shock to hear them claim to be conscientious objectors. As tank crew members they had taken part in all the training exercises, lived in the dirt with their fellow Marines, sweat with them and grumbled with the best. This was not a training exercise. All these Marines would be shooting at real targets, manned by real men.

Now that we were in Saudi Arabia, we suddenly have two men that want out, do not want to do the thing they had trained so hard for, months prepared for. Why suddenly now?

I believe the underlining reason was, they were both

married, one with a newborn. They perhaps thought that they were not going to get back home and their families would have to carry on without them. That is something they shared with all Marines in the Gulf. They were not alone.

Since they had now declared officially to be conscientious objectors we took away their pistols. One of them had expressed an interest in the fact that he wanted to shoot himself. The two were packed out of the area quickly, as there was a general fear among the troops that they might get hurt, somehow. When you have a large group of eighteen and nineteen year olds, all keyed up for war, you know someone just might take it upon themselves to do something rash about these two.

Give credit where credit is due; someone higher up decided not to send them home, kept them in country with us. As we deployed out into the sands, they deployed along with us. Someone found them work that kept them busy.

As we later broke through the berms those two conscientious objectors drove buses forward to collect those masses of prisoners. They stayed in country the entire ground war, in some way being productive and useful to the Marines. When we eventually deployed home, they deployed home, not getting the early ride that they had expected.

Concerned with the public's view of the Marine Corps, the entire incident was kept rather quiet and generally speaking, everyone was pleased with how these two men were managed.

The Warehouse
Port Complex of Al Jubayl

Location of the off-load of the MPS (Maritime Prepositioning Squadron) ship. This warehouse held the MEF (Marine Expeditionary Force) after deployment from the Stumps (Twentynine Palms) and before deployment to the sands.

Photo by C. Freitus

Chapter 3
RCT Deployment to Al Jubayl

After declaring the MER combat ready General Hopkins deployed RCT 7 in accordance with the 7ᵗʰ MEB Op Order 003. The mission given to the brigade tasked it to deploy forces north in its sector no earlier than 26 August 1990. On order the brigade was to conduct operations to disrupt, delay, and destroy attacking Iraqi forces in order to protect vital facilities in the vicinity of Al Jubayl. The brigade's mission included coordinating with Saudi Forces in the sector. General Hopkins intended to carry out the mission by using marine air to attack and delay an advancing enemy, the ground defense was oriented to prevent the enemy from being able to come within artillery range of the important oil facilities at Al Jubayl. Hopkins wanted RCT 7 (Regimental Combat Team 7) deployed to battle positions to create a screening and covering force. If the Iraqis attacked, General Hopkins expected the Saudi Army to delay the enemy and effect a passage of lines through the Marines defensive forces, the Marines would then employ long-range weapons and tank killer teams to further delay and channel the enemy's advance. A second handover would follow to the main defensive positions in the main battle area. The main battle area consisted of battle positions of tank hunter-killer teams, supporting arms, direct fire weapons, obstacles, and fixed strongpoints.

At the time of Op Order 003's writing, the main battle area was so close to Al Jubayl that no fallback positions existed. Hopkins informed the ground force that there would be no withdrawal. There was no place to go.

The move to the big sand box, the desert that is, was made somewhere on the 9th or 10th day of our stay in Al Jabayl. Of course we expected the entire Iraqi 6th Armored Division to be waiting just beyond the gates of the city when we set out. Not too over wrought! Rumors and some trickled-down Intel had the crack Iraqi Armored boys, the ones who supposedly had originally invaded Kuwait, well rested, replenished and just itching to go head to head with the Marines. They wanted to kick our tails all over the Saudi desert.

We had heard stories that the Iraqi brass were telling their folks that in order for us to join the U.S. Marines we had to kill our own mother. Yeah, right! I suppose this was a technique to stiffen the backbone of the Iraqi grunts serving in the line. Whatever the purpose it did not lessen our fear of driving directly into combat!

Not knowing how true all this was, we anticipated anything and everything once we cleared the warehouse complex at Al Jubayl. Not certain just how many men and tanks comprised an Iraqi Armored Division, and rumors abounded as to the number, most of the men felt that with the reported 15,000 plus men of the Brigade we could slap the Iraqi's about for some time. We had enough food, fuel and ammo for some 30 days, so who knew.

Getting to the assigned area, just outside Al Jubayl was no easy task. Obstructions did not help us a bit.

"But you cannot drive onto the highways with your tanks during the daytime. You will scare the poor local folks with your fearsome, big tanks and cause much congestion and many accidents with the motoring Saudi public."

Okay, so we made the big move at night, which was

probably a better idea. After all, we did not want to go about crushing Mercedes, Caddies and whatnots with our tanks. Not good PR, you know.

The big question quickly made itself known: How do we get to this place? Where is it? Uh, check the map, right? Why didn't we think of this, it is so simple, right? Not so, for only Company Commanders were in possession of said map. So it quickly became a game of follow the leader and do not lose him!

Despite the lack of maps, we finally moved to a position just outside the Al Jubayl military airfield. The moon was full, which helped us with the move, but we worried about being easy night targets. Upon arrival we secured the area and just hunkered down to await daylight. Shortly after being in place I decided to check on my people and walked the perimeter, speaking softly to each tank crew. There was no need to remind them to stay awake and alert! Believe me they were alert!

On the way back I had one of those National Geographic moments. Aware of nightlife that roamed the California High Desert country, I began to sense someone or something stalking me. I walked a little faster. I walked to one side then the other, never in a straight line; it did the same, following me exactly where I went. I stopped and made my ears listen real hard, nothing moved, not a sound. I walked a little further and there it was again, but not a sound.

Finally I arrived at my tank and hurriedly jumped onboard. I turned and peered into the desert darkness and could see nothing. At the time I was unsure of what it could be, nerves, stress perhaps, but I did not think so. There would be many adventures of this type awaiting us all.

No one really slept, for all night we listened to the roar, rumblings and the sound of aircraft on the move at the Saudi airfield. When the sun finally came up, there, in all its splendor, was the Al Jubayl military airfield, with transport aircraft landing every few minutes. It was glorious for us tankers to watch these huge transports, knowing they were ours because it meant troops and supplies were arriving. Gave us a warm feeling to know we were getting backup. It seemed the moment one landed one would take off. Talk about incredible air control systems! When we looked about it became evident that other than the airport, we were in the middle of just about nowhere, except that out there in the middle of nowhere was the tough as nails Iraqi armor, at least that is what they thought.

We actually held what might be called the high ground of the area. All around us were the classic undulating sand dunes, the type one expects when they find themselves out in the desert. The view was unimpeded for many klicks about, with the exception of the airfield, and it was nothing but sand! We could see the nearby highway with its constant stream of traffic, auto and truck. Where'n hell were all these people going? Were they aware there was a war going on?

Sometime around mid-day we could see what looked like a recon platoon making its way toward us. It soon turned out to be from the airborne unit already there. They came into our base with several M113 tracked vehicles and their good-ole standby, the famed Sheridan Tank. The Sheridan is their airborne, droppable light tank they ride into battle. As they pulled up, they looked totally lost, shell shocked.

When they stopped, the platoon commander dismounted and came over to us. He asked if we had some water and some meals, if we could spare it. He had had no contact with his command structure and was not certain where they had moved. Several of his vehicles were running on jury-rigged parts, the track had been short tracked, road wheels had been removed, arms had been smashed, and one was towing a personnel carrier that was not functioning. Of course he asked for spare parts, which we either did not have or could not offer because our systems were not compatible.

All we could finally do was give him some meals, and tell him what direction we thought his HQ was, and send the poor guy on his way. It became evident that these guys were expected to be the trip wire in case Saddam decided to cross the border into Saudi. It appeared that no one really knew much about them, nor seemed to care. We did not appear to have any word on them and, at that point, I was very glad I was a Marine.

We spent the days catching up on the vital maintenance of the tanks, making certain that we had everything in place that needed to be. Somewhere by day three or four in the desert we were notified by radio, the BBC from good-ole London town, I believe, that we Marines were part of something called Desert Shield, the guarding and protecting of the Saudi Holy Land. Whoopie, that sounded really impressive. During the next several weeks, while supplies and more forces continued to arrive, we continually moved in and about the Al Jubayl area, constantly waiting for an armed force to come crashing out of the desert, especially at night.

It did not take us long to understand that we were in fact providing a security force and a checkpoint for the Al Jubayl airfield. We settled into the routine of maintenance, eating, sleeping and staying alert for the sounds of Iraqi armor!

News, or should I say rumors, trickled out to us that the 1st Marine Brigade had arrived along with the remaining elements of the 1st Marine Division. I suppose they were not as rushed as we were when we arrived, so therefore missed all the fun we enjoyed getting our raggedy selves into the field.

It felt pretty good knowing we were our nation's premier Rapid Deployment Force. We felt we caused Saddam to lose his window of invasion opportunity. Still, there was little to stop him from trying. We, along with some airborne types, stood between him and Saudi Arabia.

The Bob Hope Show

Although Mister Hope did not bring the scantily-clad girls, he did bring a much needed morale booster. Pictured also is baseball legend Johnny Bench.

Photo by C. Freitus

Chapter 4
The "Cement Factory" Defense Line

In September 1990 the 1st Marine Division had too few AAVs (Amphibious Assault Vehicles) and tanks to conduct the active defense that later came to characterize its deployment. General Myatt took advantage of one of the few natural obstacles that existed between Al Jubayl and the Kuwait border. RCT 7 (Regimental Combat Team 7) moved 50 kilometers north of Al Jubayl to establish the third Marine defensive position. Drawing its name from the large structure of the cement factory complex that dominated the surrounding area, the new defensive position was centered on an elevated ridgeline and a series of gravel pits that bisected the north-south coastal highway at that point.

Eventually we deployed to an area north of Al Jubayl, a place called the Triangle. Shades of Vietnam and the Iron Triangle! This triangle was basically an area where the coastal road joined with a road that went deep into the interior of Saudi Land. We moved into a location called Manifah Bay, very near the coastal highway.

We immediately became involved in the usual tanker maintenance and kept an eye over our shoulder for Mr. Saddam and his thugs. It soon became impossible not to see the incredible amount of traffic that was heading south along the highway.

Although Saddam had supposedly sealed the Kuwait/Saudi border, refugees were still streaming through, taking everything they had with them. Almost every car that drove through was a Cadillac, Lincoln Continental or a big, and I mean big, black Mercedes sedan. People had all their worldly possessions strapped onto the roofs, trunks filled so that they could not be closed, and all of them waving to us, yelling and smiling. Yeah guys, you are saving our country and we are bugging out, running for our lives. Ah, yes, thank you very much American Marines! See ya later!

While the auto traffic surged south the truck traffic moved north toward Kafji. We finally moved within range of one of the largest factories in the area. It turned out to be a cement factory. That figured, with all the sand surrounding the place. Later on, one of the platoon Sergeants, Staff Sergeant Mummey, who we liked to call Mumbo, seemed to know all about it. Seems his father was a cement worker and had sent Mumbo an article from a trade magazine. Thereafter, Mumbo became our resident authority on the cement factory. Everyone stood around gazing at the place, impressed at its enormous size, which made it stick out like the proverbial sore thumb. Of course we were deployed about it, a good sighting target for the Iraqi cannoneers!

Before the week was over we had settled into a routine once again of maintenance, sleep, eat and move about the area. One day it was announced that a Congressional Fact-finding Committee would be stopping by to see after our welfare. Someone with the PR folks decided that we would put on the usual Dog and Pony show, something every Marine likes to do.

Some explanation is required for this tale. Prior to the arrival of the Congressional Committee, that included John Kerry, the good senator from Massachusetts who just happens to be an old Navy man from the Vietnam era, and highly decorated at that, we had problems with getting mail. When we first deployed to the Gulf the main purpose of all transport was "Guns and Butter". This is an age-old process and well-used to explain how the military was operating at the moment, "Got to get enough bullets and food to the Marines already in the Gulf!" sounds good. Our location had changed so many times that apparently, we thought at the time, it was difficult to get mail through to us. Some mail did get through to us while we were at the warehouse complex, but after we moved to our positions at the Al Jubayl airport, the mail took a real nosedive. Any person who has served in the Armed Forces anywhere in this small world realizes the value of receiving those loving words from your wife or sweetheart from back home.

Being far from home has an unsettling effect on anyone and an even greater effect when expecting soon to be in a shooting war. Mail is the only means of keeping your memories of family and friends alive. So there we were, a reduction in mail and no packages. Our frustration level began to rise. I remember stating this fact to my father in a letter home. He, on the other hand, wrote that he had been sending packages and they had been returned to him along with small package envelopes notifying the sender: "Patron should seek refund. Restriction X Applies: Mail limited to letters and voice tapes, 12 oz. Maximum."

Knowing my father as well as any child can, I knew he would not let this stop him from getting us packages. One of the items we dearly needed was good-ol' soap. Constant maintenance of the tanks and blowing sand made for grungy Marines, but with soap this is simply a drill. I mentioned this in a letter home. Letters seemed to present little or no problems; packages were the problem.

My father's mission therefore became how to get soap to his Marine in the Gulf. Senator John Kerry to the rescue! Now what my father did annoys any and every brass hat in any branch of the service, he made a great deal of noise. I am certain that Big Al, the Commandant of the Marine Corps, General Alfred M. Gray, USMC, was annoyed with him. After some discussion with a few local Congressmen, he was told to contact the good Senator John Kerry, as he was heading to the Gulf on one of those much dreaded by the brass fact-finding missions. "Uh oh, here they come again to stick their noses in where we don't want them."

After some discussion with the Senator's office, arrangements were made for my father to sneak a small package of soap into their travel luggage. Not just any soap, but one that was not made from animal renderings, one that was used in hospitals throughout most of the world.

We were newly moved into our operational triangle just south of the cement factory, a very prominent terrain feature, and word filtered down through the chain of command to provide a tank for a Dog and Pony show. Word eventually filtered down to Battalion, then to Captain Ed. "Ed, have Charlie Company put on a great Dog and Pony show for some fact-finding Congressmen." Because we were newly into the field and everyone was trying to get their act together, I let Captain Dunlap know that I, his XO, would take the Dog and Pony show tank. He gave us our mission order to where we should be, and so off we went.

We clanked off toward the cement factory and took a right turn onto the highway, trying to drive carefully in and among the many Caddies and Mercedes. Finally, we got to a small side road and we clanked away until we get to our grid coordinates and stopped. Sitting there was an LAV (Light Armored Vehicle), a hummer (HUMVEE, replacement for the famous Jeep) with a TOW missile variant, and a few other military vehicles.

"So, any ideas?" I asked, being the senior officer present. After some brief discussion suggestions were made to dismount and seek whatever shade was possible. Good thinking.

How the individual that set up that show ever found that particular patch of wondrous desert, I shall never know. What we turned up was hard packed-sand, not hard-packed like the beach, but hard-packed like cement. There was no way we could penetrate that stuff to rig some camo netting and produce some badly needed shade. We had no idea how the Congressmen would handle the intense sun, but for us seasoned, hard-bitten Marines, it was going to be shade, one way or the other!

Not even the durable engineering stake could be driven into that hard ground, all of which meant we would have no shade. After some wrangling we managed to get some camo netting rigged and we proceeded to beautify the place in military fashion. The PR (Public Relations) folks would have indeed been very proud of those Marines that were not good enough to be seen on TV! We even managed to get ourselves cleaned up; we did not want the PR folks to see us like the raggedy Marines that tankers can be.

After much ado, we were ready to meet the great fact-finding committee and do the Marines Corps proud!

We waited. And we waited. And we waited some more. After a fashion, it seemed like a very long fashion, a couple of squeaky clean HUMVEES came dashing across the desert trailing the usual fine plume of Saudi desert sand. They pulled up; Marines got out followed by some slick looking civilians. Ah, this must be the Congressional Fact-finding Committee searching for some missing facts.

Very quickly the Congressmen started to filter, pressing the flesh. "Hellooo there, what state are you from, son?" After some introductions and discussions most got a kick out of the fact that I was from Alaska and here in the great Saudi sand box.

After a while a Senator walked up to me and said, "Hello, I am Senator Kerry."

"The Senator Kerry?"

"Yes?"

"Sir, my name is Chris Freitus."

"Your dad is Joe Freitus?"

"Yup, that's him."

"Well, well, seems I have a package for you," he grinned. The Senator had been carrying this package all the way from the States, across the Atlantic, Saudi Arabia, the desert and here he ended up at a Marine Dog and Pony show to deliver a package from my father. Talk about a twist! The good Senator arrived with his own Dog and Pony show and I ended up accepting it, the presentation of my package. How the Gods work!

Senator Kerry went to get my package and when he returned we sat down and shared the wondrous delights of an MRE (Meal Ready to Eat), over which he looked most enthusiastic, but I suspect he popped a Tum or two thereafter. He handed me the package and I thanked him profusely. The Congressmen loaded into their vehicles and roared off toward the south, soon disappearing into the forever-sands of Saudi Arabia.

I opened the small package to find packets of liquid soap not made from animal fats. We could not afford to insult our Saudi hosts. At this time and place, with no PX available, we were unable to obtain the few items we needed to keep ourselves sanitary. The few supplies that we had brought were just about exhausted and these packets of soap would serve us well. We hoped to find a PX in the not too distant future. After that incident I was very careful about mentioning things to my father; I knew his determination.

Our stay at the cement factory was one of our longest stays in the area.

We had many grunts (Infantry folks) accompanying us and one of the first tasks that all good grunts do is construct earthen fortifications. All along the ridgeline and among the gravel pits they dug trenches and constructed fortified bunkers. It was September, miserably hot during the daylight hours, and not much better at night, maybe a little cooler. Some! If it was too hot to dig during the day, the grunts dug all night and rested during the noonday sun. And with our tanker tasks we followed the same procedure.

It sounds like a nice arrangement except that exhausted as anyone may be, flies, blasted flies, swarmed all over us while we tried to sleep. They crawled at the corners of our mouths and eyes, seeking any available water that might be there. It seemed as though there was little we could do to escape them. I tried pulling a towel over my face and that just made me sweat more, attracting even more flies. Eating was a similar exciting experience. Flies!

What was finally accomplished was an interconnecting system of fighting and communication trenches with emplacements for the arty (artillery) folks and we tankers. Somewhere out in front, Marines from Task Force Shepherd had established emplacements as outposts. We were ready for almost anything Saddam might throw at us.

While all this feverish activity was raging we were constantly bombarded by media from all over the world. Since we were there, ready to stand up against any Iraqi attack and somewhat nearby, we were news.

One of the tank crews was interviewed by a German reporter, a rather beautiful fraulein. The resulting article ended up in a German magazine. We even got a copy of the magazine sent to us, which we all thought was very decent. It was a good story and we were all pleased with our publicity, raggedy as we might have been. We could not help wondering at the time, how many former Afrika Korps vets read that story and pined for their days of glory.

Once we got all the digging and fortifying out of our

system we eventually moved further into what we called the Triangle.

The Triangle was a large expanse of the sand box north of Al Jubayl. It was bordered on the east by the coastal highway and the intersecting roads west of Manifah Bay. We actually replaced elements of the Saudis or other Arab groups that had been responsible for the area. On a map it represents a sector of the Saudi/Kuwait border that was called the Heel. Until December, we performed moves in and about the Triangle which were defensive in nature and designed to blunt any attempt by Saddam's troops to run into Saudi. We would set up our BP (Battalion Perimeter) about four square kilometers, then move about every two or three days, still within the confines of this very large triangle of roads.

In November it was three months we had been grunging in and about Saudi land. 1st and 3rd Tank Battalions were the only armor present in the KTO (Kuwaiti Theater of Operations) except for a few Arab units, so-called Saudi National Guard. It was not until after Thanksgiving that the Army finally got its 24th Mech (Mechanized) formed up. This gave us another viable tank force that could engage the Iraqi tankers should they make the decision to come and pay us a visit.

Personal transistor radios were not very common so it was difficult to know just what was happening in the real world out there, the big picture. With our few small, battery-operated radios we were able to pick up Armed Forces Radio and of course that sterling radio personality, Baghdad Betty. She was a real joke because no one believed anything she had to say. So we lived on scuttlebutt (rumors).

Somewhere during our stay within the Triangle, we had the British attached to us. They were very welcome, especially their tanks! The British troops were always a constant source of amusement because they were so British. When they first began to arrive in Saudi, it soon became apparent that they wanted nothing to do with the American Army. They wanted to be with the Marines. I am not certain why this was so, maybe because we were warriors from the sea; but we were very happy to have them aboard. Perhaps they had gone sour on the U.S. Army due to their long association through NATO.

When the British "Desert Rats" appeared in Saudi, they very quickly formed an excellent working relationship with the Marines, especially with us tanker types. These Desert Rats had not operated in the desert since their fame of WWII. They quickly picked up on its limitations and worked to correct any of their deficiencies. The Marines with open arms welcomed the Brits and started to do exchange programs with their officers and NCOS. We cross-attached personnel on several days and did maneuvers with them, we in their tanks and they in ours. We together established the usual daily routines of just moving an armored unit about the desert. It was a situation where we learned from them and they from us.

Their squadron commander was the equivalent of our company commander. They joined Charlie Company one night and I had the dubious honor of being acting CO. The Major was great, joined me on my tank and assumed the duties of the loader. I must say that this is what the tanker's community is really all about. He was friendly and easy to get along with, totally unpretentious. He even helped take down the camo net, just an all around nice guy. Afterward we sat around and chatted with his regimental officers. What a wonderful impression they made, and left, with us.

For us Marines in general it was a new experience to be with the British. For me in particular it was a type of renewal; when I had trained in Norway, I did so with several Royal Marines and they too were extremely good folks.

Meals were another new experience. Whereas the U.S. Army and Marines received the standard MREs or the larger Tray Packs that fed several men at one time, the Brits did meals differently. Their infantry had their usual lightweight meals, but the tankers received their meals in a big box with all their food in a large can. The food in the box is enough for a single day and the preparation of the meal was strictly up to the crew. Compared to our MREs they had real food, like jams, puddings, stews and the like. We are talking real chow here, not stuff that came out of little foil packets. Of course it seemed like real food to us, but to the Brits it must have seemed very like our MREs.

Every time they came to one of us they would bring cases of their food to swap for a similar amount of our famed MREs. We had a difficult time understanding why they wanted our food, but never dared to ask. However, there was one typically British food item that our Marines shied from and that was Bully Beef. I would eat an MRE before I would eat Bully Beef, yet the Brits relished it.

Then, along came the glorious green apples. Someone managed to procure fresh fruit for us and it came in the form of green apples, like the Granny Smiths back in the States. When our green apples had been eaten our old nemesis dysentery struck like the black plague of old Europe. Man oh man, and we had a minimal amount of toilet paper, rolled or otherwise. Actually most of our toilet paper was obtained from the small packets within our MREs. I am uncertain who decided that this small amount was all a male warrior needed. Once stricken we soon ran out of toilet paper and developed a routine: roll out of your cot, run into the desert, evacuate from both ends, clean up, bury the stuff, and return to your cot and lie back down completely drained. We each shared the experience. We had all eaten the green apples so the entire Charlie Company was struck. Actually half the Battalion was incapacitated, unable to function. If we had had to move at that point it would have been very difficult. Like so many, I went down with dysentery and massive dehydration. The corpsmen had a delightful time sticking the

XO with needles.

If Saddam had gotten wind of our condition and decided to make a move against us, he could have rolled through us just like the dysentery. After this encounter with the apples no one ate another.

Sometime after this glorious experience, the ARAMCO (Arabian American Oil Company) folks came on the scene. They were slowly moving north, staging barbecues for the various Army groups they encountered as they went. They had to leave their oil rigs and fields when the Iraqis showed up on the scene, but now that we were there they slowly moved back into position to keep the oil flowing.

These wonderful folks originally began holding these feeds for the Army, who did not seem to appreciate what the oil folks were doing for them. Mind you, these civilians, these ARAMCO folks who saved their foods and their rations, cooked them up and served them to the Army types. They had watermelons, hamburgers, hot dogs and all sorts of good-ol' American back-home type foods. Their old- fashioned cookout was their way of saying thank you for being in Saudi, saving us from the Iraqis. They did this with a couple of Army units, but found the response to be less than desired, shall we say.

Army, "Where are the chips, the ice cream, the Cokes and so on?" "Hey man, these are burgers; where are the steaks?"

So, the ARAMCO folks said fine, packed up and came further north until they found us Marines. Talk about a grateful bunch of men; I was never so proud of my Marines as on that day. ARAMCO loved us because we said thank you, helped unload and reload everything. Not only the quality but also the quantity of food was outrageous. Somewhere in all this I sent a Polaroid to the folks back home.

These folks took pictures of us, gathered our addresses and sent our pictures back home. They did not use the military mail; they used civilian mail. Military mail was much slower.

ARAMCO continued to treat us to these fabulous cookouts until the CENTCOM folks decided to put a stop to it, figuring that a terrorist threat or something might come of all this generosity. Yeah, right!

The media kept up its usual blitz on us, constantly interviewing Marines, probing for whatever dirt they could uncover or generate. CNN was most notable. They seemed to be everywhere and anywhere. I must say that the Marines handled the interviews very well, never complaining about anything, not because we had been ordered to remain quiet, but because the spirit was there. No one wanted to air any dirty laundry with the press. We were a tight band of warriors.

As our stay in the desert continued, we watched the full moons come and go. The full moon, with a clear night sky, offers the best chance for a desert invasion. There is a werewolf concept that was associated with our stay. Apparently when Saddam Hussein invaded Kuwait, he did so during a full moon. His technological ability did not center on thermal imaging as did ours. His nighttime optics centered on infrared and passive night sights, similar to the M60A1 tank that we employed.

Simply stated, the werewolf concept involved the possible attack by Saddam during the full moon. Months passed and no attack. The full moon, with a clear sky, would occur, tensions would mount, and stress levels would increase. Everything had to be checked and double-checked. The full moon would come and go, so the entire episode became a big joke, the werewolf will get you!

Dealing with full moons soon became a part of our desert humor and daily life. The deployment from the cement factory site to the Triangle settled down to become a daily routine of waiting, making small moves about the area and making rotations to the rear for a little R&R.

Chapter 5
Digging in at the Ridgeline

One of the tasks facing the Marines of RCT 7 was the construction of a series of field fortifications along the ridgeline and among the quarries. September was miserably hot and Colonel Fulford, Commander of the RCT 7, immediately established the schedule, dig positions at night and sleep during the day. While that helped, the experience at the cement factory defense line remained in memory as one of suffocating heat and exhaustion. Daylight brought hordes of flies that made sleeping and eating difficult. Temperatures often soared to 120 degrees Fahrenheit. Night was scarcely better for even a 20 to 30 degree drop in temperature was still hot.

Nevertheless, RCT 7 completed a system of interconnecting field fortifications with positions for tanks and AAVs. Behind the defense line were the M109A3 and MI98 155mm howitzers of 3rd Battalion, 11th Marines and RCT 3, which was in the process of receiving its equipment. In front of RCT 7 were the mechanized 1st Battalion, 9th Marines, and Task Force Shepherd as general outposts. The Iraqi attack never materialized and as RCT 3 moved to the field, RCT 7 began shifting battalions farther forward. By late October, the entire division moved beyond the cement factory positions and began rehearsing mobile defensive operations. Though never entirely abandoned, the cement factory line receded in importance and later became a staging area for 2nd Marine Division units.

Basic life in the desert was something that we were prepared for. Our constant training at Twentynine Palms was done full time in the California desert, the Mojave, and that could get really hot, but the humidity was much less. When we finally got to play in a real hot desert, such as in Saudi, we discovered many weak spots in our training. It may not have been hotter in the Saudi desert but the amount of moisture in the air at any given time was higher and constant, very tough on us. At Twentynine Palms we trained in 100-degree weather and it was not too much of a strain. We just had to get used to it. I believe the proper military terminology is acclimatizing.

Getting used to the Persian Gulf environment was a trick unto itself. At 120-degrees, and in the sun, the tanks became incredibly hot. Working on or in them was next to impossible. Just learning to operate there was a lesson we had to learn very quickly if we were to survive in fighting condition. We simply learned not to move quite as fast and the Marine Corps changed our working times to coincide with the cooler nights.

We kept something such as the camo bush hat on our heads at all times. It acted much like a towel absorbing considerable amounts of free running sweat. Whoever designed that hat and decided on the material to be used certainly understood the conditions we were operating in. I wondered if the folks back at the U.S. Army Labs in Natick, Massachusetts had anything to do with it.

Maintaining a running sweat meant that we were all right, but if not careful heat stroke could hit us without warning. That meant we had to drink lots of water, usually warm water. Water, water everywhere and not a *cold* drop to drink!

The flies were another constant annoyance. Never in my wildest dreams had I anticipated the hoards of flies that engulfed us every minute. It was impossible to sleep during the day without netting of some type. Let me say again; when we covered our faces with a towel we sweat even more. Moisture seeped through the towel, and flies quickly gathered. When we first encountered them the question was, "Hey, XO, how do these flies survive without moisture, you know, water?" After a few days the answer became obvious, our sweat.

Some mention should be made of the Company Commander's tank. The Marine Corps Air Ground Museum in Quantico, Virginia contains the artifacts that the Corps has used in its 220-plus years of taking the fight to the Nation's foes. This last expedition into the sand box of Saudi and Kuwait provided more artifacts for the museum, including the first coalition tank to cross into Kuwait. Parked outside one of the metal quonset huts that house the museum is a sand-colored M60A1 tank with the name Genesis II painted in black lettering on the bore evacuator. How did the name come to evolve? Let me describe an episode of our days of high adventure.

When our tanks were removed from the MPS ships, the bore evacuators were as virgin as the driven snow. Tankers are always ready to leave their mark on the world: "When I move the ground shakes. When I speak people die," all that good stuff. More important, we want to tell the world who it was that left the mark. So the name on the gun tube is a very important facet of the tanker's world, similar, I imagine, to the nose art of the fighter and bomber crews in WWII.

The CO's (Commanding Officer's) crew is no exception to this rule. His gunner was concerned about the lack of a namesake gracing the main gun tube of his beast. The gunner in an officer's tank crew is very similar to that of an aircraft crew chief, ensuring that all is kept in ready preparation for the arrival of the officer and starting of the engines. The gunner assumes many of the tasks of the TC (Tank Commander), allowing the zero officer to go about his zero business.

Our CO's gunner, Corporal Sean Pulliam, was growing

concerned about the void gracing his main gun. I, being his Platoon Commander, XO, and HQ (Headquarter) Platoon Commander, it was my sworn duty to provide guidance.

Captain Ed Dunlap was a most correct officer, concerned with his professional military appearance, in garrison his high and tight provided an example to those he lead, as did the lack of any facial hair. Yet, upon venturing forth to the land of the Arabic cat box, this Marine became decidedly, politically incorrect. For what should appear, no not the tiny reindeer and the guy in the red suit (supposedly a patriot would have blown them out of the sky), but a moustache! Well, with his upper lip somewhat fuzzy, and the growth of hair on his brain housing, he began to resemble a certain Rock star, Phil Collins of Rock group Genesis. Our leader, the stalwart Company Commander, began to look more and more the same. Now, for those who are of the Rock flavor, the number of band members in the group Genesis and the number of crewmen in a tank are the same. So, with hints, Corporal Pulliam soon had the name "Genesis II" emblazoned across the main gun tube of C-51, the CO's tank.

Sometime in October or November, so difficult to remember when you are having fun, who should appear but a reporter from CNN. He wanted to interview some of the Marines in Charlie Company. Good show, we will be famous now. Even better the PAO (Public Affairs Officer) was nowhere to be seen or heard, so several Marines were interviewed by the older gentleman, who had been a tanker himself in Korea. I wish I had been able to catch his name. He was not one of those that went to Baghdad to see the light show. He asked no dirt questions and treated the Marines like professionals.

The last to be interviewed was the head hog-jaws, Captain Ed Dunlap. Standing tall in the turret of his mighty war chariot, he was George Patton himself, deftly fielding the questions posed by the media. Then the question that the XO had whispered to the reporter moments before the interview cropped up, "So, Captain, how'd your tank get the name "Genesis II?" The Captain looked aghast. The Marines commenced to guffaw, and the mighty warrior looked off camera to his trusted second in command with the look that Medusa would have been proud of. Genesis II now stands a silent watch in Quantico, but to me the memory will be of Captain Ed Dunlap standing in cupola with that look on his face!

During and since WWII the preeminent military newspaper has been the famed *Stars and Stripes*, the military newspaper that tells all without ever saying anything of importance. We knew that we were in Saudi because the *Stars and Stripes* said so. They ran an article about the flies and the Afrika Korps during WWII. When the Brits and the Germans were interviewed during that time, both were asked what the most horrendous moment of the war was for them? You would suppose it would have been something related to combat or the fear of being captured. Not so. It was the flies!

The Marines, always looking for entertainment of any kind, held contests capturing flies. When we emptied a water bottle, we would try to see how many flies we could kill. It was not uncommon by mid-day to have a bottle half-full of buzzing, irritated flies.

Eating was another major problem, one that none of us ever really solved. The flies would gather on your food, around your mouth, wherever there was a hint of moisture. Each spoonful provided a mouthful of flies. Eating soon became a real challenge, and we tried all kinds of methods to eat without enjoying a mouthful of flies!

Regarding the food there were no real complaints. Oh sure, there are always the jokes and the few who would complain about anything, but in the end the Corps tried mightily to serve good food, plenty of it, and it was usually hot. It sounds strange to want hot food in the hot desert, but it really tasted that much better when it was served hot, and the Marine service units did just that. They worked hard to truck hot food out to wherever we were hunkered down. The task was not a simple one. They served hot morning and evening meals; the noon meal always consisted of the wonderful MREs. The meals were the typical military energy food, high in grease, low in taste, but at least it was always there after the first month or so.

At first, eating only the MREs was tough because the mails were not getting through; therefore, no care packages were arriving from home to supplement our tasty MREs. When packages began arriving from home, and the Marines began serving food on the line it was great. We were supplied with fresh local fruit, and at one point we even received Arabic Coca Cola. No, it is not like the American Coke we all know and love, but it was great to have a taste other than Cool Aid or coffee.

We craved liquids of any type, color or flavor. We continued to receive bottled water, which we kept strictly for drinking, warm or not. Being Marines we scavenged and hoarded whatever drinking water we could. It may have been psychological, but water was always on everyone's mind. We soon understood that a sweating Marine kept cooler with his clothes on, yet a sweating man meant loss of water, and possible dehydration. During high desert temperatures a resting man could lose up to a pint of water per hour just sweating. Because we carried on continuous maintenance, our water intake was tremendous and constant. There were also some humorous situations.

We had a water bull (water tank on wheels) that contained potable water which meant that it was heavily chlorinated. We used it for drinking purposes if we really had to, and of course minor washing chores, clothes and dishes.

We also utilized the standard military Lister bags which when filled with water would evaporate thereby cooling the water on the inside. We had them in Twentynine Palms, but there we did not have dung beetles! In Saudi we had all colors and sizes of dung beetles. After they had munched down on the abundant fecal material so generously provided by the Marines and camels, they were thirsty, and would head directly for the Lister bags, crawl in through some small openings, and have a decent drink. Before we knew it, more dysentery visited us. Away went the Lister bags and we thereafter relied on the bottled water and the water bull.

Arriving in the Saudi desert we were re-introduced to scorpions. This 2-5 inch little eight-legged beast of the desert we had seen before in the desert of Southern California. There, if one of them bit you, death was not inevitable, just a swollen mass of flesh and a pain that lasted for a few days. Here, in Saudi Land, we were not so sure, so we took all kinds of precautions.

Active mostly at night when it was cool, they sought shelter in our shoes, clothing, sleeping bags and whatever. It seemed they were everywhere. One soon learned to shake clothing and empty boondockers (boots) and helmets before putting them on.

Still lacking entertainment, the Marines soon figured out how to make scorpions a center of attention. Scorpion races and scorpion fights attracted the attention of every bored Marine. Scorpions do not kill each other with their poisonous stinger, but they sure can raise the roof with each other in a fight.

Snakes added another diversion, especially the so-called Egyptian Cobra. These beauties ranged from 4-8 feet long and could be as big around as your arm. They are the guys that expand a hood-like feature on their head and can spit their venom at you. Everyone remained alert when on night guard for this is when they moved about, seeking a meal or two. Silent killers, they usually stalk their prey and hiss just before striking. We had very few encounters in the beginning.

When it came to recreation nothing really beat simply watching the camels. Remember, the camel is a horse designed by a committee, and it certainly looked it. Our first glimpse of the beast, this so-called ship of the desert, was during our first move north from Al Jubayl military airfield to the cement factory. Our tanks traveled along the coastal highway with Mercedes whipping in and out around us. I looked over to see this guy passing us on what looked like a horse, but the rider sat way back on its haunches. Then I realized that the beast was the fabled camel. The Arab sitting way back on the rear in a saddle, was beating the poor camel. Its legs were all over the place to keep up the pace, running faster than we were.

All our moves occurred at night when it was cool, and also so Saddam could not see us. When we arrived to establish a new camp we went to sleep with nothing there. The following morning we would wake up in the middle of a herd of camels, all kinds of camels, old ones and young ones. We noticed that each of the camels had a tag in the ear, similar to cattle in the States. We assumed that this identified the owner. At first, the camels would not interact with us, staying a distance away, but eventually they slowly would walk up to us, chewing their cud, and belching horrible stomach gases. They soon found our delectable camo nets.

Camo netting is a kind of plastic canvas material, with a string that holds the entire thing together. The object of the camo netting was not to see a tank hiding in the desert, but to see a tank with a camo netting hiding in the desert. It became a constant battle, chasing the camels away from the netting they found so delicious, but eventually we were able to cure them from eating it.

The camels found other things to eat, some things we thought only goats delighted in. We had managed to scrounge a few picnic tables to eat on and use for writing letters. It rarely rained in the desert, so we thought we could leave our plastic eating utensils and condiments on the tables at night. We still knew little about camels, or jamels as the Bedouin pronounces it.

One night I awoke to a strange sound. The desert has its own symphony of sounds, but the particular sound I heard was more like munching noises. Reaching for my trusty flashlight, I carefully probed the darkness and there were several camels standing near one of our tables. One of them was busy chewing a mouthful of plastic forks, knives and spoons. It was a strange and wild sight, to watch him happily munching away and then, after a fashion, just swallow the entire mess. Their digestive system must be fantastic!

The more we became accustomed to the presence of the camels and how they react, we began to have a little fun with them. We used to empty the Kool-Aid packets from the MREs onto the fender of the tank. A camel would saunter by, stop and sniff the air, grumble a little in typical camel fashion, then walk over to the tank. Leaning over, with its large tongue, it would slurp up the colorful powder. Of course, we saved the grape or cherry colored packets for their bright color.

Not only would the camel slurp up the entire Kool Aid powder, but also would proceed to run his enormous tongue over his lips. Great! Then he looked like a horse designed by a committee with a smear of bright red lipstick! It was hilarious to see. Then the camel would turn away and head off toward the Arab encampment causing his master great concern! His prized camel had these enormous red lips. We did not win any hearts or minds in that campaign!

Constantly on the alert for water, it was not long before the camels caught on to the water bulls. The story goes that camels can smell water miles away and so they could smell where the water bull was positioned.

At first they had no idea how to get at the water. They would stand around belching, grumbling, groaning, butting their heads against the steel tank, frustrated at their inability to get at the water. However, one morning we awakened to find that the water bull was about half-empty. We found traces of the missing water in the sand below, and it did not take us long to figure that the camels were the guilty culprits. But none of us could figure just how they managed to get at the water.

It took one of the night guards to actually catch the camel pilfering the water bull. They had learned that they could spring the metal hatch of the cover. There were two covers on each water bull, and each hatch or cover had a spring-loaded toggle, similar to the old Jeep hood latches. Just pop them and the cover or hatch would open.

Well, each of the camels had figured out how to pop the spring-loaded hatches and would take turns slurping at the water by reaching their heads and long tongues down into the tank. After a fashion they also learned to use their tongues or noses to release the spigot and while one camel pressed on the faucet one would slurp away. By the time morning arrived they had finished off half the water in the bull. The fact that water was chlorinated did not seem to bother them. Water was water! Despite all this they were a great source of entertainment and amusement.

Goats, more great watching, were everywhere. I never really understood what they were until I wrote and asked my father. Were these sheep or some new mutation of a desert animal that had gone astray? They turned out to be Angora goats, which explained their long kinky black hair. We would move into an area one night, and the next day some of the usual camels would show up followed by the foul smelling goats. Phew! The next morning tents and sheep appeared as far as the eye could see. There we were in the great Saudi sand box waiting for Saddam to show up with his mother of all armies, and there were these Bedouin tribesmen and their bleating sheep, goats and camels.

It was not uncommon to see a small boy, a really young

lad, with a bell in one hand and a shepherd's crook in the other, leading thousands of sheep. One instance comes to mind, and had I a camera at the time, the photo would have served as a cover for *Time Magazine*.

We were involved in one of many counter attack rehearsals, making long flanking movement to the right which would eventually turn into a wedge formation, then move straight ahead. As we turned into the wedge formation, the left flank units were moving into position when a little boy, with his ever present bell and crook in hand, and followed by his sea of sheep, came along and moved right across the Company's flank. A tank company takes up a lot of space, especially in a desert scenario. There can be some 300-500 meters between tanks and there are some 12-15 tanks.

The little boy walked out right in front of the left platoon of Charlie Company and so Captain Ed Dunlap stopped the entire company. From my tank I looked over to see what the hold up was. At that moment I wished I had a camera. There was this little boy with his huge flock of sheep stopping the might of several enormous fully armed, battle-ready, M60A1 Marine Corps tanks. It was an incredible sight, one small boy with his bleating sheep holding up the might of an armored column. This incident says a lot about the Marine tankers sitting there quietly in their tanks watching the sheep slowly move by. It probably speaks for Americans in general.

Camo nets were mentioned as a food source for the passing camel. It soon became a part of their food chain. Imagine a pool table with its green felt top. Place a white pool ball on that green, flat surface. What do you see? Why, a white pool ball sitting on a flat green table. Now place a small green net over that white pool ball and what do you see? Why, a green pool table surface with a white pool ball under a green net. We kept putting up these stupid camo nets, orders you know, and the chopper pilots kept telling us we looked just like tanks hiding underneath camo nets on the desert sands.

We did not have yhe engineering capability to dig in the tanks at the time. We did not want to use the only M60 blade-tank we had because we were afraid it would blow the transmission, and we badly needed that tank, so we continued to set up those camo nets and the nets continued to come flying down because of the constant wind. When the big winds, the Shamals, came we put up the nets again and again, all day long.

We had to use the camo nets as the material supposedly had been treated with some exotic infra-red, radioactive, counter infra-red, signature-seeking chemical that was supposed to hide us from any and all electronic eyes the Iraqi might have. One net was supposed to cost somewhere in the vicinity of $10,000. The aluminum poles had plastic tips, but the poles would bend under the weight of the net. Some wizard rocket scientist failed with his calculator and never did get the weight-to-pole ratio correct. The anchoring devices we had were foot-long engineering stakes, and these would not hold the net down to the ground, especially if the sand was soft. The nets were constantly blowing down and we just as constantly put them back up. Nice game!

About the first of October we got the reactive armor tiles for the tanks. When we got the tanks off the MPS ships we never realized that half the tanks had dummy tiles and not the reactive armor they were supposed to have.

Prior to the ground war, the Marine Corps possessed a tank that the Army believed to be obsolete. The modern battlefield had evolved such lethal and nasty methods of killing tanks that the older generation armor of the M60 series tank was no longer survivable on the battlefield, thus the newer generation of Chobum armor with its layers of ceramic, steel and depleted Uranium (not to worry, none of this is classified; it is even on the Net!). But what was the Marine Corps to do, as Big Al, our Commandant, had told us we did not need the new

M1A1 battle tank. The answer was easy. We shall turn to the Israelies, gurus of tankology. The Israeli use many of the M60 series and even older tanks, and maintain their survivability by modifying them.

Thus blazer armor, or reactive armor as it is better known, works as follows. To defeat the armor of a modern battle tank, the chemical-energy, explosive warheads use a principle called the Monroe Effect to focus the energy of the blast to defeat the protecting armor. A shaped charge generates a highly concentrated stream that bores through the armor. To defeat this in turn, it is necessary to trigger the explosive charge prior to impact with the armor. Thus, a standoff layer of armor with an explosive charge to blow back into the Monroe Effect is used to advantage. A series of explosive tiles is attached to the outside of the tank, approximately a foot from the tank's armor. This gives the tank the standoff ability to defeat chemical energy munitions directed against it. This is a very effective asset.

With all these mind-boggling scientific digressions, the tanks of 3rd Battalion had no modifications with the reactive armor. In my two years with the company prior to deploying to the Gulf, we had trained with reactive armored tanks on only one occasion, when we did amphibious operations at Camp Pendleton and used some of the 1st Battalion's tanks. Thus, only a handful of us had any experience with reactive armor.

Upon arriving in the Gulf we met the MPS ships and our tanks. We were surprised to learn that fully half the tanks had not received the necessary modifications, even though we had been briefed otherwise. Only half of the tanks were equipped with reactive armor! Apparently not all the ships had had their maintenance cycle, thus, all the modifications had not been completed.

It gets better! When the tanks rolled off the ships even those appearing to be equipped with reactive armor tiles were not. You see each tile is crammed full of composition B, a nifty high explosive. The folks that sail the MPS ships got a little nervous about having a bunch of tanks lying about with explosive tiles bolted onto them. So the tanks came with empty training plates mounted in the racks. Looks impressive, but the plates wouldn't stop a bullet from passing through!

We sat in the warehouse waiting and fearing the expected Iraqi invasion, with half of the tanks missing the reactive armor modifications and the other half clad only in hollow training tiles. Right! Bet they never told you that one on CNN. The training tiles were eventually replaced with the explosive-filled version; a process by which the hollow ones are unbolted and replaced one by one. Trust me, there are a bunch of those tiles and it is not a fun job working in 120- degree heat. For those of us without modifications, it would be several months before the process would include us. Oh joy! Understand it makes a person feel naked to know that a couple of Iraqi Divisions are running about the Kuwait desert, looking to blow you to pieces, *and you ain't got no tiles!*

The modification included welding a steel framework onto the turret and upper hull of the tank. Onto this jigsaw puzzle tiles are then mounted. Welders were brought into Saudi Arabia from the United States to do the welding at a cost of about fifty big ones per hour. Here I am making a lot less, the troops a lot less than me, and these guys are making $50.00 an hour to weld some funky looking rack onto my tank. Well, at least they did a good job. Thanks guys! The tiles of course are not all the same size. They come in two flavors, square and rectangle. The trick is to get the combination that will fill the rack correctly, yet not block optics or the turret ring. Easier said than done. There is no magic number or pattern because each tank is slightly different, depending on how the man with the torch places the supports. You would think for $50.00 an hour that they could get them alike. It was not until just before the air war started that we finally got the tile count and placement pattern unscrewed! I am just glad we did not have any serious challenge to the reactive armor. Bring on the Iraqis!

During the month of November, it became apparent that Saddam and his friends were not about to leave Kuwait, so we began to think offensive plans. We did not at the time have the assets for that but we had been briefed by the admin folks that we were to get mine plows, mine rollers, an assault bridge that could be placed across the open span of a ditch, and so on. The number of toys seemed endless.

Captain Ed Dunlap, at this point, decided that we would place all our engineering assets in one platoon and so I traded the blade tank I had with Gunnery Sergeant Schofield. Marine Corps doctrine required one blade tank per company and it was usually assigned to the company XO. It was I, therefore, that had been driving about the shimmering desert sands in a blade tank until then.

Captain Ed Dunlap wanted to have a hasty breach element. He also wanted to avoid targeting his XO as a command element. The blade that stood out from the blade tank called attention to the command element housed therein. The blade tank went to the 3rd Platoon because Gunnery Sergeant Schofield was the most experienced tanker in the platoon.

As the mine plows trickled in we placed them also on tanks in the 3rd Platoon. We then began planning breaching techniques and the assets needed to accomplish that mission. Every step is in order and each is necessary and sufficient.

The longer we stayed in the field the more serious the morale problem became. We were not getting mail, especially the care packages, and that demoralized the married folks. When all of a sudden it started to arrive on a more regular basis, up went the morale. Mail always does wonders for lifting morale. The long sought after care packages from home, the Dear Serviceman letters and mail from loved ones arrived by the bag full. It was also wonderful to get mail from folks we did not even know and to receive their encouragement. I was writing up to 24 letters to individuals back home and telling them what we were doing in the great Saudi sand box. We began receiving care packages from folks we did not know, which helped augment the basics we were living on. Some American companies sent us all kinds and types of goodies.

Our maintenance chief had received a small box of Folger's coffee, the small individual bags, that resembled old-fashioned tea bags. He received them from his brother or sister back home. He wrote them a letter saying the coffee bags were a great invention and fulfilled a need of the Marines in the desert. They sent back a case of the coffee bags and told him to share them with his fellow Marines. That was typical of the generosity and thoughtfulness of the folks back home. All this attention boosted our morale considerably.

Then there was the radio station in Los Angeles. They made up a wacky Iraqi tape and if you sent them a request they would send along copies for free. They also included a large decal that had a picture of their party pig on top with the station call numbers and letters. The party pig was obviously their signature. So, we sent for and received all those goodies and in turn placed the large decals on tanks. They looked just great.

A continuing aggravation for the tanker crews was the lack of shoulder holsters for the pistol we carried. Carrying an M-16 was a little awkward in a tank environment. A tanker's weapon is a 9mm Beretta pistol because the pistol allows you to exit and enter a tank much easier than carrying a rifle, an infantry weapon. The hip holster issued to us got in the way, bashing your hip each time you went through the hatch of the tank.

Standard operating rules called for a tanker to be equipped with a shoulder holster. When we deployed to the Gulf most tankers did not have a shoulder holster. We were told to requisition them. Well, it was sort of like a Cinderella story, Cinderella had a better chance of going to the ball than we did of getting a shoulder holster. We found out that when you went to the rear, all the folks there were wearing the shoulder holsters we were supposed to have. Must sound familiar to every vet who has fought in the front lines in a war to know that the rear turkeys were always so well armed and equipped. They were all walking around with the new desert boots, boonie hats and shoulder holsters. Real warrior types those rear-echelon studs. They had gear that we never saw until the air war started and I guess the decision was then made that we would have to go into Kuwait on the ground. Then and only then did we get what the rear echelon already had.

A U.S. Cavalry catalog fell into the hands of 2nd Platoon Gunnery Sergeant Codero. Well, with that little gem in hand, we ordered some fifty odd shoulder holsters. We paid Gunnery Sergeant Codero and he purchased the lot using his credit card. Good-ol' US CAV, they mailed all the holsters to us at a reduced rate. We now had a shoulder holster for everyone in our tanks. No more getting our hips beat up getting in and out of the hatch and bouncing about in the tanks. We never turned them in when the war was over because we had bought them; we owned them. It aggravated the supply folk when they wanted us to turn them in. Of course we told them to take the traditional long walk off a very short pier.

We also had a somewhat regular supply of sunglasses from home. Guess folks realized that the sun was rather bright in Saudi land, so we must need them. Since most sunglasses were plastic, just the act of wiping off a lens scratched the surface due to the fine-powdered sand on them. We all went through many pairs of sunglasses and the sun was indeed bright in Saudi land!

At one point the folks in Groton, Massachusetts sent us a few cases of sunglasses, not packages, but cases. They never arrived. We thought the ship sank, or the plane that was transporting them went down, or the boys in the rear got them. Everyone had to declare a customs ticket on the outside and of course everyone could see what was supposedly in the package. There must have been quite a few lads in the rear wearing those sunglasses from Groton, Massachusetts. We are sorry, folks, but we did appreciate your sincere effort to help us.

Meanwhile, all this time we were still moving about the desert, watching the crazy camel antics, flocks of sheep and goats, and the Bedouin encampments. We kept on the move so that we did not offer Saddam's troops an easy target. It seemed that every time we moved in a given direction, someone on the other side was also keeping up with us. However, they seemed to have a much larger number of folks on the move.

Life in the sands became a more or less routine existence after a while, as routine as living on the uncertain edge of a razor ever gets. The sands blew, the politicians came and went, the waiting continued. And then came the Commandant. The Commandant of the Marine Corps has very little to do with his forward troops once they leave the land of the big PX. CENTCOM and the multi-levels of strata have operational control over all deployed units. Yet, it is good for the little green monsters, or should I say in this case the little sand colored monsters, to see their Commandant from time to time. So, word came down that General Gray, our Commandant, is Saudi-bound. There was joy that day.

At this point I must digress with a bit of background. Those who are familiar with General Alfred Gray, Marine Corps Commandant, already realize how big a part he played in reshaping the Marine Corps of the late 80's and early 90's.

The Corps war-fighting doctrine and recharging of the warrior spirit within the Corps are generally attributed to him. However (always got to have one of them howevers in there) there does exist one group within Uncle Sam's misguided children that does not have fond memories of Big Al. Yup, it is the tank community.

Big Al did not approve the procurement of the latest toy for the tankers, and it is because of that that yours truly ventured forth into the great sandbox in the older and less capable M60A1. Now, the M60A1 is a truly capable weapons platform, but when your Battalion is facing Divisions, the newer, high-speed, low-drag piece of Star Wars technology was looking mighty good to us. So, when Big Al turned down the procurement of the M1A1, it did little for the hearts and minds of the armored community. Those same hearts and minds are fully aware that the Commandant must make decisions based on money, as well as the benefits of state of the art weapons. Trade-offs! Back to the cat box!

The Commandant approached. The question: where shall we assemble the warriors of the sea, now beached? If Mohammed was coming, bad pun given the geographic location, we needed a mountain. So, the troops were assembled around one of the higher terrain features in the next several map sheets, little more than a knoll but beggars cannot always be choosers. Who was to protect this assemblage of the different representative units of the Regiment? Why, the very creatures that were slighted during the procurement phase mentioned above, the Tankers.

Thus the word is received down the chain of command from the levels of rarefied air for Charlie Company of the 3rd Battalion of Tanks, to move to a certain grid coordinate, and with dispatch encircle the key terrain located there. The key terrain in this case being a wannabe mountain from which the mighty one would address his minions.

Mounting our mighty metal steeds we quietly clanked across the Saudi wastes, encircled the towering knoll in a ring of steel, and utilized the approved interval of dispersion to create a safe haven for our minions and our leader. The minions arrived by five ton, and assembled to hear the word.

Tankers are by nature a rather creative lot. When left to themselves, they will not dig like the grunts, rather they will strip down to their skivies (underwear) and work on their suntans. Have to look good you know! Why we had to look good in the middle of the desert, I have no clue, but it is tradition, and one thing any Marine, past, present or future, knows is tradition. Am I right? So, pretty soon the perimeter of steel turns into a perimeter of sunbathing lizards seeking to up their RAD (radiation) count.

In the midst of this a helicopter appeared bearing the Commandant, himself. Off the bird steps the General, to the welcoming throng, his minions, mostly grunts. Soon the echoing tones from the loud speakers are carrying the stirring words across the sands. Questions are fielded and answers put forth. Occasionally one of the alert, sun-bathing, perimeter lizards moves to scratch at a fly or move binoculars around to get a look at the general. He looked taller in the posters the PAO types sent around back home.

Then occured the question that would come to haunt the Commandant; the question about USO shows. How did the leader of the Corps reply? Words to the effect that we did not need USO, the Marines have no morale problem! Reality check. Life at the moment was a morale problem. Five hundred Iraqi tanks poised to pounce on us seemed to our iddy-biddy brains a definite morale problem. I will not continue.

Well the media picked up on this and ran the extra mile as they always seem to do. I don't think that the Commandant meant ill by his statements but the results were the same. Several newspaper articles sent via the mails proved that to be so. Here was the Commandant telling us no USO and out there, photos eventually are produced showing Marines being entertained by Bob Hope! Of course, by then the Commandant was back in Washington and it just so happens that his 2nd Tank Battalion, his choice A Team, of the 2nd Marine division, was transitioning through its training. With the man's A Team now in the Gulf, USO was all right. You figure the rest!

Despite Big Al the USO did come to the Gulf and the Marines vastly enjoyed it. When we received word that Bob Hope was in the area with his traveling show, I guess this was, to me, a turning point. When you stop to think about it, Bob Hope usually toured with his troops in the area where men were about to go into combat! That spoke volumes to all of us.

I had not made arrangements to see any of the other personalities that had come to the Gulf to entertain us, so I decided to go and see Mr. Hope. When we finally got there we were located directly down front, almost on the stage. I could have actually reached out and touched the man. We saw the entire show and enjoyed every bit of it. If I remember correctly, he had Johnny Bench with him and between them they certainly entertained all of us. Hope did not have his usual entourage of girls with him because the Saudi did not allow that "sort of thing" in Saudi Land! I suppose to the Saudi officials that was sacrilegious infidel kind of stuff. So, here we were, Raggedy Marines being a part of history, being there when Bob Hope gave a USO show.

M60A1 USMC 506042

This M60A1 shows the left profile of a very similar version of the Executive Officer's tank, C-52.

Photo by K. Gee

Chapter 6
The 2nd Division Cometh

The 7th Armored Brigade became part of an expanded British force, the 1st Armored Division. On 20 December General Boomer outlined an essentially defensive plan to cover the buildup period. While all units were to prepare for offensive operations, for the time being General Boomer envisioned a mobile defense with the 1st Marine Division stationed in the northern sector as a covering force, 1st Armored Division as a mobile maneuvering element, and the 2nd Marine Division in reserve.

A warrior does not really expect to celebrate holidays while waiting to enter the dead zone of combat, but we did our best to do so just the same. Labor Day was a bust because we worked right through it. Everyday is Labor Day in the Corps. Hurrah! Thanksgiving was perhaps the most interesting holiday I have ever spent. It would not have been much of anything but the same ol' same ol' if it had not been for my dad and the folks back home. Seven weeks prior to Thanksgiving we started to receive package envelopes and boxes of goodies, so we built up a feast by the time the holiday came around. I had received cooking utensils, pots and stuff, which we set aside for the great feast. The day to celebrate arrived, and we awoke to a great wind blowing like crazy, a Shamal. But, what was a little wind?

We were not deterred despite the fact the rain came at us on the horizontal.

We broke out all our stuff, the food, the pots, our tanker stove (a small Coleman type) and all the other good stuff. We also cranked up our hobo stove which was an ammo can with holes punched in the bottom, then filled with good ol' Saudi sand and doused with a liberal amount of aviation fuel. The hobo stove is a wonderful cooking device.

We cooked up a feast and my crew really enjoyed themselves. Later that day it rained and it continued to rain heavily. The Marines brought out the pre-cooked Thanksgiving meal, in an absolute downpour. I remember being served my meal poured into a canteen cup. Slurp. Anyway, they did their best and we all appreciated that fact.

Christmas was another special holiday. Once again the folks back home outdid themselves sending us, a bit at a time, goodies that we could enjoy during the holiday. Of course we squirreled them away inside the tank for safekeeping. No Iraqi was going to have the opportunity of finding our cache. My sister-in-law, Pam, sent candies. You know the type, the little candy corn kernels you get at trick or treat time and a jar of peanut butter. My sister Beth sent jars of her homemade jams and jellies. She said that when she packed the goodies, she went to the hospital, where she is still employed, and threw the package off the roof to see if it would survive a trip to the Gulf. It did!

Somewhere in Saudi Land we managed to scrounge a loaf of ol' white bread, sliced. We were doing a night op and while we waited we sat on the tank eating peanut butter and jam sandwiches. Just outrageous!

When the holidays rolled around, we certainly enjoyed everything my wife and family sent to us. It made a world of difference at Christmas when packages started to arrive, and I mean boxes and boxes of good things. We received boxes of goodies from my father's students and that cheered the Marines greatly. We got a small Christmas tree and I set that up back at Camp 13, the real area. My sister-in-law sent a little tree just a few inches tall, with Christmas decorations adorning it, sort of doll-like furniture stuff. We placed this on top of the tank and it became our decorated Christmas tree in the field.

We listened to Christmas carols played over the Armed Forces Radio all day. We had our Marine Corps Christmas Day feast. The Shamal blew like crazy again, but we still managed to have a good day, mainly because of the goodies the folks back home sent us. It was terrific for morale.

A non-denominational Christmas Eve religious service was announced and those who wanted to boarded a truck and drove to Divisional HQ. Here was a scooped-out emplacement that engineers had dug, covered with a camo net. It was a brilliant star lit night, and they passed out candles to everyone. We lit the candles and had the services by flickering candle light. It was humbling and wonderful at the same time. We all stood there softly singing Christmas carols that were familiar to everyone.

This church service took on a whole different meaning. Here we were, in the Middle East, the birthplace of Christ, getting ready to celebrate Christmas with all the Marines softly singing Silent Night, knowing we would soon be in battle and many might die. It was a very special moment.

Eventually the infantry, Marine grunts or crunchies as we tankers so labeled them, were assigned to the 3rd Tank Battalion. The Germans proved during WWII that tanks without infantry were too vulnerable to other infantry, so we got our covering infantry. During Desert Shield time was spent introducing infantry folk to the versatility of the armored vehicle; i.e., what to expect from a tank.

As Desert Shield gradually began to wear toward Desert Storm various cross-attachments began to form with other units.

This meant the ground-based infantry was to be assimilated into the assault vehicles.

The AAVP7A1, an amphibious assault vehicle, was utilized to move large numbers of infantry from the ships to the beaches. It is not necessarily designed as a land based fighting vehicle, but being the only personnel carrier the Marine Corps had, it was called upon to conduct large-scale ground warfare. The Saudi sand was like having one large beach to clank around on. So why not use the AAVs like the Army does its APCs (Armored Personnel Carriers)?

The infantry climbed into their Tuna Boats, as the tankers liked to call them, and clanked their way across the wastelands of Saudi. Of course, we had always thought that this was the reason for the existence of the U.S. Army.

At this point the Battalion was at full strength, having four maneuvering elements, four companies: three tank and one mechanized (infantry). When we commenced maneuvers to move around within the Triangle, we constantly worked our way north in preparation to push into Kuwait. We moved from one position to another conducting counterattacks, always forming a Battalion perimeter. The perimeter usually involved about four kilometers, with each unit taking up an area of about a square kilometer. Infantry was no exception.

The difference between a tank company and an infantry company was that the infantry always dug in wherever they went. It is a tradition, a way of combat and thinking. No self respecting infantry unit wanted to be caught unprepared out in the open, and so they dug!

When we first arrived in country each tank company had its own blade tank, with its steel bulldozer-like blade out in front. The tank is not really an armored bulldozer, rather a bulldozer blade in front of a tank. It was strictly designed to push around dirt. The problem: push too much dirt, too heavy, too often and you quickly blow the transmission. So, after we dug a few holes here and there, the Battalion folks decided that we should no longer dig-in tanks. No need to burn out perfectly good transmissions. Later we dug when we received a true excavator, thereby saving our blade tank transmissions. The tankers may have stopped digging in but not the infantry; they continued onwards and outwards.

If the infantry was left to themselves long enough they would dig condominiums, a small-sized underground city. It always amazed us that they managed to scrounge the timber used to shore up their bunkers.

Later on when I became an infantry instructor at TBS (The Basic School), I would become more versed in the world of grunt excavation and the science behind it. I observed that they began by digging two-man fighting positions along with appropriate listening posts and sundry other posts. The posts were then provided with overhead cover, fighting positions connected with a trench. Finally they would dig toward the front and tie in the listening posts if they had the time. And we always had thought that ants were the great diggers with their maze of tunnels.

As usual our encampments and perimeters did not last long, perhaps four days. One might think four days is not enough time to dig an elaborate maze, but give credit where credit is due; the Infantry will live up to their usual standards. Just give them a shovel and they will dig all over the place, any place, and create what looks like a prairie dog town.

Add to this those inhabitants of the desert that followed us where we traveled and there is bound to be humor. We would move from one position to another, and in a matter of a day or so, the usual camels, goats, sheep, tents, the BFOs (Black Floating Objects) and all those things associated with a Bedouin encampment, would suddenly appear. The question of course that comes to mind is where did all these people come from and what are they doing way out here? We could move from one side of the maneuver triangle to the other and they would show up. How? We never had any contact with them, no trading, no barter, not a thing.

Along with all the animals and tents came the family, and this included the one member of the family that particularly interested the Marines, the female. One usually saw this blob moving about the campsite, gliding over the sands, and turning out to be the female. They would be covered from head to foot leaving much to the unhampered imagination. It is difficult to explain what we saw to another person unfamiliar with the culture of the area.

The females dressed in a black sack, a large body bag with vision slits cut in the top end. Dressed in a black robe and black veil they never resembled a human being. They appeared to float over the ground in the shimmering heat; therefore we labeled them BFOs, Black Floating Objects.

Very early on we had been instructed to respect the BFOs, considered very important by the male Arabs who considered them property, like a car or a camel! No one messes with property in Saudi Land as the consequences are too severe to contemplate! If you mess with a BFO you are going to be in a bucket of trouble. During our stay at Al Jubayl, after the Major got into trouble with his camera, we were constantly warned: STAY AWAY FROM THE ARAB WOMEN!

Let us place this in proper perspective. Here we are in picturesque Saudi Land, no booze, no women, no nothing except the sand. All we saw was an occasional camel chewing on our camo netting, plenty of scorpions fighting each other, and slithering snakes. In other words, ZZIPP!

One night we did the usual by pulling up to wait and see what the morning would bring. The infantrymen began their ritual of digging. Morning found the Arab encampment was out in front where the infantry was busy digging up the sands, and of course the usual BFOs floated over the sand, doing whatever they do to keep their men folk happy.

Colonel Alphonso Diggs, our esteemed leader of the 3rd Tank Battalion, being the good Battalion Commander that he was, decided to make his rounds and check the perimeter. As he drove around the area he noted that the infantry was very busy at their usual digging and that was good because digging Marines are busy Marines and busy Marines are happy Marines that do not get into trouble. On day one of his perimeter check he noted that they had dug forward.

Day two of his perimeter check revealed that the Marines had dug forward even further, and so into day three. It did seem a bit unusual that they had neglected to dig the usual connecting communication trenches, tying their fighting holes together. Day four, Colonel Diggs noted that they had dug forward even further, and so the good Colonel studied the matter for several minutes. The secret reason the Marines kept digging in one direction was soon revealed. These busy folk were working their way toward the Arab encampment. But why?

Well, it turned out that the object of their energetic endeavors was to better observe the BFOs. It seems that any time a BFO had to answer the call of nature, she moved outside the encampment and hoisted her robe to squat. Our brethren of the infantry Marines were simply digging to improve their ability to observe. Colonel Diggs understood and stopped them from digging any further from the camp. No one wanted to interfere with our Arabic brethren.

Mention should be made of the arrival of the famed Marine Corps A Team, Big Al's saviors of the Middle East, the 2nd Marine Division. The term A Team comes from the designation of an Army Special Forces Operational Team familiarly referred to as Green Berets. They are highly trained and extremely competent force multipliers. The Army A Team is given impossible missions that somehow succeed, and they generally are at the highest rung of the warrior ladder.

Commandant Gray's association with the term derives from a speech he made at Camp Lejeune when addressing the Marine 2nd Division. He called them his A Team during a pep talk, not a bad thing to do, very inspiring. But it was picked up by the media and promulgated widely, and there lay our problem. We smelly ones who had been surviving in the desert for months without creature comforts or amenities, and who expected probably to die, did not take kindly to the implications of the A Team's arrival. We had endured a life of deprivation and hardship, had been whisked away from our families on short notice, had survived extreme temperatures, and we had held a thin line in the sand. We were proud of that. Then came the word that the varsity team would save us. We were agitated.

Shortly after moving out of the port complex into the lush green fields of Saudi, rear elements of the 3rd Battalion moved into a former base camp of ARAMCO (Arab American Oil Company). It may be worth noting that the largest percentage of the Battalion consists of the H&S Company, the Headquarters and Service Company. It is this element of the Battalion that allows the trigger pullers to close with and destroy the enemy. The H&S Company is the resting ground of the higher echelon maintenance and logistical support of the line companies. Without the butter, bullets, fuel and bolts provided by the H&S Company, we riders of the steel behemoths become useless. Of course, we still referred to them as REMFs (Rear Echelon Marine Forces)!

Anyhow, the rear area of the Battalion moved itself from the port facility into the former oil company camp. Now, this is not a camp in the fashion of a summer vacationland that many boys and girls go off to, tying knots and learning about bugs and canoes. This was the great sand box, and the Saudis were dealing with infidels in the Holy Land. They want the infidels around to help with the oil, as it is Allah's will that the Arabs have the money from the oil, but the infidels must stay out of sight when not working in the wondrous sandy wastes on the oil platforms.

The solution was to construct a high-walled compound with all the facilities needed, i.e., chow halls, laundry and dormitory spaces with showers and flushing heads (toilets). It sounded like a great place to allow the infidel warrior Marines to take advantage of a little R&R. We little sand-colored monsters cannot stay in the sands indefinitely; the Arabs did not want us running amuck in the populated areas; stick them in a camp somewhere. The 3rd Tank Battalion and RCT 7 as a whole shared this rear area delight, known as Camp 13.

Periodically, depending on the training and movement schedule, about one-third of the company rotated to the rear and occupied a dormitory building. This allowed for a rotation every 8-10 days, with the promise of a shower and air conditioning at the end of the period. The camp offered a change of scenery with greenery everywhere. Saudis planted lots of green things for the infidels. This wondrous place offered the opportunity to write letters and sleep without flies zooming up your nose. The camp also provided one of the most important facilities of all, a telephone. Here were public telephones.

It was not until the later stages of the operation, during November and December, that the telephone centers began to appear in more forward areas of the rear. During the initial stages of standing up against Saddam, mail was the only means of communication. So a rotation to Camp 13 allowed for the use of a pay phone. This usually meant taking one's place in a line of always over fifty Marines. All would show up with the all-important gas mask, reading and letter-writing material. As Marines would take their turn on the phone, the line would slowly but surely advance to the phone. Waits of 3-4 hours were not uncommon, and in all that time, I never once heard of a fight or tempers flaring in the phone line. It was as if the telephone place was sacred ground, and no one wanted to raise the wrath of the phone gods!

The saying states that all good things must come to an end, and they sure did! Shortly after Christmas, good timing, word was received that we were to pack our belongings and do the sea bag drag to Manifah Bay. Elements of the 2nd Division would be moving in and they needed the Camp as a staging area. Now wait just a #$%<f&@*@#@ minute. Some of us had been forward deployed for five months now, one month short of the time to qualify us for the SSDR (Sea Service Deployment Ribbon), for all you non-naval service types, and we are being booted out of Camp 13 so the new guys in town can have the flush toilets! Not to worry, oh you smelly tankers of tattered uniform, you now have shower stalls in the field, easily accessible to your needs. So what if the desert is barely above freezing during the day; now you must make room for the famed 2nd Division to acclimate. Acclimate? Acclimating happens in August when it is above 100 degrees at midnight, not in December when the weather requires a coat and a sleeping bag!

Being good grumbling Marines, move we did. It would be three months before I had a hot shower that was not exposed to the wind and weather, three months before I would sit on a commode that did not have to be burned at the end of the day. How did this go over with the 1st Marine Division? Let me illuminate. Just prior to the start of the air war one of the corn gurus, Corporal Flores, and I ventured to the rear to perform a much needed errand of logistical importance, i.e., fool around, and pulled into Camp 13. We arranged to meet at the Hummer in a couple of hours, and I proceeded to the Pakistan-run odds and ends shop. On the way I spied a couple of fellow, tattered, desert cami-clad Marines, approaching the store. After six months of harsh field conditions, our camies were by then falling apart. Who approached at the same time but several green cami-clad, polished-boot Marines (I had not seen polish in months).

As we two groups approached the door at the same time, one of the green team jokingly stated, "Don't worry, boys, the A Team is here now."

I am not certain what about that statement sent the cami-clad Marines off, maybe months of flies, months of MREs, months of living with the looming specter of death on the horizon. All I know is that one hit the green cami so fast and hard no one had time to react. Amongst the teeth and blood, the desert-clad warrior Marines walked off leaving me with a lasting impression of how the little sand colored monsters felt about the issue concerning the 2nd Marine Division and Camp 13. We may be all one Corps, but there exists a division as real as the line that divided the North from the South during the Civil War. Yup, Big Al's A Team had arrived.

Right after Christmas our mind-set began to change. We started reorganizing equipment but still practiced maneuvering for defensive war. New engineering assets began to appear, such as the armored excavator (armored bulldozer) and the towed assault bridges. All this increase in assets just did not fit the defensive role we had been practicing. It did not take a rocket scientist to realize that we were going to invade Kuwait and tangle with Saddam and his mighty army. Remember it was heralded as the mother of all armies. Right!

We realized that with the increased rhetoric used by Mr. Bush, as reported on CNN, we were getting ready to do battle with Iraqi forces just across the wire.

We continued to move from place to place about every 72 hours and each move was one of a tactical learning situation. We would be attacked by LAVs (Light Armored Vehicles) then counterattack, a drill on how we would fight that particular type of situation against the Iraqis.

We did most of our movements at night, a good thing because later it provided us with a lot of good night-training experience. The Marine Corps has always preached, "If you own the night, you own the battle."

There was not a lot of live fire training. Prior to the ground war we perhaps squeezed the gun triggers two times. The first was to zero in the main gun after we got the tanks away from the MPS ships. The second was at a range complex where we maneuvered and fired. That was basically it because we were restricted from shooting the main gun. We did fire the small arms many times but not the crew-served main battle weapon.

Dealing with the Saudi military was very different than we expected. Although they were happy to have us there, keeping the Iraqis behind the line, they treated us like snake-oil salesmen. It was very obvious how they felt about our being there even though we were supposed to be part of the same coalition forces.

When we first got the tanks off the MPS ships, the vehicles basically were in good shape although missing some items like the armor tiles mentioned before. These were good tanks compared to the broken down relics we had at Twentynine Palms. Do not misunderstand, the maintenance folks took tremendous care of our vehicles and not enough can be said or written about how hard they worked to keep everything moving, but when a tank gets old, malfunctions and other things happen far too frequently.

The problem was multifaceted. When you fire the main gun, when you move the tank, when solar energy works on that gun barrel, new relationships develop. Where the optics point and where the center of the gun barrel points generally become different. The question on our minds: where and when do we shoot to re-align these very important elements?

We bore-sighted and did anything we could think of short of shooting, of pulling triggers. This problem for a tanker is crucial. You need to know where you sight. Alignment of the main gun barrel with the sight must be one and the same when you have to pull that trigger in combat.

Then we discovered there were no practice rounds, these being like the actual combat depleted uranium rounds in that they are designed to give a visual mark when they hit their target. What? No practice rounds? Well, you will just have to forget about zeroing your main gun.

Excuse me!! We are about to go into tank-to-tank combat and you yahoos don't think we need to zero in our main gun. Oh joy! We knew that we needed to get a kill with the first round fired; those guys thought we did not have to zero our guns.

The actual comment from the logistic source was, "Too bad you don't have any training rounds. The MPS ships don't have any and there are none to be had at this particular time."

Words must have been uttered by those in the know and who had some pull with the higher ups. Evidently they were able to make those who did not understand realize that we could not survive in combat without zeroing our main gun. We did not get our training rounds, but we did get to utilize so-called Black Bullets, the depleted uranium rounds, which made us nervous. Think about it, depleted uranium!

We finally moved to a nondescript section of Saudi Land, lined up the entire company of tanks and commenced to blast away with real honest to goodness live ammo! I feel certain there were a number of three or two-footed goats running around when we got through!

It was a spectacular sight to see that line up of tanks, all blasting away, for it was photographed and of course made many national magazines and newspapers throughout the world, the mighty Marine warriors zeroing their outdated M60A1 tanks getting ready to do battle with the mighty Saddam! The Old Breed Marines leaped to their aging feet and trundled off to re-enlist. Hurrrah!

Now that we had our main gun zeroed in we were ready

for combat. We had battle positions we could go to, especially at night, for we had calculated that Saddam would decide to cross the border and have at us at night. The bean counters never really thought we had a chance of stopping the Iraqis. I guess everyone, including the brass, thought we were going to get wiped in glorious living color. Well, had Saddam, the Wunderkind, made his move at that time with all his traveling circus of clowns, it might have happened just that way.

A close companion to intelligence, or lack thereof, is that entity known as the scud missile. According to the intelligence briefs given by our purveyors of military knowledge, the scud missile was a short range surface-to-surface missile capable of carrying a limited payload of conventional explosives, or the rather unsavory and unconventional chemical or biological types of warheads. The accuracy of that missile was never clearly defined, but omnipresent powers indicated that said missile system was an area weapon rather than a pinpoint delivery system. Thus, the scud threat was born.

I cannot speak on behalf of those multitudes of rear area dwellers that occupied the all-important hotels, rear area tent camps and the other assorted dwellings that rear area types inhabit (sorry, I lived off a tank fender for seven months and saw a flushing commode less times then you have fingers; except if you are a former combat engineer type, then maybe I flushed the arable commode more times then you do have fingers), but for those of us who spent the excursion to the sand box forward deployed, the scud threat was less of a threat and more of an amusement.

In the case of missiles being launched at Israel, the scud was seen in a very different light. Those were a threat, for if the Israelis decided to respond we might all be glowing, or be up to our armpits in Arabs that were our former allies. When the word came from CNN that a scud had been launched in that direction, we sat up a little straighter and paid closer attention. Yes, the word of attacks on Israel came across CNN faster then through our channels; what did you expect?

In the case of domestically targeted scuds, the case was a wee bit different. I do not recall any daylight scuds, seem to remember them being thrown up after dark. So my memory is one of either sitting around with the HQ tankers, or with the 1st Sergeant and Top Sergeant listening to the evening radio shows when Armed Forces Radio played the Lone Ranger, Buck Rogers, Gang Busters, etc. The Marines loved them. Without TV, we little sand-colored monsters used our imagination, and some one would yell "look at that" or "hey" and we would look up to see a streak of light heading from north to south. They looked just like the shooting stars that we would see back home in the stumps. But a little different in that the little bugger would not burn out as it passed.

Well, as the little shooting star thing headed south another light would shoot up from the horizon in the south and there would be a dull flash over the southern horizon. Every one would kind of "ooh" and "aahhh" at the fireworks, and return to what they were doing. If a radio was close at hand we would tune in to the CNN to hear where the thing had come down. We always figured CNN was staging the thing because they had an answer for everything.

About ten minutes after the fireworks were over, and we were all listening to a reporter telling us he was on a roof in Dhahran under attack, we got some flash traffic on the field phone. "Hey XO, flash from higher. Scud attack probable!" "OK!" So we would go back to listening to the CNN broadcaster going on about a possible chemical threat and how he is under attack and all. About another ten minutes would go by, and the phone would ring again. "XO, scud attack imminent." "No kidding, Thanks!" Change location to some other reporter on a roof in Saudi Land with air raid alarms wailing in the background, going on about how many scuds had been launched, and how many Patriot missiles had countered. (Hmmmmm, only saw one heading south, other ones take the turnpike?) Ye ol' faithful phone would once again do its thing. "XO, would you believe we are under scud attack, missiles inbound?" No, really, never would have guessed. Get out of here.

By this point the reporter standing on the roof was getting a little old. Think about it, everyone else had secured for condition zebra and got out of town or into a bomb shelter. Who would be on a roof waiting for a good-sized piece of the blown up scud to land on him. Tell me CNN was not choreographing. But the only game in town kept us listening.

All good things come to an end, and so do scud warnings. Another ten minutes would pass and the tired phone would once more summon the energy to do its thing. "XO, we can secure from Scud attack now." Oh good, back to the Lone Ranger!

I guess if my tour of duty in the big kitty box had involved my being in the rear, scuds might have been a bigger issue. But, with my carcass living off a tank in the middle of nowhere, scuds provided far more entertainment than threat. To those who lost their lives to the scuds that did make it through the Patriot umbrella, I feel truly sorry. I at least had the chance to fight back. They did not.

I am glad the Isralies respected Bush so much, and did not shoot back, definitely glad.

We knew that the air war was going to kick in before we actually got involved on the ground. The flyboys were there to win the war for the coalition. All one had to do was ask the air bubbas and they would tell you so.

The night the air war started, I was sitting up on the tank with the crew. We were in the usual philosophical discussions Marines are famous for. The moon was almost full, the Marines were at 25% alert, and I decided to turn in and get some sleep. It was a restless sleep because a lot of aircraft were passing overhead. This was unusual because we saw aircraft only rarely. Once in awhile we would see one streaking across the horizon, hurrying somewhere, and there were the ever-present Marine choppers, kicking up the desert sands, but few jets.

Jets were now flying, in large numbers, high overhead toward what we assumed was Iraq. Eventually the Assistant Communications Chief, Corporal Flores, came over and said, "Hey XO, just got flash traffic; the air war has just started." I lay there with my back against a wall of sand thinking we were not about to be heading back to the MPS (Maritime Prepositioning Squadron) ships without something major happening on the ground.

As a ground pounder, I never thought the air war was going to win all the marbles. No one ever thought that Saddam was just going to pack up and leave. "Gee, there are so many planes, I am overwhelmed and so now, I take leave. Adios, amigos." No way was that about to happen.

After the air war began we restricted most of our movement to the shadows of the night. Tank movements progressed steadily north and west out of the Triangle area. Movements no longer emphasized a training value as we prepared to kick off the ground war.

During one of the many moves north, I was introduced to my FAC (Forward Air Controller) for the first time. Captain Jeff Butler, call sign Mumbly, was a Marine Harrier pilot we had trained against back at the Stumps. There during one of our field exercises with fast movers (jets) one of the fast movers was piloted by none other than Mumbly himself. Small world!

FACs work either with an infantry or a tank unit. Of the two, an armored unit is preferred because the FAC does not have to walk around with a radio strapped to his back. With tanks, he rides! Now, that is a big job-enhancement factor. Up to this point, I had played the role of Forward Air Controller, and now we had our very own FAC. We knew for certain that the cow-puckie was about to strike the whirring multi-bladed device.

With the addition of Captain Mumbly, we now had additional radios to deal with and that meant more antennae sticking up from the tank.

There is a basic rule in tank warfare: the more antennae on a tank, the more important that tank is. Therefore the tank with the most antennae is the tank shot first.

Chapter 7
The Chemical Situation

On the mind of every Marine who served in the Gulf War was the fear of the unknown effects of the many chemicals encountered, from both our side and that of the Iraqis. In this age of high-tech warfare, where missiles seek each other, even in the dark, destroy at a distance beyond the capability of the human eye to see; penetrate armor of unbelievable thickness and hardness; it was the little bug, the germ, that frightened warriors the most. This type of warfare is difficult to deal with because the enemy may never be seen or detected, unless you are very alert or very lucky!

Doing combat with a foe who would employ biological and chemical devices involves counter-germ warfare and anti-chemical warfare, vaccines, gas masks and chemical warfare clothes. Shades of WWI. Therein lies the problem for the Gulf War vet.

Pre-Persian Gulf War, NBC (Nuclear, Biological, and Chemical) training was a joke. How do you prepare for a nuclear strike? The usual answer was, "Bend over, put your head between your legs and kiss yourself goodbye!" How do you prepare for a chemical strike? Repeat the aforementioned instructions. The NBC officer for the Battalion accomplished the training goals for the Battalion. He was very knowledgeable. He, as with all the NBC officers, cared about the training and what was presented. It was not the Marine Corps, but the Armed Forces brass that had neither the necessary resources nor the inclination to better prepare for a real chemical or biological threat. When the time came to deploy to the Persian Gulf it suddenly dawned on everyone in planning, "Hey, those Iraqis have a stock pile of chemical and biological warfare stuff!"

Everyone, military and civilians alike, knew that Saddam had utilized chemical warfare, even against his own people. That should have spoken volumes of what we were up against, at least to the good ol' boys in planning. Here we were deploying to the Gulf with the mission of being ready to go directly against Saddam and his army, and a vast array of chemicals and biologicals. Of course the scuttlebutt was simple, "He won't dare use the stuff because the world certainly would crucify him." Right! Certainly there would be some harsh words thrown his way!

A lot of brainstorming and jury-rigging went into planning how to combat this situation, utilizing the resources we had on hand. The MOPP Suits (Mission Orientated Protective Posture Suits) we wore probably dated back to the 60's. That gave us a wonderful, warm, fuzzy feeling of confidence. The only time we had ever used them was inside a gas chamber for familiarization. Once or twice on a CAX (Combined Arms Exercise) we donned them for a few minutes and then turned them back in. We had no real experience with suit utilization, not even suit decontamination procedures.

We all felt the threat was ominous, discussed its ramifications at great length and decided to take it seriously. I will not state that there was a fear among the Marines, but there were many unanswered questions that made us feel somewhat uncomfortable.

When we showed up in country we went through a series of briefings about the threat. The media quickly picked up on these and ran wild with it. "Saddam is armed with chemicals and biologicals; Saddam will do this; Saddam plans to do such and such; and so on and on. By the time the media got through sensationalizing the chemical warfare situation my gas mask never left my side, the same for other Marines. It went everywhere I went, my constant companion. After the Gulf War, back at home, occasionally I had nightmares, awakened and found no gas mask beside me. Bummer!

The threat portrayed by the media was so great that we felt we were going to get wiped from the face of the earth by a devastating chemical attack. I am not sure we ever really believed we were going to get chemically flogged, but it seemed everyone else thought so. We had no idea of just how we were going to decontaminate ourselves. Given the material we had on hand, and the situation of being in the desert with water a premium, there was no way we could deal effectively with this. This was not a situation of how well the marines would fight their way through this mess; they would give their all. It was a situation wherein the Marines had not been given the proper means to be effective.

The media continued to have a reporting field day with the biological and chemical aspects of this war, but then the air war started. This gave the ground pounder a real chuckle when the flyboys informed us we had no worries because they were going to win the war single-handed. They saw our role as going in and mopping up the stragglers. Sure, how often has that statement been made and in how many wars? Since the advent of the airplane ground forces have been told they were no longer necessary. We knew you can bomb the living stuff out of the enemy, but until you put a tanker or grunt on his ground and take the war to his backyard where you enforce the rules, you have not conquered.

It came down to knowing that Saddam was not about to throw in his hand and give it all up. Lessons from the Vietnam War taught Saddam that the American people would not tolerate another war like that, especially if there were horrendous casualties. With this supposed mother-of-all-battles, we were all to become casualty figures, and fast. That was the implication.

We knew that we would have to punch through his defensive barriers and give his army a bloody nose in some fierce combat, but we also believed that he was determined to fight and would resort to the use of chemical and biological warfare.

Not to worry is the by-word of the day. Not to worry young man or woman serving your country, we have everything necessary to protect you against the abominations of the microbial and chemical world. Because we are looking out for your well being, we have all the necessary drugs and chemicals to combat whatever evil Saddam can throw at you!

These drugs will build up your immune systems, strengthen your body against these chemicals and biologicals, and allow you to continue the mission.

I do not remember any of this mentioned during peacetime. I do not remember any of it at all! There was the standard treatment for nerve gas agent that was presented in training exercises. For this we knew there were autoinjectors of Trypanchloride and Atropine. Added to this was a third offering of Valium. After you have gone through the process of sticking yourself six times you were to inject the Valium. Is not Valium a relaxant, a tranquilizer? One day I asked a very senior Hospital Corpsman about the added Valium. I had enough chemistry in college to make me ask questions. The public information reasoning was that so much Trypanchloride and Atropine acted as a heart stimulant; therefore, Valium was needed to reduce or counteract the reaction.

The senior Corpsman responded, "Sir, that is simply to put you out of your misery. With that much Trypanchloride and Atropine running hog wild through your system, there is no way you can survive."

Being my usual self, I viewed with a jaundiced eye all

this information about being protected from chemical and biological warfare through the miracle of modern chemistry.

After the air war had commenced and the aviators were whipping the poor ol' Iraqi, we were finalizing our plans for the ground war. We were one move away from the final assembly area, a matter of miles from the Kuwaiti border and the first of the obstacles.

While we waited, we were given our last minute attachments (added personnel for special purposes). We formed up, marched to an assigned area, and heard about an option. The option had a very long string attached.

"You know the air war is doing a great job up there, taking out any chemical launch systems and any vehicles that can launch chemicals toward you, but (there is always a but) we are still faced with a probable threat. We have this wonder drug, this remarkable vaccine that we can shoot you with, and you will not have to worry about it."

"Since Saddam may use anthrax or some other such stuff, we are prepared to give you a series of two shots that will prevent any problems, should you be exposed. We want the officers and Staff NCOs first because we want leadership by example."

All the PFCs, Lance Corporals, and Sergeants were looking at the officers and wondering, are you guys doing this thing? If you do it, then because I trust you as an officer, I will too. It is Marine Corps doctrine and tradition that officers lead the way. You either lead, bleed or get outa the way! Sound familiar, Old Breed?

"Sir? Just sign here."

"Wait a minute, what's this?" I ask.

"It is a standard waiver, sir."

"A waiver? Are you giving me a wonder drug so that if I get into a situation where my rear end is being handed to me by some little bug or chemical, you want me to sign a waiver?"

"Yes sir. No waiver, no shot."

Some situation! I was standing there, the Company Commander was standing there, along with other officers, and we were all thinking the same. We were to sign a piece of paper that basically states that I am not going to hold you liable or responsible, forever. However, if I don't sign this scrap of paper, those Marines behind me might not take the shots. Hey, if the XO won't, why should we, right? Whatever your Lieutenant does has to be right. After all, he was made an officer by an act of Congress.

Many thoughts ran through my head. What happens when we do roll through those breaches and we do get zapped with some exotic chemical? A good number of fine Marines might lose their lives for something that I did not agree with, or did. However, if it smells like, tastes like, and feels like snake oil, it must be snake oil!

Drummed into every officer and NCO was the doctrine that you were to safeguard your Marines to accomplish the mission. You do not waste lives!

So there it was, the result of all that indoctrination, all that superb training, the XO of Charlie Company, along with the CO and other officers took their shots, signed the papers, and the Company lined up like good little sheep because the officers lead the way. They trusted us to see to it that they would not be harmed. In the end, we really did let those good Marines down. When I see today how many are suffering, I know we let them down. It surely was snake oil! I don't remember how many days later we got the second shot but I do remember they issued us our desert boots at the same time. We finally got boots like the boys in the rear had all along. We got our last shot and desert boots two days before we went into combat. We hardly had time to break in the boots.

I got my shots and signed that paper, but never received a copy. They were stacked nicely, whisked away, and we never saw them again. Later we found out that the drug was not even approved by the FDA (Food and Drug Administration), and folks back in the States that had been given the drug for test purposes had turned up very sick. They gave it to us anyway.

They also gave us another neat little pill. We jokingly called it the birth control pill, looked just like it. These packs of pills were labeled Pyridostigmine Bromide, nerve agent pre-treatment tablets, to be taken every eight hours. To this end I would set the alarm on my watch.

We got an experimental vaccine, a nice little pill to take every eight hours, and one more preventive measure. Just in case the Iraqis dropped a dysentery bug, we had to have Cepracol, an anti-diarrhea medicine. Nothing like having more than half the Marines running into the sands for relief in the midst of battle. Sigh, we took that one as well. I do not hold a degree in biochemistry but with all those chemicals running loose in my body, I wondered if they were having synergistic effects. Did anyone else ever think about this?

We were not through yet. Add to this mix of elements the use of depleted uranium. My college chemistry memory says depleted uranium is a metal residue that is left when the natural uranium ore is processed and refined. Someone figured out that it could be used in artillery shells, rockets and bombs designed to penetrate the armor of tanks and such. It could be used to form shielding for armored vehicles. Remember our missing protective plates?

It is stated somewhere that depleted uranium is relatively harmless, especially when sealed in the artillery shells, rockets and bombs. It seemed to me that just like regular armor steel, the depleted uranium oxidized (rusted), especially in the humid Middle East. We also noticed that the metal burned and oxidized into minute particles when a round was fired or exploded against a target. We inhaled the stuff. Uranium, processed or not, is toxic. More snake oil!

I wonder just how many Marines and other military folks were exposed to depleted uranium? I know of a few who were hit by friendly fire. Those were depleted uranium rounds that ripped into them. Even if the uranium fragments were quickly removed from their bodies, they probably have kidney or liver problems.

It was a tough situation, one that left every Marine who served in the Gulf wondering, "Just how competent are the individuals who manage our military? Do I dare marry and have children? If I am already married and have had children since the Gulf War, will there be problems with my children?" Tough situation, tough questions, indeed!

Eventually, as we know now, the air bubbas did not win the glorious war as they anticipated, so we were committed to the war on the ground. Charlie Company became the lead company, of the lead Battalion, of the lead Regiment, of the lead Marine 1st Division. We went through the obstacle belts, berms, mines and all; and that night outside of Al-Jaber Air Field, in the pitch dark, the FOX vehicle (chemical sniffer) sounded an alarm. The FOX vehicles were our mechanical hound dogs. Ours sounded off several times during the night. Chemical sniffers went off in other units, too. Later as an instructor at TBS (The Basic School), I was able to talk with other Marines who had been there. They assured me that they had similar experiences.

The FOX vehicles sounded off because of the sulfates and other impurities that can be found in the roiling smoke from the burning oil wells. The FOX vehicle was one high-tech vehicle. It could sniff out multiple chemical substances at the PPM (parts per million) level, screen them, and differentiate between chemicals. That sniffer went off a few times behind me and whatever it was must have gone through me like the well known Cheese Whizz.

When the sun finally came up, all that passive NBC tape

that we had plastered around the tank had blisters. It was not just my tank; others surrounding me also had blisters on their tapes. We held up our little chemical identification card to see what these little blisters meant. None of them matched the chemicals found in the burning oil wells! There are petroleum distillates and other large molecular compounds formed as the result of burning. The little legend card showed none of these.

Finally, after we packed up and went home. An entry was placed into my military record that this Marine spent time in the Al-Burqan oil fires. I was hocking up black stuff from my lungs and wondered what might be going on. I had been injected and stuffed with several other chemicals. What were these chemicals doing in my system? The Defense Department, in all its wisdom, stated that there is no such thing as Gulf War Syndrome. Okay.

My experiences remind me of syndromes after the Vietnam War, no syndromes there either, and some very unhappy feelings rise to the surface.

I do not have enough information about what happened to me, to us, while in the Saudi Sands. Was I exposed to chemicals? Yes, starting with those plugged into my body by my government, and those inhaled from burning oils wells and unknown chemicals unleashed during the night. What happens in the future? We all worry about that, about cancer for example. It takes so long for some biological damages to show themselves somewhere in the body sacred. This is the unknown that may cut my life short from my family. We will always wonder. The already large number of identified victims, increasing each year, leaves me wondering if I will see our sons grow to adults.

Lieutenant Chris Freitus

Executive Officer of Charlie Company and Tank Commander of C-52. See photo on page xxxiv.

Photo exerpt by A. Martinez

Chapter 8
Final Preparations

The Iraqi offensive against Kafji hastened the northern movements of division units. Within hours of the assault, Colonel Fulford had Task Force Ripper on alert and ready to maneuver north.

Once the excitement of the first large engagement subsided, life for most of the Marines returned to the familiar routine experienced over the previous months in the desert. They awoke each morning to an almost featureless landscape, washed themselves, brushed teeth, ate what were known as MREs (Meals Ready to Eat) or food sent from the United States, shaved as best they could, and trained, performed their duties, and otherwise went through another twenty four hours in the desert.

Like anthills, the Battalion larger camps came alive each morning. Vehicles drove in and out taking officers to meetings, picking up or delivering supplies, or carrying individuals simply on their way to do something different for a few hours on one pretext or another. The turning point of each day was the arrival of the truck carrying the "Cooked Meal." Though some Marines grew fatalistic of ever again experiencing good food on a regular basis, the food truck signaled the shift in activities to preparations for another night.

It was February in Saudi Arabia and the weather got

*cold and wetter. Tents collapsed in the night from a combination
of rain and wind, which resulted in frantic cursing, confusion
and a sudden effort to put them back together. Infantry, tank,
and mounted battalions, which long before dispensed with all
tentage except for their command and control centers, simply
suffered that exposure as they had the heat months earlier. As
each day in February passed, Marines got progressively more
weathered in appearance and noticeably thinner. The long
anticipated offensive was about to happen.*

With the ground war becoming a possibility, we were
transferred to an enormous Saudi range complex. Not only did
we clear our weapons and live-fire the main guns, which had
been done only once since we had arrived, but we could now
advance and fire at targets, exactly what tanks do in combat. It
was a good experience, an excellent rehearsal for the ground
war, and one badly needed.

We also rehearsed clearing berms, knocking down the
berms, passing the tanks through, and clearing simulated obstacle
belts. We also practiced crossing deep ditches, heavy coils of
barbed wire and the inevitable mine fields. Reality turned out to
be different. Reality was less barbed wire, a few shallow ditches,
smaller berms, and only a few mine fields.

We practiced with the new mine plows, which was an
experience and then some. It took some getting used to their
intricacies. During one particular practice, Lieutenant General
Boomer and other high-ranking officers came to see how we
handled all these new toys. We ran a tank with a mine plow
over a live line charge, Boom! Great show!

The intelligence flow, or lack thereof, became a sore
point. As usual we were like mushrooms, kept in the dark and
fed a continual diet of you know what. For example when we
deployed in August, we did so without cold weather gear. So,
questions began to surface, "When does it begin to get cold

here?" "How cold does it get in Saudi land?" No one seemed to know the answers.

What plants and animals were considered dangerous and what else should we be aware of? I knew there were poisonous plants and animals in the region, but this basic information never reached the Marines in the field.

The Battalion Intel Officer was a great guy, but even he could not get answers from other Intel (intelligence) sources. Just before the air war kicked off and someone figured there would be a ground war, Intel began to trickle in a bit at time. We could turn on CNN and pick up more needed intelligence than we were provided through regular channels. It was from CNN we learned about the Iraqi units on he other side of the wire from us, their possible strengths and compositions.

For instance, we knew that the main Iraqi battle tank, the T-72, was a Russian-built tank, an excellent weapon with a low silhouette, but not equipped with a long-range gun. The Soviets generally did not engage in long distance standoff battles.

Since the Russians had trained Saddam's massive army we had an idea of what to expect in combat. We knew the T-72 to be an excellent tank, but we wondered if the M60's 105mm main gun could penetrate the sloping, armored front of the T-72? The answer came back an unqualified no. The pucker factor (degree of tension in sphincter muscles, sometimes a euphemism for fear or apprehension) just went up another notch. Later, during our actual ground war, the answer was proven to be wrong, but we had to learn that during live combat.

This small but valuable piece of intelligence was known by the Army folks at their Aberdeen Proving Grounds, had known it for years. I learned so after the war was over when I was sent to Aberdeen as the Armor Officer at TBS, Quantico. Yet, this Intel was never made available to us. We had a capability we did not realize until the ground war commenced.

I had my own personal Intel services, seriously. My

father, an old Navy type who had been in the area once before, fed me bits and pieces of intelligence he thought we should know. Good things we really needed. From books and other sources he mailed a constant stream of information, including charts and pictures, headed our way. We learned about temperature variations, the famed Shamals, full moon dates, the wonderful Egyptian Cobras, scorpions and lizards. How else did I learn what kind of cobra there was in the area?

When the ground war was about to get underway, he provided information on the city of Kuwait; we wondered how he knew where we were headed? CNN?

He provided us with Intel on the width of Kuwait streets the physical layout of the city and outskirts, where the water towers were located, and where we could swing the main gun on the tree-crowded streets. He had friends who were the architects that built the City of Kuwait and they could provide anything we might ask for. The humorous story he tells is that one of the engineers when leaving Kuwait, stepped forward to the CIA and offered all this Intel. They told him they already knew all this and there was no need for him to become involved. Perhaps they knew this Intel, but it never reached down to us. Like I said, we sometimes felt like mushrooms.

During one of the moves from the Triangle, all officers were sent to Battalion where we listened to a Naval Officer, a medical doctor. He had been a Navy Corpsman, a "Doc" as we call them, in Vietnam. One of the survivors of his Corpsman Class, he had no trouble getting our attention for one of those talks not given to those who were homeward bound. The good doctor tried to make us understand that after we had made all those tough decisions that would affect many lives, we would eventually have to try and fit back into civilian life and lead a normal life. We knew we were headed for combat. It did not look like we were going home soon.

This would be one of many so-called pep talks we

received. The talks started off with Major General J. K. Myatt, our Division Commander, coming in to clue us in on the big picture, what our role would be, and which divisions made up this thrust into Kuwait to take it away from Saddam and his troops. Of course, when you are going to be the tip of that spear which is about to be thrust into Kuwait, you do not quite share the same enthusiasm or perspective. You are more worried about the shaft from behind!

General Myatt, Big Mike, gave us a big hurrah talk, including Ripper's position. Ripper was the call sign of the Regimental Task Force, or 7th Marines. Tiger Three was the call sign of the 3rd Tanks.

We had all the arty folks telling us how they were going to manage the war. The air bubbas still were telling us they would have someone on station every six minutes, so all our FAC (Forward Air Controller) had to do was call to bring someone on station in less than a minute, raining upon the enemy below. Sounded great!

A giant sand table caught my eye; it was enormous. There was no place better to have a sand table than right on the Saudi Sand. It was decorated with blue arrows and General Myatt, utilizing his four-foot pointer, occasionally stabbed at something on the sand table. To describe it as impressive is an understatement. This was the coach giving us a real pep talk. Finally we were dismissed.

Three days later Ripper wanted to talk with us. Colonel Fulford from Regiment spoke to us. We did not relate to Division when we were the point of the spear, but Regiment was a different story. That we related to. Colonel Fulford got right down to reality and specifics we understood.

He gave a good hurrah talk, got everyone pumped up. We felt he knew what was happening. We spent about a week at the training range and then moved back to the Triangle area. After a short stay, we made a series of three moves, road marches, the last being to an assembly area at the border just before moving through berms into Kuwait.

We continued the routine of constant movement within the Triangle, never allowing the Iraqis time enough to determine where we were. There is a kind of novelty about seeing marines in the desert, as most folks associate us with the island-hopping battles of WWII, the mountain fighting during the Korean War, or the jungles of Vietnam. Now we stood up for months in the desert of Saudi Arabia, and we moved about every few days.

The Army moved about the areas utilizing HETTs (Heavy Equipment Tank Transporters). The Iraqis, when they hauled out of Kuwait with their tanks, did so using some HETTs. Not so with the Marines. When a Marine tank moved, it was done either under its own power or towed behind the tank retriever.

From the day they rolled off the MPS ships, to the day they were parked and forgotten at the back gate of Al-Jubayl, the fourteen tanks of Charlie Company moved only under their own power. The Corps had no organic HETTs. I can count on one hand the number of times we operated the Company either on a paved road or actually within sight of a paved road. The move from the port complex and the move to the Triangle area were two of those occasions.

After moving into the Triangle area, a period of approximately six months would pass before we had occasion to cross over a paved road. Company personnel operated extensively on the coastal highway and intersecting roads in the area, one leading to Camp 13 and another to Al-Mashab. These operations were conducted with the Company's wheeled vehicles, no tanks.

As the time came close to the dawning of Desert Storm, the tempo of field operations picked up. This raised the logistical concern of running the tanks to the point of breaking them. Obviously during the bleak times, when it was two battalions of

Marines Corps armor and the trip wire of the Army Airborne against divisions of Iraqi armor, we did not train as much in order to save the equipment. As the Army got its act together and stood up its units, the training definitely picked up in tempo.

Soon we were training with multiple battalions on the playground, ultimately conducting regimental exercises with Ripper, as a whole. Eventually the air war kicked off, and the nature of our training took on a deadly seriousness. A couple of trips about mid-January to Al-Mishab, Battalion rear area, had shown me a great deal of activity. It was nice to know that the Army was really there after all. We never moved on roads at this point. We really had become desert rats, living like them and looking like them.

We were worn about the edges, a little worse for wear, yet we kept ourselves as clean as possible and our area policed in good Marine tradition. Not all our coalition buddies shared that tradition. On one of our moves we stayed in an abandoned Saudi National Guard position. We had done that only once before, when we were moving all over the place during Desert Shield. The abandoned Guard position was a litterbug's dream. The food and trash all over the place reminded me of a sanitary landfill. No one had bothered to police the area. There were snakes, Egyptian Cobras and rats everywhere possible. I assume Colonel Diggs pushed the issue with the Brass because we never encamped in a position like that again.

Snakes! Ah, so many stories to tell about snakes and so little time. But there is the tale of our good Colonel and the snake. Our Battalion Commander was the right man at the right time and the right place! The old saying, "I would follow that man to hell and back should he lead!" applies to Colonel Diggs. If the Colonel ordered me to go forward I would go forward without question. The higher echelon wanted to divide the tanks among the infantry units, but Colonel Diggs managed to prevent the breakup and keep the tanks as a single battalion, as they should be in fighting a desert war. Those who understand tank warfare understand this principle.

However, the good Colonel had an aversion, the slithering, undulating, crawling, lurking, skulking reptile, the snake! He just did not care for our slithery brethren in any color, length or character. Did not like them in the Stumps. Did not like them in the great Saudi sand box.

With this in mind, I see the landscape, a giant kitty litter-box in the middle of a pool table. I see the tanks in place. I see the total darkness of the desert night, the desert creatures, even us bedded down in our sleeping bags. I imagine our dreams that have nothing to do with tanks or the Marine Corps, some most likely lewd.

A lone sentry walks among Headquarters Company vehicles. Because we had set a perimeter watch it was determined that we really did not need a full watch in the HQ area, as we were located directly in the middle. The thinking was, if something should get by the perimeter folks we needed to get ourselves in motion and take action.

In this particular case, a certain staff NCO was manning the watch. This Gunnery Sergeant, now a Master Sergeant, had with him a SAW (Squad Automatic Weapon). Somewhere along the way we had acquired this light caliber machine gun, usually considered an infantry weapon. This weapon was assigned to Headquarters and as the night watch rotated stations, the weapon was passed around. It had a lot of firepower and it looked good. If you look good, the enemy tends to leave you alone.

So, Gunny was armed with that magnificent weapon of mass destruction that made him look good, the good ol' John Wayne, Sergeant Striker image. He walked his post from flank to flank, taking no backtalk from any rank, when lo and behold what should appear but a slithering reptile, a snake. It was sneaking across the wondrous Saudi Sands, heading for some unknown destination, perhaps an unsuspecting helpless night creature hiding in the dunes.

The mission of the Marine Corps, loosely paraphrased from multitudes of manuals and reference books, is to locate, close with, and destroy the enemy.

The Gunny had definitely located and identified an enemy and was closing with him. He was about to fulfill requirement number three, destroy the enemy. He was not about to take evasive action. Quickly he removed the safety from his awesome weapon of destruction and proceeded to fire a long burst into the slithery intruder, ripping it to bloody shreds.

Except for the duty guards, everyone was snoozing, tripping carefully through dreams, when all of a sudden, BBBBBBBBBBBBRRRRRRRRRRRUUUUUUUUUUPPPPPPPPPP, bullets flying everywhere!

Pandemonium! People were leaping out of their dreams into trousers, grabbing their weapons, grabbing gas masks, running around, jumping onto and into tanks, striking the camo nets, powering up systems. We were under attack!

That was not just one round fired. That was a burst from a machine gun, a whole bunch of rounds being sent down range! I rolled onto the ground, not one thought given to snakes, grabbed the ever-present gas mask and handy 9mm pistol and yelled to the guard. "Sound Off!"

Not a thing! Silence! I was not out on the perimeter but a few hundred feet away from the blasted machine gun. I was sleeping in the sack dreaming XO dreams, and a machine gun went off real close to my head! Now I was up and alert, but someone had interrupted my sleep, and so I was slightly cross. No, I was really mad!

No one answered me when I yelled for a report. I quickly looked around, took stock of my crew, and found them all up with pistols firmly in hand, wondering what was happening. All my people were accounted for.

I shouted again, "Who's on guard? What's going on?"

This meek voice, the Gunny, replied, "It's okay, XO. It's only me, Gunny."

Hmmm, "Gunny, you just shoot a snake?"

"Ah, yeah."

"You just shot a snake!"

"Yes sir."

"A big snake, Gunny?"

"Sir, not really."

"A big cobra snake?"

"Sir, not really."

"What'n hell did you use the SAW for?"

"Sir, it was all I had."

While the Gunny and I were having this discussion in the middle of the night, in the middle of the great Saudi desert, I heard a sound in the background, the ringing of the field telephone.

Our Company Commander, Captain Ed Dunlap, was not present because he was in the rear at Camp 13, having a refreshing shower, drinking cold beverage stuff, having hot meals, and sleeping on a soft bed under a real roof that keeps the rain out. That left me, the XO, Acting Company Commander. That is why the telephone had dutifully been placed on the fender of my tank.

I knew who was on the other end of that phone, Battalion Himself. Oh, there was no joy in Mudville that night.

"You going to answer that, sir?"

"Yeah, I'm gong to answer that."

"Gunny!"

"Sir?"

"The weapon is on safe?"

"Yes sir."

With a cringe I picked up the phone. "Charlie Company."

"What 'n bleep is going on?" came a voice from our Battalion Command.

"Sir, we just shot a snake."

"Snake," he blurted.

"Yes sir. The situation is secure, sir."

This was the moment that the entire Battalion was standing itself up, preparing to repel the vaunted 15th Medina Guards Division.

"You shot a snake?"

"Yes sir."

"Excellent. Carry on," he muttered and hung up.

You know, I know the Old Breed knows, any Marine knows, that was not how situations work out in the Marines. We know that. That was not to be the end of the incident. Over at Battalion CP, under his tent, sleeping on his cot, dreaming Marine Corps Battalion Commander dreams, was Colonel Alphonso B. "Buster" Diggs, Tiger Three, himself.

The good Colonel was sound asleep on his cot, away from the snake he despised, when the machine gun exploded. Colonel Diggs unzipped his warm sleeping bag, leaped from his cot smack into a thick briar patch attired only in his BVDs! He gave the world a fine dressing down, forgetting the snake that was dead.

Gunnery Sergeant, now Master Sergeant, Codero, learned a lesson and will no longer shoot at snakes with an automatic weapon.

Marines, all combat personnel, want their body to be identified so we carried ID Tags in different places on our bodies. I had one around each ankle and a set around my neck, on a small chain. I had also placed my wedding ring on the same chain around my neck. It seemed the logical thing to do as it is not advisable for tankers to have too much jewelry on them. It might make contact with the large variety of electronics onboard the tank and zap!

I was walking across the sands one day, when I suddenly felt the absence of the ID Tags, ring, and chain about my neck.

I stopped and felt around the inside of my shirt. No tags. I then felt around the bottom of my trousers and could feel the lost tags. I didn't have the trousers bloused but the strings at the bottom were tied, which kept the missing tags safely inside. I quickly opened the bottom of the trousers, very carefully, letting the chain and ID tags fall into my hand, but no ring!

With several members of the company I must have spent three or four hours looking in the sand. No wedding ring. We never found it. Marine warriors are not superstitious folk, but right then with the air war raging overhead, battle order maps going up, and us getting ready for a ground attack, the loss of my ring served as a bad omen. There was no other way I could look at it. This was the wrong thing to face battle, but that ring was the single physical connection I had with my wife, and now it was missing.

Our next move was a temporary one so we did not bother to dig in the tanks as usual. The bulldozers came around and built a small berm around our tank, and the pucker factor intensified. These were not stationary emplacements; just short stays on the way to the barrier, which meant the Saudi-Kuwait border. We approached from the south, near the Tap Line road, and would eventually cross it heading northwest. It was also at this time we received our infamous anti-bug shots and vaccines along the way.

Captain Ed Dunlap called me and said, "Why don't you get with Captain Mancini and see what is happening here."

Captain Mancini was the skipper of Alpha Company detached to 1/7 (1st Battalion of Infantry, 7th Regiment, or in total, I MEF). By means of a cross detachment that basically gave 3rd Tanks three tank companies; Bravo, Charlie and Delta, and one company of infantry meshed with armored assault carriers. The cross gave 1/7 three companies of meshed infantry and one tank company. The organization was going to place Charlie Company as the lead tank company. It had been decided that 3rd Tank Battalion was going to lead the Regiment through the obstacle belts with Charlie Company in the lead. Once we closed with the obstacle belts, we would set up a protective umbrella on the Saudi side. 1/7 would then move up through the tanks, pass through the belts, proof those lanes for mines, work our way up to the next obstacle belt, and repeat. The Battalion would simply be two companies up and two companies back. Through all this Charlie Company would remain one of the point units. The pucker factor just went up another notch.

At the same time, Alpha Company would be passing forward through our lines. What we were doing is a long established Marine operation. This was the typical beachhead invasion; establish the beachhead and drive your forces through a narrow point, then expand the beachhead once the objective was taken. The beachhead in this case was the Iraqi side of the barrier and once we were there we would begin to spread out. Today tacticians call it maneuver warfare. Of course, when an obstacle belt is faced, one begins to wonder where the maneuvering part went.

"So, XO, find Captain Mancini and bring him back so we can have a little chat."

I hopped into my HUMVEE and buzzed off into the wilds of the desert. All of a sudden I came across a giant trail. Most folks have seen National Geographic and have seen the narrow dirt tracks or paths that camels and a few vehicles use in the desert. This was no narrow, camel or utility dirt trail. I later learned this was the Khanjar Expressway. I saw trucks, armored vehicles, water tankers, fuel tankers, cargo transporters, dragon wagons, self propelled guns, and the first M1A1s (battle tanks) I had seen to date either with the Army or the Marines. This was to be one of the biggest armored engagements since the great tank battles of Kursk from my perspective.

I knew the Israelis and the Arabs had fought with some pretty large numbers, and George Patton and his armored corps ran about Europe, covering an area the size of New England. Still, it boggled my mind to think of the size of the overall Desert Storm Operation, and what an insignificant number we were in comparison.

But then, I remembered, for the first few months this small Marine Regiment was the only force we had in country, and we were expected to stop the mighty Saddam.

I scooted through three or four lanes of several tanks and finally managed to find 1/7. Captain Mancini agreed to meet with us and hold a discussion. He did come over with his XO and others. We all hunkered down and I remember looking around at the faces, realizing we had done this one before.

Each time we moved we went through basically the same discussions and meetings. Every time we had done so in the past it was always with a controller, the military referee with the white band around his helmet from the TECG (Tactical Evaluation Control Group). I remember thinking that this time no referee was going to tell us how to get through a minefield. This time there would be people out there that wanted to stop us, kill us, to prevent our tanks and equipment from going through. During this discussion we listened very intently, not missing a word or inflection.

I watched the intensity with which all the officers and NCOs listened. With all the time we had spent in the desert, we were now ready to have at the Iraqis and see just how good their capability was.

The Marine Corps of today likes to portray itself as the most professional organization of warriors ever to grace the face of planet Earth. To a large extent this is true. Today's Marine is high-tech oriented, better educated, and a well-read tactician of the battlefield who uses all the latest in gadgets, gizmos, and satellite wizardry. Today's Marine has a better knowledge of his adversary.

Communications are encrypted and secure from the

listening ears of the one we are trying to destroy. Radio frequencies can hop around more times a second than politicians can change their minds on what ROE (Rules of Engagement) should be. Yet, many things remain the same. The more things change the more they remain the same an old saying goes. Among these things are the notorious call signs.

All units are given unique call signs that identify it on the radio net. Each call sign changes daily, providing another layer of security. The reality is that small units, such as companies, do not always abide by the assigned call signs while using internal radio nets. Collective call signs arise.

Charlie Company had several collective call signs to identify the various platoons and command elements. I could never find out how long these had existed. They seemed to be handed down over time. For example: the First Platoon was Red, Second Platoon was White, and Third Platoon was (can you guess?) Blue. The Company Commander was Gold and yours truly, the XO, was Silver. We even had one for the tank retriever, Heavy Metal. Thus, while using internal nets we did not need to constantly revise and update our call signs.

A dilemma arises, how to get the entire Company to respond or execute a command. An example is the short count to start all engines in the Company at the same time. This is a technique to mask individual engine sounds in order to help conceal how many hogs you have. During a staff meeting this topic was brought up, and became the center of a heated debate. A voice was heard to say, "How about Gang Bang," referring to the initial deployment to the Gulf during Desert Shield.

Thus, the Company Collective was born. The procedure is, "Gang Bang, this is Silver, Short count in 5 minutes." Simple and direct.

I am not sure how Battalion felt about this colorful, if not original, company collective; but in a way it served as a statement as to how we viewed the world in which we found ourselves. Guess today in this world of political correctness and the fear of sexual harassment this would be viewed as being inappropriate. It only gets better, or maybe worse!

Graphic control measures such as Control Points, Fire Control Lines and Phase Lines are as important to armored warfare as the entrenching tool is to the grunt. When moving large armored formations across the map, command and control becomes much more complicated. By placing onto a map the control features common to all players on the battlefield, command and control becomes much easier. "Red, move to phase line Green and hold." Usually, the words *phase line* would not be spoken. Thus, command and control is simplified and maintained all in the same abbreviated transmission. Phase lines were assigned to the two obstacle belts that Ripper was tasked to breach. The first belt was named Saber (phase line Saber).

How does a phase line work?. When an element reaches or crosses over that line placed on the map, the unit's higher Headquarters is notified. When Charlie Company crossed through the minefields, yours truly, in accordance with Captain Ed's battle plan, radioed, "Battalion (the appropriate color)."

Within the Company we kept matters simpler. As the Platoons, or CO, or retriever crossed through the breach sites, each called me and informed me, "Home Free," meaning, for example, all members of the Platoon are across the breach. Although I knew we had a long road ahead of us, it was a good feeling after the second breach to call the CO and let him know, "Gold, this is Silver, all Gang Bang is Home Free!"

With the increasing number of artillery firings, raids across the border, and aircraft aloft, we continued to build our plans toward crossing the border. We all knew where we were going, what we were going to do, even though the actual OP-orders had not been drawn up and given to us. President George Bush had given his famous speech with an ultimatum to Saddam in effect, "You can throw down your arms and start walking north and we'll call it quits." We wondered if he and the General Staff thought that Saddam would really throw down his weapons and beat it out of Kuwait.

At this time, Master Sergeant Graham, or Top Graham as we say, was the tank leader (OPs Chief, logistical coordinator, Charlie Company). He began to have these strange nightmares. So did I. We had signed for an incredible amount of gear, munitions, ordnance, all very expensive electronic wizardry. If Saddam and all his Iraqi friends decided to take the Prez at his word and go home, someone would have to account for all these military items we had been playing with for the past several months.

I could see it all before me. "O.K, XO, Top Graham, where are the 27 M25 anti-tank mines? Where are the RXM3J-6000563456789 hoozzi-whats, which by the way are worth $18,500 each." Top Graham and I began to wonder how to account for all that stuff. We didn't want to start looking and accounting. When we realized the ground war was actually going to happen and we were going to be shot at, we discussed which was the lesser of the two evils, accounting or war. We determined it was war.

On the last move to our final position before jumping into Kuwait, I had an accident. I was riding in the tank with my head stuck out of the hatch as usual, goggles on my helmet (Rommel effect?) and the sand scarf around my neck. We were suddenly hit by one of those frequent dust devils, those mini-tornadoes. I did not blink just at the right time and got sand in my right eye. One of the Saudi grains decided to tear its way across the surface of my eyeball, scratching the delicate tissues, and causing the eye to weep and swell. It looked awful. I irrigated it as best I could, but by the time we got to our destination, my eye had closed. I went to the skipper and said, "Sorry to do this to you, but with this eye I need some help."

The CO sent me to the armored retriever, which also

acted as our armored ambulance, among other things. The corpsman looked into my eye and proclaimed, "Sir, you need to go and have the Battalion Surgeon look at you. There is little that I can do for you here."

On the way to the Battalion aid station, I was literally overwhelmed with the horrible feeling that the doctor was going to look into my eye and say, "Comfort." Comfort was one of the Navy hospital ships that stood by at sea. He could even send me to the hospital located at AI-Jubayl.

During the early days of Desert Shield that situation could have been a welcome relief from the tedium of the desert sun and fun. Pretty nurses, good food, and those clean sheets to sleep between. Ah, the good life. But, with a jump-off time of 0200 hours the next morning into Kuwait, and I could not see out of my right eye.

I envisioned myself with the Company going into combat with me comfortably tucked away in the rear. My Company and my friends would be in combat, and I would not be there with them. I had been with Charlie Company for three years and had gotten to know everyone and all the problems that go along with being a part of that unit, a team. I did not want to be taken out of the game.

I arrived at Battalion; the surgeon treated my eye, irrigating and carefully cleaning it.

"Well," he said, "that is about all I can do for you." Looking directly at me, he asked, "What do you want to do?"

I answered, "Go with the boys."

He placed a patch over my eye and commented, "Twenty four hours," and dismissed me for duty.

During the day and on into the early night we went through a series of checklists, preparatory work a unit must accomplish before going into combat.

Previously I had written letters to my wife and my folks, but had not mailed them yet, personal things that had to be written because of the possibility that they would never get written otherwise. Listening to the radio we had become very aware of the numbers game and our survival did not seem to be a real probability.

I also wrote a letter to my two-year old son, Kyle, and asked my wife, Venus, to hold the letter for later. When he decided that he was angry because he did not have a father around, she could give him the letter, which would explain things to him.

As it had for many months in the desert, darkness finally enveloped us. I remember climbing up the side of the tank and standing there, looking off toward Kuwait. It was still twilight, but what greeted me was an enormous wall of black smoke, so intense it blocked out the setting sun. This is where we were heading. Every so often the ground would tremble as the air OPS were still pounding the awaiting Iraqis. I looked around at the assemblage and thought, "Just get me home, Lord, so that I may serve my family." I remember thinking about Kyle. I had not given him much of my time as the Marines required most of it, I wanted to be able to go home and be with him. I remember praying, which was not new to me.

We waited for the Chaplain, a Lutheran, I believe. He was a wonderful man, always there when a Marine needed him. He had just arrived from Okinawa when we deployed. Welcome to 3rd Tanks, padre. As the communion wine was unavailable, his wife was sending it to him in Scope bottles and dutifully dyed green with food coloring. Couldn't have booze in Saudi land, you know. One could say that the Reverend was having a good ol' Irish mass, green wine and all.

He presented a no-nonsense, non-denominational mass, or service. We all sang a couple of hymns, said some prayers, and heard a to the point sermon. He blessed us and sent us on our way. We wanted our God to know that our hearts, as warriors, were in the right place and that we prayed together, because later there would not be time to do so. Some of this seems a bit corny now, but it did not seem so at the time.

Just before we kicked off for Kuwait, we picked up a correspondent from the Marine Corps side of the house, Staff Sergeant Vaughn. Can't remember his entire name, but he joined Charlie Company that afternoon. He took a sizable number of human-interest pictures of all of us getting ready for war. He spoke with everyone he could, asking about their feelings and what kind of preparation they were doing. He ended up riding with the assault engineers, as did the Kuwaiti translator. Man-o-man, we were all set now.

Captain Ed "Phil Collins" Dunlap
Commanding Officer, Charlie Company
Photo by C. Freitus

Chapter 9
G-Day

On the evening 22 February General Myatt, Colonel Fulford and Colonel Hodory calculated that the hints offered by developments along Task Force Grizzly's front suggested the Iraqis were not enthusiastic about fighting. Later that night, Task Force Taro and Task Force Grizzly reported by radio that the area between the two obstacle belts was neither heavily nor resolutely defended. That agreed with intelligence and nothing happened during the night to alter the impression. By the time Task Force Ripper launched its attack, Marines in the waiting assault vehicles felt they were going against a defense that already seemed to be coming apart, at least along the first obstacle belt. At 0405 Task Force Ripper began the drive that would confirm that suspicion.

The attack began at 0001 with receipt of the code word, Coors, meaning Task Force Ripper to depart the assembly area. Radios came to life, vehicle engines were started and the task force began moving to its attack position. Colonel Fulford put the two mechanized infantry battalions and the tank battalion in a task force wedge formation. Using night vision devices, the drive forward was slow and deliberate, as expected for a night movement. At 0125 Task Force Ripper crossed Phase Line Black on schedule. Scouts saw no sign of enemy, although thirty minutes later Colonel Fulford received an aerial surveillance report indicating the existence of an enemy: four tanks, six BMPs (Soviet-manufactured personnel carriers), and a suspected command post in front of the task force.

While moving to its attack position, Task Force Ripper picked up its FAC (Forward Air Control) teams, artillery observers, naval gunfire teams, a SAT (Surveillance And Target) acquisition platoon, and its mine-clearing tanks. Colonel Fulford deployed these elements on 23 February to check and mark the route, secure the attack position, and make last-minute adjustments to ensure the assault went smoothly.

Unit movements were controlled through the use of phase lines. The lack of identifiable terrain features meant that for the ground offensive, Division's phase lines were tactically placed lines on the map, reference points. Commanders used a combination of PLRS (Position Location Recording System) and GPS (Global Positioning System) to provide them with their unit's exact position.

Phase lines were generally named after colors, going from Black at the Kuwait border to Red just south of the Kuwait International Airport.

Ripper's advance, well rehearsed before the ground offensive, proceeded well, arriving at its attack position at 0200, an hour ahead of schedule. Engines idled in the darkness then were shut down as the task force settled in to await division orders to attack.

At 0359 General Boomer informed General Myatt that G-Day and H-Hour had been confirmed. The division attack was preceded by a B52 strike and at 0410 Myatt told task force commanders to execute the attack plan. An hour later General Myatt directed Colonel Fulford to send Task Force Ripper across the line of departure near the first obstacle and begin the main attack.

After we had obtained the battle graphics, each of the

tank commanders, separately went to Captain Ed Dunlap's tank and made copies for themselves. The most prominent features of the graphics maps were the obstacle belts, one primary and one secondary.

The area that we were to breach was of regimental size by intelligence estimates, supposedly determined by Recon groups that had sneaked and peeked.

Minefields were originally buried in proper military fashion, but now many were exposed due to the constant strong winds. Wire barriers had been inserted to prevent frontline Iraqi troops from rushing over and surrendering en masse. After the air war began, maintenance of the wire became almost nonexistent because the Iraqis moved around very little, trying not to reveal themselves.

Later in the day we assembled at Captain Ed's tank. It was not one of those meetings to study a training exercise or discuss a mock battle with a hypothetical Iraqi division or battalion. This was it for us. Everyone was very attentive, quiet and asking good questions. We had rehearsed and practiced, and now Captain Ed issued the Go Orders. The meeting was not long but very productive and, of course, up went the pucker factor again. I returned to my tank and met with our FAC (Captain Mumbly) and the HQ (Headquarters) tankers to go over the orders. It was a walk-through, no surprises.

The company was to appoint a Recon (Reconnaissance) mission. We needed an individual in charge of the mission who would become explicitly familiar with our planned route. With me still somewhat done in with a bad eye, Captain Dunlap selected Gunnery Sergeant Cochran who had been an Army tanker in Vietnam and had considerable experience. Gunny formed up the Recon unit and went to the berm to survey. Later he would brief everyone on the passage that would occur during the night.

Recon positioned on top of the berm and surveyed the-belts that lay beyond. When Gunny returned he briefed us on his observations, including a burned-out T-55 tank pointing toward the Saudi portion of the force line. No need to shoot it as it was already dead. It was probably left over from the Kafji firefight. The pucker factor went up again.

From this point we played the waiting game. Courtesy of the FAC our crew was able to listen to the air war as aircraft passed over our heads on the way north. He was able to tune to the controlling agencies on his TACP (Tactical Air Control Party) radios, and gave us a blow-by-blow account of the big game. We even listened to a tank strike just to our north.. That one kind of hit home for us.

To the north of us B52s were engaged in what was called Arc Lights in Vietnam, when they dropped enormous amounts of ordnance on an area. We could not see the results but we certainly could feel the earth tremble with the weight of the explosives. All that stuff must have torn the Iraqis to pieces.

I remember sitting atop the tank and thinking that there was some Iraqi soldier hiding in his sand hole trying his best to kill me, and at the same time he was doing his best to survive the awesome power of hundreds of bombs falling about him. It was a paradoxical situation. I felt sorry for him in a way but, at the same time, it was he who overran Kuwait, not me. He would try to kill me and I in turn would try to kill him. I tried to remember the scene from the movie *Lawrence of Arabia*, where the French representative said something like, "War is the breakdown of politics." Sounded about right, but someone should have added, "It is thousands of nameless souls who must fight that war, not the politicians who caused the breakdown in the first place."

Toward evening the wall of smoke in the distance became more evident. It was similar to Dante's Hell, with all the oil wells ablaze. The smoke appeared to be a giant, roiling, living curtain in the twilight sky. Maybe Saddam had ordered the torching of more wells, or maybe its growth just seemed to grow in portentous foreboding of deaths to come. It felt ominous to know that was where we were going.

As we settled down we pulled off the camo netting for the last time. We celebrated removing that cursed net. Yeah! This was the last time we would need this foolish thing we had come to dislike so much. Then we thought about it some more. Did we really want to take this big awkward thing with us? Did we want to travel into a raging battle with this stupid camo net tied on the backside of the tank? Silly question!

The camo netting becomes a big object when it is secured inside its canvas bag. It reduces visibility for the tank commander when the tank is buttoned up for combat. Naw! We jettisoned the blasted thing right there. $10,000 worth of netting and poles, the whole nine yards, were heaved overboard.

I went over to wait out some time with the skipper, Captain Ed. We had little to say, just stood near each other and rambled once in a while. We were really trying to support and reinforce one another. I respected this man greatly. He tried to make me a Marine tanker and leader of men and I looked up to him for the effort. History will judge how effective he was. We discussed the IR (Infra-Red) beacon that had been placed on his tank. The IR beacon, a little device invented by some fellow from New Hampshire, was set up to flash an infrared light about every three seconds. Unseen by the human eye the beacon would act to warn coalition forces with IR detectors that we were friendlies.

Due to the several friendly fire incidents, it was decided that the forward units would carry wide international orange panels on top of the tanks so that the flyboys would identify us and not shoot us up. We also had added the notorious inverted V on the sides of each vehicle. We were for anything that might reduce the possibility of getting shot at by our own side.

Captain Dunlap had his orange panels displayed on his

tank and in the middle was his IR beacon; his was the lead tank. I remember thinking at the time, Captain Ed would be out front, lit up like a Christmas tree and therefore a perfect target for any sharp eyed Iraqi gunner with decent night vision and an IR sight. I realized that if someone smoked him I would end up being the Company CO, under those circumstances, something I did not want!

Captain Ed Dunlap provided me every opportunity to act as company CO, giving me the chance to flex my wings while still the XO. The timing of the Gulf War gave us a unique opportunity; we had a much longer relationship than most COs and XOs have. Most Company Commanders at the time held on to their command for about a year, then rotated into a staff position at Battalion. When the Gulf heated up, Charlie Company was almost at the point of changing its Company Commander. The Gulf gave Ed a chance to hold on to Charlie Company for almost two years. That gave us opportunity to work out the occasional bug in our working relationship, and I think it gave me the opportunity to become a more effective XO.

Ed's confidence allowed us to do something unique although not quite doctrinally correct. The Company Commander, according to the manual on tankology, calls for the CO to maneuver his three gun platoons, coordinate the indirect fire of the company, all the while answering the never-ending demands of the Battalion radio. This is akin to parting the Red Sea.

The Brits have a rather clever solution to this problem. They have the Battle Captain. The British CO, termed a Squadron Commander in accordance with traditional British Cavalry, has an officer that monitors the command net, and acts as a relay and call talker. This arrangement frees the CO to shoot and scoot, run the business of war. The Battle Captain relays all sitreps (situation reports) and passes on instructions as the situation allows. Good system, but not doctrine for our way of fighting.

During several of the training OPs into the sun-baked wastes of the Stumps, Ed Dunlap let me fill the role of Battle Captain for him. I was able to free him to fight the company, yet he was able to monitor the net with out the need to respond. Another advantage was that the extended period of command gave him trust in his XO (Extraneous Officer).

When we packed up our battle plan and took it on the road, the plan worked well, with Battalion allowing us the flexibility to operate as Ed saw fit. During the ground war I handled most of the radio communications that were exchanged on the Battalion net, notifying Ed when Battalion wanted to speak to the CO himself. To those think-tank types at Fort Knox who write doctrine it worked well regardless of what the FMFM (Fleet Marine Force Manual) says!

Back at the tank, I caught a short nap and suddenly there it was, time to get the show on the road. About 2350 we did the short count, which meant that all the tanks fired up at the same time. The noise was deafening! We fired up the beasts, reported to Battalion that Charlie Company was ready to go, and began to move. How do you spell pucker factor?

The actual move to the berm took little time. Tank Commanders wore their NVGs (Night Vision Goggles), keeping an eye out front and back. We moved through the first breach, with Captain Ed Dunlap going through first. My heart was racing and I assumed it had a lot of company.

When we passed through the berm there was that ghostly looking Iraqi T-55 tank, gutted just like Gunnery Sergeant Cochran reported on the earlier Recon. It lay there completely burned out, totally destroyed.

Once through the berms and about ten klicks south of the minefields, we ranged out into attack positions, just as we had rehearsed so many times. Darkness at this point was still our concealing friend on this desert pool table. The company arrayed into its formation of company wedge, modified with a right echelon. By that I mean a wedge with the tip to the front, the direction of our intended movement. Gunnery Sergeant Cochran's 2nd Platoon was the tip; Lieutenant Croteau's 1st Platoon made up the left side; Lieutenant Gonsalves' 3rd Platoon had the longer right side in an echelon right formation. Two platoons up, 1st Platoon right front, 2nd Platoon left front, 3rd Platoon to the right front in echelon along the right front flank. We had no flank security.

The Battalion was to be the pointy end of the spear that we would thrust into Kuwait! Task Force Ripper was composed of the Regiment itself, Headquarters, 1st and 2nd Battalions, 3rd Marines; 1st Battalion, 5th Marines; 3rd Battalion, 9th Marines; 3rd Assault Amphibian Battalion, 1st Combat Engineer Battalion, 3rd Battalion, 11th Marines; and, of course, 3rd Tank Battalion, with three tank companies and a mech company forward, leading the task force through the obstacles, the tip of the spear.

As we started through the berm there was little talking, only occasional chatter on the air traffic radio, with the tanks maintaining radio silence. That was it for us; we had started the ground war and there was no turning back. We had committed.

Just before we jumped off we listened to the CNN and BBC news. They discussed the last minute posturing by the Russians and others to delay the ground war, and we just chuckled. While commentators were highly optimistic that Saddam would come to realize his evil ways, repent, and suddenly announce he was withdrawing, we knew we were going to war.

The HQ tanks were arrayed behind the two lead platoons, and I was just behind the platoon on the right side, with the FAC (Forward Air Controller). We expected to encounter something in this position and it would give us a better chance to call for air support if needed. The CO let me position my tank where I thought we needed it and from time to time I would swing back and forth along the line of attack.

When we arrived about ten klicks from the Iraqis, at our appointed position, we stopped and shut down. With all the noise an armored unit makes, I am certain every one of those nervously awaiting Iraqis knew we were in their neighborhood and knew exactly where in the neighborhood we were.

We were in MOPPS (Mission Orientated Protective Posture Suits), along with our ever-present gas masks, body armor and weapons neatly tucked into shoulder holsters. Orders were to expect a chemical attack as a last ditch effort on behalf of the Iraqis. We would cross the berms so prepared.

Waiting in the bitter cold for the other units to pass through the breach and form up behind us, I was glad we had worn the MOPPS. To catch a few ZZZZs I got on top of the sandbagged turret, behind the loaders hatch, CVC helmet on, and blithely drifted off to slumber-land. I had an entire, armored company surrounding me, so despite the location and the circumstances, I felt quite secure. We were off to see what color the elephant was, and I was falling asleep.

A little later a tank crewman awakened me. It was time again to do the short count. We fired up the tanks and moved north. This is usually described in tank warfare as the movement to contact. We had no idea where or when we would make contact with the Iraqis. We knew the geographic location of the enemy, but not how he would respond. When he did respond, in the classic sense of war we would close with and destroy him.

As we closed with the first obstacle belt, one of the reasons I got rid of the camo net became obvious. To store the netting we would have to secure it to the sponson boxes, and this made traversing the main gun difficult. It always got in the way, a fact we learned during our many rehearsals.

Sergeant Fitzpatrick, from the 1st Platoon, had stored his netting on the right rear sponson boxes, because the actual storage decision was left up to the individual tank commander. He knew what his equipment and space capabilities were. The bulge of the net, being on top of the armor, would interfere with the operation of the main gun. The netting wound up getting entangled in the drive sprocket of Sergeant Fitzpatrick's tank and he was forced to stop and perform an emergency netectomy, tearing the net all to pieces and finally just throwing the thing overboard! I was glad my net was gone!

It was uneventful when we moved up to the first belt. With the help of the GPS (Global Positioning Satellite) Captain Ed had onboard, we knew we were right on station. This was quite different from desert tank warfare during WWII. The Polaris system that all Army tanks used was constantly on the fritz. I was the only one in Charlie Company that had this system, and I can report it never worked the entire ground war! However, when we were about to depart Kuwait, at the end of the war, the foolish thing came back online and worked perfectly. Maybe it just needed a few good whacks.

With Captain Ed's GPS working, he led us through the desert darkness right up to the edge of the minefield. I wonder what it would have been like without the GPS and shudder at the likelihood of a lot of destroyed tanks and men!

1/7 moved up with Alpha Company tanks leading the way, and worked on punching breaches through the minefields. Once the lanes were cleared and proofed we geared up for our move. As practiced, combat engineers punched two lanes through the belts, and our approach showed both lanes open for passage.

We did what we had practiced so many times. Tank crews buttoned up all hatches, and one by one the steel monsters of Charlie Company passed through the breach points, each platoon letting me call out when it reached the far side. Though buttoned up, as the tank commander, I could see out through the vision blocks of my cupola, and in the early morning gloom I could just make out the mines sitting ominously on the surface of the sand. When we reached the far side of the breaches, and unbuttoned our hatches, we could see wire entanglements lying about. Some positions appeared to be hastily made bunkers. Scattered about were burned vehicles, many rolled over on their side.

As we reached the first obstacle belt and Captain Mancini's Alpha Company began moving through, the FAC indicated that he had lost his encryption capability on his air radio. He no longer had secure communications with the overhead AWACS (Airborne Warning And Control System) that relayed messages for us. He would have to communicate in the open, and so would all those he spoke with, not good! So I jumped from my tank and ran across the sands to the CO's tank to get the KICK, a device that holds the encryption cipher for secure radio communication. I ran back to my tank and Corporal Scott immediately installed it; the FAC was ready to rock and roll. The Arty was slamming stuff into the ground ahead of us, messing up someone's day.

Breaching the first barriers went pretty much as rehearsed. Combat Engineers set off across-the-line charges, destroying mines in the area. Captain Mancini's company moved up and through, and cleared the minefields with their mine plows. Bright, international orange identification panels were laid out for the air movers so they would know us. The 2nd Platoon went through first, then Captain Ed, followed by the 1st Platoon. I passed through with the FAC and the 3rd Platoon. We had two lanes laid through the minefield allowing the Marines to pass through without being channeled into a dangerous single lane. Two lanes helped prevent the company and those that followed from being wiped out.

Clearing the first barrier established a Phase Line. I notified Battalion with our code word Home Free. This meant the entire Charlie Company, tip of the spear, was safely through the first obstacle. We were well in advance of what I believe Ripper expected us to be.

The process worked well. As Gunnery Sergeant Cochran's Platoon went through he called, "Home Free." As Captain Ed's tank went through he would inform me like the others, "Home Free." When everyone was Home Free I passed the word to Battalion who in turn notified Regiment, and so up the line.

The weather began to turn to moderate rain, making visibility a little difficult. During part of the clearing operation the FOX chemical detection vehicle was called in to investigate a possible chemical or biological mine. This made us nervous. When the detection equipment indicated it had located a chemical mine Battalion ordered us to MOPPS Level 4. This meant we now had to wear the complete chemical suit, gas mask and gloves. Those in the immediate vicinity mine clearing operations were the first ones needing to suit up.

While 1/7 was busy clearing our right flank we fanned out to cover the forward point. Within minutes of clearing the minefield, we ran into trouble. Murphy's Law! Unlike the simulated combat missions of the Stumps, we did not have the luxury of the number of radio channels we were accustomed to. This was due in part to the volume of units operating in the field, or should I say sand, at the same time. Not since Vietnam had the Corps operated as a Corps with two divisions in the field at once. Big Al was lonely back there in CONUS; all his little green monsters played together in Saudi land!

In the process of moving forward with badly reduced radio capability, our speed began to slow. Someone may have been trying to straighten out the FEBA (Forward Edge Battlefield Area, better known to the forward edge forces as False Enthusiasm Bad Attitude). We stopped to consolidate, to make sure all the Tonka toys were in the right part of the giant litter box.

The level of indirect fire began to increase, nothing major. The occasional round landed in front, one to the right, then one to the left, and then one behind. What is this? I remembered almost aloud, talking to myself, "Hey there, genius, think back to indirect fire support classes that TBS drilled into your little brain housing: those rounds coming down are spotting rounds!"

For armchair tankers, a fire support lesson follows. When one has lots of arty tubes, big guns of the artillery battalions, waiting to pummel one's enemy, it is necessary to tell those tubes where to point. Start by throwing out one round and see where it lands and what kind of response you get. A forward observer like the good Corporal riding in Captain Ed's tank then examines the ensuing kaboom and makes adjustments, moving the next round, and any others necessary, laterally or inline. The target is thus bracketed; range and direction is known, and the arty boys know where to throw every thing they've got.

When we realized these spotting rounds were targeting us we knew someone out there was alert. That was bad because it meant the enemy was not getting properly smacked from the air. So much for, "Rest easy! With the mighty air armada that will be circling over your helmeted brow, no arty will be able to trash you. We shall be on them in a matter of minutes." One problem with pep talks, where now was the guy who gave us the talk?

Well, if some one should see us, remember their FO (Forward Observer) has to see the kaboom to adjust it. If he can see us, then we should be able to see him. On top of a sand covered pool table their is no advantage of terrain or elevation from which to spot. Even knowing the little trouble-maker had to be close at hand, where to point? Suddenly the infernal smoke curtain shifted and we sighted a huge water tower, a great big mother of a water tower. This was one of those towers the architect warned the Intel boys about, but no one ever told us. The tower was too far away for our tank's main gun, and several attempts by the TOW critters (anti-tank missile platforms) revealed it too far out of range for them, too.

Unlike the CAX (Combined Arms Exercise) of the Stumps, these guys were not allowing us lengthy deliberations. Indirect fire was creeping steadily closer. Our FAC (Forward Air Controller) called the air boys, but visibility was too reduced for the fast movers. Tell me again how wars are won by superior air power!

Our FO (our eagle-eyed kaboom spotter, not theirs) was scrambling to get a fire mission started, but he was behind in the spotting process. It is considered bad form to acknowledge one is taking indirect fire because that may provide a snooping opponent with the knowledge that his rounds are having an effect. Thus, a brevity code was used. I called Battalion with the brevity code Snow Storm. Snow? In the desert? Oh, well! Battalion's reply was, "Affirm, we are working on it. Out." I can state that was not very reassuring.

The Marine Corps defines initiative as the implementation of action without direct orders, doing something without being told to do it. Up in my cupola watching the show, I remembered we had two definite assets several klicks behind us, the two Cobra AH-1W gun-ship helicopters operationally attached to Charlie Company. These two missile-packing babies followed Charlie Company in trail, waiting for word of something we needed blasted.

During the days of Operation Desert Shield an idea was developed of necessity, maybe some desperation, to mount a MULE (Modular Universal Laser Equipment) and slaved TOW (Tube launched, Optically tracked, Wire guided) sight in the tank carrying the FAC. This would enable the splashing (illuminating) of targets with a laser beam for missile homing. Never been done, not possible, said the experts. Oh, yeah, let's call in an NCO to see if that is true. Captain Mumbly delivered MULE and TOW equipments, along with their multiple cases and cables to my tank, C-52. Sergeant Jeff Welsh reported to me, the XO, to assess the impossible. Sergeant Welsh examined the equipment, the tank's wiring, and rendered his verdict, "Piece of cake!"

Impossibility became reality and I had MULE and a TOW sight on my tank. I could splash a target for the Cobras to launch a Hellfire (laser-guided missile). We had demonstrated some of the good ol' Marine Corps initiative.

I called for Captain Mumbly to whistle up the Snakes (the Cobra Squadron) and had Lance Corporal Florence move us forward. We rumbled past 3rd Platoon, Staff Sergeant Walters' tank being the closest, and stopped out in front of the Company. We were then the lead element of the Company, which meant that we were lead element of the Battalion, the lead element of the Regiment, Ripper itself, lead element of the Division. I had the view that lead platoons normally get, but I had a whole lot more antennas than they did! XOs do not belong in front; they belong in back.

Meanwhile we had the Cobras up and closing on their firing position behind us. The FAC was on the TACP (Tactical Air Control Party) net, and he was warming the MULE for a laser splash. About that time I was praying that the good Sergeant Welsh had wired the thing correctly.

The Cobras pulled in to position about 500 meters to the rear of the Company, and with the FAC ready to lase, popped up to about 300 feet in the air. I waved to the tanks around me and pointed to the Cobras. When the FAC lased the target I called out a warning to the Company because the optics of our antiquated M60A1 tanks were not laser safe as they were in the newer M1A1 tanks, and the birds let loose with Hellfires. I arched my arm and pointed to the tower.

We watched the missile exhaust trail lead right to the water tower, and saw the explosion. I looked back to the other tanks and took a deep bow. Everyone hanging out of the hatches was yelling and clapping. The TOW critters looked pretty pumped as well. I thumbed the intercom and had the driver move back behind the protective steel curtain of Charlie Company. I had no idea where their snoop was on that monstrous water tower, but with that direct hit, indirect rounds slacked off. It was safe to assume there had been an enemy observer somewhere on the tower.

With the quantity of coalition air that was standing above, any time the Iraqi arty fired, slam, down air would roar and commence a little urban renewal in the desert. Those Iraqi gunners weren't stupid, and they figured out real quick that if they pulled the lanyard, they disappeared. Good thinking!

Captain Ed not only had the honor of having his tank the first coalition tank to cross into Kuwait, but also of having the first direct fire engagement with a tank's main gun. Although the CO had led to the attack position, he had followed in trail of the lead platoons, as did the conservative Sagger missile magnet, the XO, since moving to the obstacle belts. The HQ tanks would close up with the lead platoons and split the gap between the tanks. That way we could have a field of fire during our frequent halts. This tactic lesson is brought to you by the FFBT(Federation For Better Tanking).

We halted when Captain Ed thought he saw two vehicles ahead of us move. He gave a fire command to his gunner and wham! The round seemed to skip over the ground slamming directly between the two vehicles. Suddenly, instead of two vehicles, up and away flew two very large crows. Well, almost the first kill of the war.

Shortly after crossing through the first breaches, the vaunted Iraqi army began to make its presence felt upon the battlefield, but it quickly became apparent that the first obstacle belt had been abandoned and that the fierce battle of entrapment between the belts was not going to be of great concern. With the exception of several indirect fire missions and the engagement of stray armored vehicles, no Iraqi super warriors had been seen.

As we approached the second belt things changed slightly. Short halts took place for coordination or to allow the Battalion front line to straighten, and Tank Commanders and Platoon Commanders began to issue sitreps (situation reports) of movements in front. First signs were of the stray soldier bolting between holes, and heads popping out of the sand then dropping out of sight again.

It was because of those first glimpses of Iraqi soldiers that we fell into a tactic leading to the surrender of thousands of the enemy's warriors.

Tankers like to keep the bad guys as far away as possible, unlike our grunt brethren who have limited range with their man-carried weapons. Tankers have the advantage of weapons with a much greater stand off distance. By using our machine guns and main tank guns we kept the ornery Iraqis at a suitable distance.

Thus, as the first heads appeared, the steel behemoths of Charlie Company sent fire down range, not engaging anything or anyone particularly, but providing the Iraqis with the definite notion that the neighborhood had just become unhealthy for those who would rally for Saddam. Once our first message was broadcast via the 7.62 and .50 cal guns of the tanks, we waited to see the response. Occasionally an armored vehicle would move, or a stray gun would return a bit of inaccurate answering fire, but those members of Saddam's legions in and about the second obstacle belt were not interested in putting up a fight.

A white flag suddenly appeared and quickly returned to its hiding place. When no bullets greeted the flag, other flags were raised and lowered. Heads bobbed up and down, looking much like a prairie dog town. One lone Iraqi soldier was suddenly propelled into view, the sacrificial lamb offered for possible slaughter.

That lone warrior pitifully ran from bunker to bunker

looking for a bolthole but found all escape avenues blocked. This was reminiscent of the human mine detectors used in the Russian human-wave attacks on the Eastern Front during WWII.

Once it became apparent to this sacrificial warrior that he was not going to join Allah's realm, his frantic scampering ceased. He commenced waving excitedly at us. Several minutes passed before the remainder of the concealed troops began to emerge into the light of day. Several more minutes were spent milling around. Many had removed articles of white clothing to wave; many had surrender pamphlets held aloft.

The flow of humanity began. In groups of tens and hundreds the Iraqis started their long march south. In disorderly groups as well as precise military formations they took the first tentative steps toward our tanks while holding high their pamphlets, or cloths, or simply their hands. Where had they keep all that white stuff hidden from their leaders?

As the groups approached, we tracked them with our tank turrets. TCs (tank commanders) and loaders trained M-16s on individuals who looked threatening. As they drew near we motioned them south. We also uttered Arabic phrases to them, instructions like, "Head south. Find food in the south."

When each group cleared, the Company advanced and we repeated the entire process again, and again, and again. Once we cleared the second belt we found the number of defenders still remaining in place drastically reduced. The unlucky few who were left did not have the option to run like those north of the belts had. This process continued throughout the day and the Battalion ultimately received credit for a capture of 8,000 prisoners of war. One thing was certain, I played traffic cop for a lot of surrendering prisoners.

From that point things went quickly. Our forces moved through the first belt, then on to the second belt, all part of our phased movement. The second belt was better maintained. Mines were concealed, completely covered with sand unlike the first one that looked like a surface-laid minefield because of sand blow off. The second belt was less exposed.

We had come about five kilometers from the first obstacle to the second belt. Our arty sounded close, it must have been pounding the Iraqis just behind the second belt. Iraqi arty was falling too, in and among us, and was getting very close. The TOW critters took some near misses. During this time we had several head-on gun engagements, direct live action fire.

The first volley by one of the platoons was actually comical. The Marine Corps has a well organized fire command procedure for firing our big 105mm main gun. Procedures were drilled, and then drilled again, until we could do them in our sleep. An individual tank fires more simply than a platoon, and a platoon has a whole different procedure for firing main guns. In either case fire discipline is the watchword; Marines adhere to fire discipline!

The first time a T-55 Russian-made tank showed itself popping over a small berm, everyone from 2nd Platoon capped a round all at once. Bingo! All four tanks hit simultaneously. With everyone firing Sabot rounds, we half expected the tank to disintegrate instantly, however, the tank only seemed to settle into the sand a little more. This was not the John Wayne version; you shoot a tank and it goes up in a ball of smoke and everyone cheers.

We moved a little closer and all of a sudden the internal rounds cooked off, tracers and main gun rounds were flying everywhere, then boom! Lesson: Do not close with a burning Iraqi tank.

So our first fire engagement was nothing at all like our practice, and nothing at all like what was ordered in the training manuals. There was no fire echelon, none! We were not off to a great start. The entire platoon had shot up one solitary target on G-Day, 24 February 1991.

Looking Good but...

This cutout reflects the serious and dedicated attitude of a warrior toward his duty despite the prediction of fifty percent casualties in the upcoming battle. See Lieutenant Chris Freitus' photograph on page 316.

Excerpt from photo by J. Butler

Chapter 10
The Al-Jaber Airfield

Task Force Ripper maneuvered north of the Al-Jaber Airfield to envelop it from the rear, wheeling along a southwest axis then closing on the airfield perimeter. By then the attacking battalions moved in semi-darkness brought on by dusk combined with smoke from the burning wellheads. Regardless, the task force maintained its formation and negotiated its way through a complex of dug-in enemy tanks, bunkers, debris from allied air bombardment, and many surrendering Iraqis. For the most part, the afternoon's artillery fire ended Iraqi resistance. However, at 1734 with visibility down to 300 meters, two T-62s attempted to engage the right flank of 1st Battalion, 7th Marines. The CAAT screening to the northwest spotted the enemy tanks and destroyed one of them. Four minutes later "Team Tank" from 1st Battalion 7th Marines, engaged and destroyed three T62s hidden behind revetments. The 1st Battalion, 7th Marines knocked out three more T-62s and three T-55s in the final push to the airfield perimeter. Iraqi resistance ceased at that point and by 1800 Task Force Ripper successfully isolated Al-Jaber.

The second obstacle belt was a scene of lots of firsts for us: the main engagements, tanks appearing out of the ground, burning vehicles and Iraqis popping up out of the ground to surrender.

One scene that day remains in my mind.

When an arty round came really close, the FAC would grab his toys, duck down into the tank and button his hatch. Now the hatch on the newer and much improved M1A1 has a feature the older M60A1 lacks. The M1A1 hatch has a rocker-mounted hinge allowing the tank commander to travel with protective positioning. The hatch rests horizontally, parallel with the top of the turret, and provides him with a gap between his post, his left and his right from which he can see out. It does not protect him from direct fire or a shell burst in the air; but it does give him a limited amount of protection from flying shrapnel and other airborne bad things.

In the M60's cupola, the tank commander's station can be in one of two positions, open or shut. If the hatch is open and unlocked, a quick stop will slam it shut, even with the commander in the hatch. There are other disadvantages to this; if there is direct or overhead fire stuff is going to rain down. Of course, with the hatch shut reduced visibility is a drawback. It seems there was a Major, in the 2nd Marine Division, the A Team, who received a Purple Heart when he was slammed by a hatch in an AAV (Amphibious Assault Vehicle).

Somewhere in our learning process Gunnery Sergeant Cochran came up with an option for the company. With assistance from Sergeant Welsh, he cleverly cut a notch in the release spring locking mechanism of the hatch. This allowed the hatch to close part way, offering protection with some visibility so that the tank commander could stick out his snout and see what was happening. He would have a little head protection and a little vision. Being blind and buttoned up in a tank can cause one of the worst feelings in the world.

Looking back, I realize that when the M1A1 takes small arms fire, the bullets pass on through. When the M60 takes small arms fire, and we did, if the turret had been facing the other way, the bullets would have clanged into the partially opened hatch, ricocheted down into the opening and smacked me right in the head. The hatch rigged this way offered me a small sense of security, but knowing what I know today, I don't think I would do it again.

There I was when an Iraqi round landed between the next tank and us. Slam goes my hatch! Through the vision blocks in my cupola, I saw two TOW critters about fifty meters away. These HUMVEES configured in an anti-armor role were mounted with TOW weapons and thermal sights. I realized those guys had absolutely nothing for protection and if a round hit them, they simply would be spam in the can. A HUMVEE is a lot of fiberglass and some metal here and there, offering little in the way of protection. I studied the HUMVEE and its small crew, watched them make adjustments to their sights, squeeze the trigger and the missile raced downrange. Just then another round of Iraqi arty fire landed between the two HUMVEES. It didn't hurt anyone, but it was amazing to watch that gunner never take his eyes off the sight and target. I looked over to my right and saw another detonation. I sat there hiding in a big steel box while those guys stood out there magnificently doing their job. After seeing that I stood in the open hatch of my tank and pretended to be brave. I was macho man but also very stupid, especially now looking back.

We passed a few more destroyed bunkers with dead Iraqis lying around on the ground. Suddenly there was a lone Iraqi running along the side of the line. He appeared to be disorientated, terribly haggard, dirty, shell-shocked and perhaps crying. Is this what we brought our great war machine to bear on, a poor wretched soldier who only wanted to surrender? Those were the poor soldiers Saddam forced to hold the front for him, his trip wire. The hard core Palace Guard was yet to be faced. I can still see this hapless trooper go by and hoped that they would all be just like him. Sherman was right, war is hell!

Navigating the breach sites, we moved onto the far side

and once again, coordination lapsed. I think we were at an agricultural station called the Emir's tree farm. It seemed strange to have a tree farm in the middle of the desert with no apparent water. It appeared to be part of an oil complex, so perhaps that is where the water came from. A tree farm just struck me as odd.

To our right, the area would eventually become either 1/7's or 3/7's area of operation. At that point we were the only force that pushed forward. Charlie Company was on the right, Bravo and Delta Companies tactically situated on the left. There was nothing else from the Battalion, never mind the Regiment. Once again we alone were Task Force Ripper.

Ripper's LAVs had not shot through yet with their Recon in force, north. We watched figures scurrying about the bunkers and we were taking direct fire at the same time. We wanted to bring in fire on them, but could not do so because that would have been shooting across 1/7's boundaries. We wondered who was running the show, the controllers back at the CAX (Combined Assault Exercise)?

Once through the breaches we were to make a left turn of forty-five degrees. That would expose our right flank! A tank's heaviest armor protection is in the front, not to the side. It is built that way for head to head combat. The rear of a tank is the most dangerous exposure, but the side is not much better. Yet, there we were about to do just that, expose our flank, a coordination glitch to say the least, one that could have cost us dearly. We wanted to bring in some smoke and screening fire, but could not do it, nor could Battalion. If there had been long range, anti-tank capability with the Iraqis, we would have lost a number of tanks, sitting there in front of everyone.

In all these problems the Marine's fire discipline deeply impressed me. Frequently our situation would find us taking small arms fire from the bunkered Iraqis. As quickly as we received fire the gunners on the tanks suppressed it with coaxial machine guns, fifty caliber machine guns, and perhaps a main gun or two. The moment a white flag waved in the air from a bunker, more or less the rule, our fire was immediately shut off. Terrific teamwork! Nobody could claim that these Marines went about the war needlessly slaughtering surrendering Iraqis!

I witnessed many fire engagements in my job as coordinator. That is one of an XO's tasks. I was not a trigger puller unless the situation warranted. My job was to make certain all went smoothly, as planned.

Fire discipline was good. I never saw a Marine shoot an Iraqi soldier who was attempting to surrender. Now, if that Iraqi was busy shooting at someone of us, that was quite a different story. This was one of the hallmarks of the Marines, together with training and self-discipline. There we were, facing someone who had been shooting at us, trying to kill us and all of a sudden he stops to wave what looks like his white underwear in the air and wants to surrender. It is tough not to want to shoot him. The Marines did not shoot and I admired them for such discipline.

All the time we encountered fire from bunkers and hit back with suppressing fire, it certainly would have been an advantage to have smoke to hide in. But 1/7 was still dithering about the obstacle belts and not really pushing toward their area of operations. It was sometime later that we heard about the screw up at the belts. When we went blazing through there had been either two or three lanes open to traffic. After we passed, it seems that one or two of the lanes got messed up which had slowed everyone else trying to pass through and hundreds of Iraqi prisoners were crowding at the breach. No one was prepared to handle such a sudden flood of people. The breaching control party did not make it on time, which just added to the severity of the problem. We all know of Mister Murphy and his many laws. Select one.

We continued pushing outwards toward the Al-Jaber

military airfield complex, our next objective. Small arms fire peppered us occasionally from the right. We fought with returning fire in the open every time some nut in the bunkers decided to take us on. After passing the two belts, we cruised along at the M60A1's near maximum speed of twenty miles plus per hour, depending on terrain and soil compactness. I was busy studying the map, playing king of the hill and trying to survey 360 degrees, when all of a sudden we came to a roaring halt, and I mean roaring halt!

From whatever logistical speed a tank is making, a complete dead in the tracks halt treats the tank commander pretty severely even if he is holding onto something that is anchored. At that time I was not. In a few seconds I found myself transformed from a Grand ol' Poobah of tankdom to a scrap heap lying atop the optics of my trusty fifty caliber machine gun. Sprawled half in and half out of the turret, with my head outside, I yelled, "Scott, for God's sake don't shoot!"

"What's your problem, XO?"

"Haven't the foggiest! Maybe Florence can shed some light and tell us what's going on! Whatever it is sure stopped us in a hurry!"

Florence, our intrepid driver, was one cool character. He had driven this beast through two obstacle belts, and never once flinched, dented a fender or scratched the prescribed military paint job. That takes talent and skill. So, I looked over the edge and there in front of us was a tan-colored object, about the size of a garbage can lid. "Land Mine."

I called up the combat engineers, those dauntless souls that will go places we tankers fear to tread.

Think of a circus clown-car. Those guys arrived in an AAV (Amphibious Assault Vehicle) designed for ship to shore movements of Marines and their gear, not for land battles. It is very big, bigger than an M60A1, and made with lots of aluminum. It is a standout target for arty folks on the other side of the ball field!

To this easy target had been added facimes, a device designed to refill anti-tank trenches. So I am describing a very big tracked vehicle with two very large bundles of PVC (poly vinyl chloride) pipe on either side. It clanked in and maneuvered until it was in front of us, and then proceeded to drop the rear assault door. Out popped several engineers who swarmed all over that mine.

They whipped out what appeared to be a stick of C-4 (plastic explosive) tied into a detonator. They did all this while we cautiously, backed the tank. When they lit that thing off, bang, a spectacular fountain of fine Kuwaiti sand shot high in the air.

I described it as like a clown car because just like in the circus, when they pulled up, it seemed that everyone inside piled outside, rapidly scurried about for a moment, attached a charge, blew the sucker and just as quickly piled into the AAV and drove off. Only the laughter was absent.

Florence and I had an intense, brief discussion after all that and decided from here on we would follow in the tracks of other folks whenever possible. No more blazing trail through the sands, playing Rommel in the desert wilderness, unless necessary! It has been a long time, but I still feel that we all owe Florence for saving our hides.

The movement of Marines from the second belt increased rapidly on our drive forward to Al-Jaber Airfield. It was not the task of the 3rd Tanks to take the airfield. We were tasked to occupy a position where we could provide a cover for our other attacking forces. We formed a blocking position to prevent Iraqi forces from possibly moving against us from the south; we knew they were still in place there. The force tasked with taking the airfield was 1/7. They would move along our right flank, push on to attack Al-Jaber Airfield, then secure it for the night. Our maneuver had a number of potential problems, but tanks provide a good base of fire, with long-range capability. The drive north to the airfield at this point included Task Force Ripper, Tiger Three, and Charlie Company.

We continued taking prisoners of what seemed like the whole of the Iraqi army. They just started popping out of the ground, in large numbers, waving something white or simply throwing their hands into the air. I think it turned out to be over 5,000 prisoners attributed to the Battalion that day.

We were engaged as we moved. Firefights, vehicles moving frenetically, sporadic and unpredictable small arms fire, and heavy arty fire created our fog-of-war environment. I remember one particular sabot round that skipped between my tank and Lance Corporal Newton's tank, C-53, a third Headquarters Platoon tank.

Normally a USMC Tank Company is organized with two HQ tanks, one for the CO, one for the XO, but during Operation Desert Shield we had acquired three M60A3s that are a more modified version of the M60A1. The Army had transitioned to the newer M1A1, but had shipped several A3s to the Gulf; three of these were given to us to play with. Each company received one, and to keep our structure intact, and because we had several qualified tank commanders without a tank, our A3 was assigned as our third HQ tank.

Another round exploded directly between Captain Ed's tank and mine.

As much fire as we received, little of it appeared to be coordinated, just random shots coming down range. It was neither organized, nor the massive counter attack we were expecting. All of it seemed to be thrown at us by a few troops who simply did not know they were whipped.

As we moved toward Al-Jaber Airfield, the most personal moment of the war occurred for me, the moment of my direct involvement in taking a human life. We were moving forward taking occasional mortar fire, easily distinguished from the heavier 105mm fire that produced large plumes of smoke when they hit. The mortar produces smaller plumes and makes a crazy screaming whistle when it sails through the air. It is when the whistling stops you have to worry. These small plumes of smoke were popping up between our tanks.

We worried that these explosions might be chemical in nature. One signature of the chemical explosion is that it tends to be much smaller than the arty high-explosive round. Continuing observation convinced us these were simple mortar rounds that do not have a very long-range capability. Those rounds had to be from somewhere nearby, maybe 3-4 klicks.

To have mortars meant this outfit must be at least a company in strength. Anything larger would be further away, like ten klicks or so, depending on the nationality of the round and how good the mortar crew is. These guys were close, too close! They were trying to destroy us and "us" includes me.

We continued tanking through the area and noted the rounds were now falling behind us. Ha! They were really nearby. If these guys decide not to give up, our trains that were moving up behind us would be sitting ducks. The Iraqis could have a field day picking them off.

The difficulty in locating the Iraqi positions was that they were dug in deeply and nearly impossible to spot from a tank. Tanking along just ten feet above the ground, a tanker's horizon is not really that great. As a matter of fact, it stinks! There is no berm, no earthen mound, or sandbagged bunker, not a thing to see. From where we sat, we might not recognize a position until we were right on top of it!

And that is exactly what happened. We ran into a mortar pit. I do not know if this was the mortar pit that was shelling us, but we almost ran it over. I shouted to my keen-eyed driver, Florence, "Hard Left!"

Florence executed a hard left forty-five degree turn and went right by the mortar pit. I looked in and probably shouted out loud, "That thing is ready to fire!" There were shells broken out, a number of powder charge increments ready for use, and bunkers leading to and from this fire pit. My eye was fixed, talk about undivided attention!

I thought I saw movement at the corner of my eye. We jockeyed down and away, and the company came to a halt. I kept looking back at that mortar pit thinking that someone, not something, had moved back there. Someone with an RPG (Rocket Propelled Grenade) would do our tank, and us, considerable harm. The pucker factor again!

Along with our tactical situation and the prisoners swarming through, there was significant confusion. We could not traverse the turret and get off a main gun round at the pit. If we faced the main gun the wrong way, someone coming up behind us might think we looked like an Iraqi tank! I could not call on others in the area to send in a round because they were not in the right position and the round might skip and we really could be in a whole lot of trouble.

We had hand grenades. Reaching behind the radio box, I pulled out a fragmentation grenade, stood up in the hatch, figured I could hit the pit from there. No one was in the way. Just as 2nd Lieutenant Freitus had been taught in Basic School, I pulled the pin, cocked my arm and threw. Dropping back down inside the tank I counted one thousand one, one thousand two, thousand three, four, five, six, and nothing! I looked down in my right hand and no pin!

I knew that every time I threw a grenade I always ended up with a pin on my finger. Oh, no, no pin! I popped up through the hatch and took a hasty look around. Okay, plus their having a mortar to play with, you just gave them a genuine U.S.-issue fragmentation grenade. Good show!

Not one to take defeat seriously again, I reached behind the radio box and pulled out another fragmentation grenade. Jerking off my helmet, I yelled to Scott that I would be right back and dove off the tank. John Wayne had nothing on me.

I was dressed in my second-chance bullet proof vest, flak jacket, my trusty gas mask on my hip, my faithful 9mm tucked into my shoulder holster, my extremely heavy and bulky MOPPS, and my newly issued desert camo boots. Looking real sharp, I began running through sand toward the mortar pit as fast as my two feet would carry me. I began thinking: You know, we have a real rocket scientist here, and in motion. Think of what you have in your hand, a simple fragmentation grenade. What if some soldier jumps up with an RPG or something with a bang bigger than my grenade? Yes? Then just what are you going to do, Lieutenant?

With this question spinning in my head, I stopped. Jerking around, I focused on the mortar pit. This was as far as I was going. Close enough. This time I made a more conscious effort to pull the pin, cocked my arm and as I lobbed the grenade into the air, there was movement in the pit! I cannot to this day say what that movement was. I know it was not a box falling over, or the wind blowing in the sand. There was the sound of metal scraping against an object, the sound a human makes when he moves. I remember watching the grenade arcing through the air, knowing that it would go directly into the pit.

I flipped around and started running back to my tank, no flies on me! When I hit the tank there was the expected kaboom, not just one but, a couple of good-sized booms, successful cook-offs. Gunnery Sergeant Schofield happened to be looking in my direction and watched as I hit the fender of the tank with my foot, leap up and duck into the hatch. He later remarked about never having seen anything quite like that in his life.

That was the first time in the Gulf that I killed people directly, the first time I was aware of. There were others, but they are uncomfortable memories. My role was to give fire commands to the gunner, direct the FAC to place assets on target, and make command decisions to platoon leaders, but none of those fire orders involved me so directly. These were insulated command situations. With the grenade in the mortar pit, it became direct and personal, the taking of lives. It needed to be done. I knew the mortar pit was still active, capable of killing us, and I could not have it behind us. If those people had any intention of surrendering, they would have stood up like all the others, waved their arms or something, but they chose to stand and fight. In the end they paid the ultimate price for their decision. Looking back I realize that the incident has changed my life forever.

We drove further inland and north into an Iraqi arty battery. I think they were less in-direct fire batteries than they were anti-aircraft or anti-tank guns. They were, of course, Soviet equipped guns. The Soviets, at that time, still believed in the gunner blasting away with his array of guns instead of the present day use of anti-tank rocketry. The use of anti-tank guns against the sloping armor of present day tanks is ineffective.

When we drove through the Iraqi position, we did not realize it was there until we were well into it. The guns were laid out in typical Russian deployment. Munitions were broken out, and had they decided to fire on us, I think a good percentage of our company would not have made it through the position. The Iraqis would have extracted their pound of flesh, and then some, before it was all over.

Just to the north of that position we stopped, and I am not certain if it was to give 1/7 the chance to catch up and move into realignment. I do not think it was because of a POW situation that we stopped; we simply stopped. I was with 2nd Platoon, the forward edge of the Company, at that point. Because of our experience with the engineers and the land mine episode, we decided to follow in the tracks of the other tanks because we were supposed to be a trailing element.

We stopped about four or five hundred meters behind

the platoon. Florence had placed us in a position to utilize the main gun, if we had to. We sat waiting for who knows what when I began to hear a voice; I can best describe it as a soft, little voice. It began talking to me from above and behind. I sensed danger. I concentrated, listening carefully. I was a college graduate, a member of the elite U.S. Marine Corps, and there I was listening to a small voice behind me. It was strange, and no, I am not superstitious.

There were no definable words, just the feeling of urgency to move, and move now! We needed to get out of there fast! If not something terrible would happen. The hair, such as a Marine has, stood up at the nape of my neck. Move, stupid, this little voice screamed.

Without giving it much thought, I keyed the mike and told Florence to move, to make a forty-five degree turn. We moved.

It takes a tank a few feet to get up the necessary momentum before it can make a turn. We did so and Florence made the turn, driving about three hundred meters. We stopped.

I turned around and looked back to where we had been sitting. An arty round, perhaps a 105mm, landed directly in the middle of our tracks, at the very location where we had been sitting! I remember seeing a plume of smoke and sand cascading into the air, realizing that if we had not moved when we did, little voice or no, we would have taken that round directly on the turret of the tank!

You can kill a tank if you are lucky enough to land a round on top of the turret. Everyone inside would have been killed, but thanks to a little voice. This was the first time anything like this had ever happened to me. I know of others who have heard such voices and were saved by them, but me? There would be other times when a little voice would speak softly to me. Perhaps there was no little voice, and perhaps I had imagined it all. Stranger things have happened in desert war, but we moved and lived to see another day! I felt exhilaration, joy, and happy as a squirrel that I heard that little voice, a whisper in the desert. I really don't care what others might think; I continued to hope the voice would keep me well informed!

The rest of the morning was somewhat of a let down as we continued to move, stop, go, stop-go, spray and wait for heads to pop up, spray some more, realign the front, stop, quickly do maintenance, go, spray, realign. Somewhere in the midst of this confusion, the Delta Company XO took a piece of shrapnel and was evacuated, treated, and then re-evacuated himself forward to join his company. This guy had guts. He could have stayed in the rear and sat out the rest of the war, away from most harm.

Eventually we closed on our objective, also the objective of Regiment. Task Force Ripper's directive for the day was to seize the Al-Jaber Military Airfield complex, which was northwest of the Al-Wafra Oil Fields.

The Battalion's objective was to seize a blocking position to provide covering fire from due south of the airport. The grunts would have to take the airfield and we would provide covering fire as well as mobile fire if and where needed.

From where I sat perched in the tank the airfield did not appear to have suffered much damage. There was some damage to the facility buildings and craters in the airstrip, but it looked as though it could easily be returned to use.

The buildings surrounding the airfield were many and reminded me of the usual congestion of urban sprawl. Fighting that would occur there would be that of typical urban, house to house, not necessarily kind to tanks. That kind of fighting raises the pucker factor to a scale understood only by those who have gone through such an ordeal.

Northwest of us 1/7 and 3/7 moved up to our right flank, and dismounted. They began moving through the airfield complex. I saw several skirmishes and firefights using Marine

Corps binoculars, and heard about more from reports by gunners in the other units. But, it did not turn out to be the brutalizing battle we had anticipated. It seemed more of a mopping up operation from what we could see and understand. It is easy for me to say that, because I was involved from a distance. We were never called upon to deliver any direct fire in support of the operation.

When the airport mission was accomplished we spent the rest of the afternoon in position and performed the usual and necessary logistic activities that kept us rolling.

There was a sign at 3rd Tanks Command Post at Twentynine Palms stating: "Amateurs talk tactics, professionals talk logistics!" That was a quote taken from the same General who commanded the famed Afrika Korps during WWII. He meant that an armored unit is only as good as its ability to re-arm and re-fuel! It can rapidly expend its ordnance and the M60A1 gobbles fuel like a starved teenager. In tanks we do not talk about miles per gallon; we talk about gallons per mile.

The need for logistics tied to a rapidly moving armored group speaks for itself. Patton's move through France is a prime example. Everyone provided me with all the necessary info to re-arm, re-fuel and bring up to standards all the other assets we needed to keep our unit rolling. When all the needs were tabulated I sent them along to Top Sergeant Graham, who was behind us in our company logistic train. Everything was anticipated, so by the time the platoon pulled into the re-supply point everything was there waiting for us.

Each platoon would take its turn returning to the designated re-supply point. That was basically a pit stop scenario and a well-rehearsed maneuver. As each tank arrived, the crew would find the ammo arranged on the ground. It would take only about five minutes to rearm. The same speed went into re-fueling. Tension was fierce due to our vulnerability. We were expecting a massive Iraqi counter attack, thinking they would not give up the airport so easily, and here we were re-arming and vulnerable to hit by an armored unit of any size. Life with the supply train is not always a cakewalk. Top Sergeant Graham reported an Iraqi had attacked them with an RPG. As luck would have it, the Iraqi was taken out before he could do serious stuff to the re-supply group.

Our re-fit and re-arm went smoothly and we moved back to our old position near the Al-Jaber Airport. I dismounted the tank, nosed around the debris, looking in the holes, and found myself looking down into an anti-tank weapon, or RPG (Rocket Propelled Grenade) site. At the time I did not actually recognize it as such. Staff Sergeant Mummey (Mumbo) thought the site was typical of Russian made RPG sites.

Around 1500, we noticed the sun doing its disappearance act, ominous for that time of afternoon. We would not see the sun again for the next several days. Of course, when we launched the drive against Saddam with the greatest armored punch ever assembled and other hurrah, we were also told we were going to have three days of the greatest weather to be conjured up by those mystics who delve into the realms of atmospherics. All we needed was plenty of suntan lotion; no sun burns during working hours!

The night we moved up into our attack positions, the sky was overcast and we were cold. The next morning it started to rain. It remained overcast, raining, and thick with the smoke of burning oil wells for the next three days. I do not believe it ever got above forty degrees. We got wet and we stayed wet. This was not like the Saudi desert we had been hunkered down in for the past several months..

One day, though a massive black cloud hung over the west, the sun tried to shine through, but the most we saw were orange hints of it. An enormous black cloud climbed ever higher into the atmosphere like a wall. When the smoke cloud shifted it gave the sun an appearance of setting in the west. I had seen forest fires burning in the wilds of Alaska and they could put out a tremendous amount of smoke, but this cloud of burning oil made those fires look like pikers. Hell could not have looked worse.

The grunts had done their job of ridding the enemy from the Al-Jaber Airport. We were re-supplied, and it was getting darker, which meant it was time to organize and setup for the night. We expected Saddam to make a stab at regaining what he had lost, and the best time to do that is night.

Word came through that we were to move northeast of the airfield to our BP (Battle Position). We could do that, we now had several months experience of doing just that. Well, not quite so simple. Just imagine a huge pool table with you on it as a very small figure. Place a bag over your head so that you cannot see and there you have the situation. Increasing darkness intensified the heavy black smoke of burning oil.

But not to fear, we had that wondrous marvel of modern technology, the GPS (Global Positioning Satellite). With such a wizard device you can find your way through anything by bouncing electronic pulses at the speed of light from a satellite positioned just overhead. What's the big deal?

I think if I ever meet the folks who were supposed to have all our technical stuff up and running, I would be tempted to wring something out of them! One must remember there are intricate details that must come into play when coordinating position from satellites around mother earth. The GPS at that time, and more than likely still, had to be triangulated. I studied geometry so understood what the rocket scientists were saying. Are you ready for this? GPS requires reception of three satellites but we received only two while expecting a counter attack at any moment from Saddam's troops.

Captain Ed, Commanding Charlie Company and attuned to all intricacies of techno-warfare, punched into the computer and found that a satellite was missing and therefore could not complete the task. Captain Ed still had the extraneous officer system to fall back on (extraneous officer system is cute for XO). Capable fighting units always have a fall back system. So his order goes out, extraneous officer, check your Polaris!

Extraneous officer checked his Polaris and replied, "Sir, the Polaris is out. I am getting a no-go sign, sir!"

"How can that be?" muttered the Captain.

"Seems the software is on the blink, sir!" came my hesitant reply. "Captain, what do we do now, sir?"

The good captain straightened his broad shoulders, and replied, "Well, we shall persevere, and move forward. Not all is lost, for this is the Marines Corps." Right!

After driving through the desert in roiling smoke for several minutes, we realized that we had not the first clue where we were going. Every one of our platoons on our flanks was having the same problem. Captain Ed quickly determined that everyone traveling in column to maintain visibility was destroying any flank security we may have. You cannot spread out if you cannot see the tank on your right or left.

The M60A1 riding passive uses a passive sight, the good ol' eyeball like the Old Breed days of yore, no thermal sight vision here. We were blundering and clanking about the desert and it would be just our dumb luck to stumble onto an Iraqi infantry unit or perhaps one of their highly touted armored units. Our trusty techno-warfare leader, Captain Ed Dunlap, de-tanked and pulled out his government issue, genuine Marine Corps compass. He took a reading away from the scrap metal that we call a tank and then began walking across the desert floor, off into the gloom and doom of the increasing darkness with a sudden thought in his head. What if the others who are supposed to be going off into the northeast direction are not going off into the northeast direction? What then?

Such a happening could result in shooting each other. We had another command conference and decided to stop and hold position. We would point ourselves north and prepare for the expected counter attack we had been waiting for ever since we had crossed over from Saudi land into Kuwait.

With atmospheric conditions of a rainy overcast night, I could almost see my hand in front of my face, could almost see around the tank, and a few meters. Seeing further was next to impossible.

To our south and west the blazing oil fields of Al-Wafra churned out thick, roiling smoke. We were not tied in with another unit so therefore we were an independent operating unit. We were alone out there waiting for the Iraqis to come charging out of the smoke and darkness to attack us. We sat for the night, and prepared for what might happen. I remember thinking what a perfect screen for an Iraqi armored unit to hide in. Naw, they wouldn't think of something like that. Would they?

Sign of the Times

Numerous signs were sabotaged by the resistance movement. Only those signs leading to Kuwait City were left standing.

Photo by C. Freitus

The Hasty Breach

Site of the hasty breach that Blue had been ordered to create on G-plus 2 so that we could get off the highway. Note the two separate rows of wire. Russian doctrine calls for mines to be placed between the rows. Glad the the Iraqis ran out!

Photo by C. Freitus

Chapter 11
G-plus 1, Possible Enemy Attack 25 Feb 1991

At 0109 General Myatt saw the Iraqi maps captured by Task Force Ripper and heard statements by several captured officers that implied a counterattack was imminent. However, for a time, he and his headquarters staff continued to focus on the Al-Jaber area; that was where the original concentration of Iraqi artillery (and the greatest threat to the division) had been. As the night wore on further intelligence reported an armored/mechanized brigade-size force and an armor brigade to the northeast. If correct, the two brigades were well positioned to strike the division's front and right flanks. Attempts to confirm the location of the enemy units failed because of the flames and smoke rising from the burning Al-Burqan oil field.

Intercepts of Iraqi radio traffic soon convinced General Myatt that the enemy was going to attempt something. He then alerted his Commanders and reassessed the division's defenses. The position was as well laid out as allowed by the chaotic conditions of the previous evening; in front of Task Force Ripper and Papa Bear, Myatt had Lieutenant Colonel Myers establish a screen with LAVs, antitank MMWVs, and scout teams. The mainline consisted of a series of battalion battle positions. Commanders placed tanks and antitank weapons to the front to favor their integral thermal and night vision devices.

General Myatt made adjustments to the division's

defenses. He judged his front to be thinly defended and lacking sufficient antitank strength. He also concluded that the division command post was too far forward in its location just south of the thinly defended lines near the Emir's farm. The placement of the forward command post at that location reflected Major General Myatt's belief that the commander should be as far forward as possible. There were practical reasons as well. Brigadier General Draude wanted to have the headquarters out of the fire sack between the two obstacle belts, and Myatt wanted to be in the best location for organizing and launching the next day's attack. Only Company C, 1st Battalion, 1st Marines occupied that portion of the line. General Myatt decided to reinforce Company C with the nearest unit available, a LAV Company from Task Force Shepherd. Accordingly, at 0645, Company B, Task Force Shepherd linked up with Company C in front of division headquarters.

We should call this the night of the long knives, or some other such sinister sounding description, for it begins what I call one of the first nights of hell. We were worried about the Iraqis who might be hiding in the burning oilfields of Al-Burqan. Radio traffic showed that the feeling was shared with the folks at Division, Regiment, and Battalion. We hoped we were ready and prepared. We waited.

Alongside and attached to Charlie Company, we had a TOW squad, about 10-12 HUMVEEs. We could use their thermal sights to keep an electronic eye on whatever went bang in the night. We occupied a space of about 800 meters across, a rather tight formation. Someone could always throw a rock from one tank to another. This was one way of supporting each other, as we couldn't quite see each other. Wouldn't you know, no one had a rock!

Some time during the early hours of the night we had movement in front of us. We could not see it either with the optics or with the thermal sights. We listened to all the chatter on the radio and followed as carefully as possible what was happening.

So, we sat and waited for the beginning of the night and the winding down of the first day of the invasion. We settled in for the night with the day's adrenaline rush slowly wearing off. The thought of fatigue, hunger, water, none of these wants had actually surfaced since we started the drive into Kuwait. I can't remember having had a drink of water the entire day. I can't remember attending to my bodily functions the entire day.

With radio traffic indicating that something might be brewing at any moment, plus the noise out in front of us, we decided on the standard fifty percent watch for the company. I took the first watch and had just settled down in my seat with earphones on when it soon became evident that Battalion was getting reports either from Regiment or from its own organic TOW assets. We had an armored thrust moving toward our direct front. In discussion with Captain Ed we decided that the attack was well in front of us and would not involve us at this time.

Battalion moved an anti-tank missile unit, a TOW platoon, forward of us. We acknowledged the move and were grateful to have the added thermal wizardry and weapons. We began to hear what sounded like the old Orson Welles' radio show, his War of the Worlds. It was eerie. I had my helmet half on and half off and there was the sound of small arms crackling fire, while at the same time the TOW commanders were issuing orders to one another. "I'm over here, man!" "Yeah, I've got you in my sights." "Do you see the bad guys?" "Yeah, I have a clear shot." "I'm clear." "Missile away." "Bingo, man, right on!"

In the distance I could see a very faint, almost subdued flash of light. I knew someone had been splashed. This was unlike training in Twentynine Palms when the TOW critters launched and the night sky lit up as the missile engine kicked in.

Anyone could see the brilliant light clear across the base, even all the way from where we were training. When the missile hit its target there was a tremendous flash of light.

Here in combat, we knew there was a battle going on but when the missile hit, there was a very faint light. I was straining to see; yet all I could make out through the smoke of the burning oil fields was a faint light from the explosion in the ever-deepening darkness.

"O.K., we've got a hit." "I'll take the next shot." "Confirmed." "Ready to shoot. Are you clear?" "We're clear. Go ahead and shoot." "Standby to shoot. Missile away!"

After a few seconds there would be another faint glow where a tank had been, and we would know someone had died. And so it went. We knew that they were involved with an Iraqi armored unit attacking our front and the TOWs were having a field day.

The Iraqi tanks couldn't return fire and hit anything because of the distance involved. With a TOW missile standoff range of some 3,000 meters, the Iraqi tank's main gun could only reach a distance of about 1,500 meters and, at night they can't fire that accurately because their sights don't go that far. The Iraqis were out there running around, and the TOW critters were literally tearing them apart. They really had no idea what was going on. I followed the battle for a while as it began to peter out, listening to the entire scenario as though it were a radio or TV show. I could see it and hear it but I couldn't taste or feel it.

My body was beginning to slow down, unwind, de-stress. Someone was dying but it wasn't me, all I could do was feel sorry for them. Dying inside a tank is a grisly way to meet your Maker. I felt almost detached from the whole scene. I only knew the Iraqi soldier, true to his Russian teachers, did counter attack, but was getting the short end of the stick.

The battle went on for what seemed like hours, although

perhaps only for an hour or two. Looking back toward the Al-Burqan oil fields the glow appeared to get brighter and more intense. During the day, when we had passed by, we could see that the oil wells had been torched, and we could see Iraqis running about their sandbagged bunkers like so many ants. The thought did occur to us, as we passed by these many bunkers, that our flanks were wide open and continued to be so. The tanks of Charlie Company and our all important logistics train were going to be very vulnerable to a flank attack. If some Iraqi general decided to put an armored/mechanized unit into that burning oil field, with all its smoke and cover... ah well, young Lieutenants are not to be concerned with such matters. The powers that lead and guide you report no armor lurking in that blazing oil field inferno, screened with the roiling smoke. Not to worry! Tank on, my son, and trust your higher leadership! As good Marines we tanked on, but disbelieved. Marines tend to ignore the mouthing of senior leaders who tell you all is well.

That night, as we sat waiting, a thought crept into my dulled mind. What happens if the Iraqis do not listen to our leadership and decide to come roaring out of the blazing oil field like Genghis Khan's hoard, but with their Russian built and trained armored units?

Somewhere to our front, in the total darkness, terrible war was being waged, but Captain Ed was taking the watch and that would let me get some sleep. I stood up, got out of the tank commander's cupola, curled up just behind the turret, and was sound asleep in about ten seconds. So much for war!

The next thing I knew I was being awakened. "XO?"

"Yeah, what?" I replied, trying to make out what planet I was visiting. Opening my eyes, I could see the twilight of the early dawn.

"Time to get up, sir."

"OK. I'm awake." I looked around trying to see how close Charlie Company had been deployed during the night. It reminded me of an administrative bivouac, we were so close. Suddenly I was hit with the need to eat. In fact all my biological needs suddenly required attention.

The sky was still overcast and for a while the rain lay as a drizzle over the company like a smothering blanket. People were up and moving about, almost in dream-like motion. It was the beginning of Day Two, otherwise known as G-Plus 1. I was still having a difficult time accepting the fact we were actually at war, shooting and killing folks. We were sitting there doing nothing but waiting. That was not what we had been trained to do, not we had been indoctrinated for, and certainly not what the Marine Corps War Fighting Doctrine was all about.

I could see the military airfield on the horizon; smell the stinking sulfur of the burning oil wells, but the fact that other assets of our armored group were more involved than us bothered me.

Battalion sent a HUMVEE over and took Captain Dunlap for a meeting of the minds. While he was gone we did the usual perfunctory maintenance on the tanks, ate some chow, the good ol' MREs, gobbled some bottled water, checked the tracks, and attended to our personal hygiene. One never knew when time for such care would arise again. A Marine must always look sharp, never knew when the Press might show up.

I had a little radio my dad sent to me. We popped that up and listened to any station we could find, gleaning whatever information possible. We were true mushrooms, living in the dark and totally unaware of what was happening to the rest of the war. The most we could gather from the radio was the fact the ground war had started and we were pushing deep into Kuwait. They knew about as much as we did.

Captain Ed returned and assembled the tank platoon commanders. Everyone seemed to have that look that we normally portrayed about the third day of a CAX (Combined Arms Exercise), yet there we were only one day into the invasion.

We adjusted positions, basically maintaining what we already had. We did not move, that I recollect, on day two. We just sat there, facing more to the northeast. I kept looking over my shoulder toward the burning Al-Burqan oil fields and wondered what was happening.

While the so-called atrocities were going on in Kuwait City, we just sat there, watching and waiting. Perhaps the atrocities could have been halted if we had been given the word to move faster. We had attained our objectives much sooner than the Division folks had anticipated, and I am certain they must have been pleased. I can imagine how CENTCOM felt about the situation; if we were so well ahead of schedule, we must have put the Army folks behind.

We spent the better part of 10-12 hours of daylight doing nothing, nada, zero, zilch. However, I did move my tank up behind the 1st Platoon section of our Company frontage.

Still, I had that eerie feeling that kept crawling up my spine because of our flank to the southeast and the burning oil fields that were supposedly someone else's responsibility. So, we went through the maneuver of repositioning our assets.

Just behind our new position was a vehicle partially covered over with the shifting sands of the desert. It looked like a Suzuki Samurai, the small 4x4. We determined that with the antennae and all the electronic gear showing, it must have served as a communications vehicle.

We were aware of the possibility of booby traps, but we reached inside and turned on the key. Bingo, the radio sputtered to life, receiving electronic signals and voice messages. It sounded like Arabic. Thinking we had an Intel treasure, we reported to Battalion that we had an Iraqi communications vehicle, one that still worked. What did they want us to do with it? Why nothing. At the moment they were disinterested, so we just left our big find in the sands.

Bored, I prowled around until I located the RPG sight.

We brought the sight to Mumbo. We examined the sight, attempting to get a better understanding of it. The RPG is a vicious weapon and in the hands of a competent warrior, can kill a tank with one shot. There are many stories about Army or Marine tankers in Vietnam being taken out with a single RPG.

Around 1400, the smoke from Al-Burqan oil fields shifted to smother us like a black shroud. It was difficult to see the face of my watch and know it was afternoon; it was pitch black. We were informed that the Marine Second Division was having problems with their breaching and would not show for some time. I suppose that was the reason we were being held in place, to await Big Al's A Team, the Corps' primo fighting unit. Brings to mind Simon's Law: Everything put together falls apart sooner or later.

Battles raged while we sat like beached whales. Listening to radio traffic we could hear small battles going on to our right, usually at the edge of the burning oil fields. Seems that 1/7 assets were busy engaging small armored units either running along our front or thrusting at us from out of the fog and smoke. Task Force Papa Bear appeared to be heavily engaged off to the northeast of us.

The darkness became deeper, an almost total absence of light. This is what a Black Hole must be like. I could hardly see my hand a few inches in front of my face, never mind the tank nearest me. I seemed to feel a mild vertigo when I tried to look outside our tank. The accompanying acrid odors overwhelmed our sense of smell, but it was our failing sense of sight that was more serious. There was no real concept of what was up and what was down. There were no boundaries of reference. I felt so dizzy my stomach became queasy. Quickly I would stick my head back down into the hatch to get a sense of reference. On the right side of the tank commander's hatch is a ballistic computer with lights. I focused hard on those lights to regain a sense of where I was, to offset the vertigo.

Eventually I turned on the FAC's thermal sight and used it to scan around through the gloom instead of trying to look outside and suffer from vertigo. I wondered what others were doing, if they had the same problems and how they were solving them. This was now the early night of day two. An entire Iraqi armored column could waltz by us and we would never see it.

We continued to sit and wait with the TOW critters lined up with us, their thermal sights clicking away, watching over us like dutiful sheepdogs. We were happy to have them. It was sheer terror to get out of the tank and go stumbling about in the void, to be so vulnerable. However, when Mother Nature calls one must respond. I actually fell off the tank trying to answer one of her summons. A tanker can close his eyes and visualize every feature, every nuance of his mighty M60A1 beast; until this day it is still possible for me to do this. How could I fall you may ask?

I was standing on the steel of the tank and could not see enough to determine where I was. The next thing I knew I was flying, through space. I had no realization I was falling because I had no reference that told me so, until I smacked the ground. It must be what divers feel when they suffer from Rapture of the Deep. It was dark! It was a good thing I had my bulletproof vest and flak jacket on or I might have cracked a few precious ribs.

Lying on the ground I could not see the tank! But first things first, I determinedly answered the mighty call from Mother Nature. That accomplished, I struggled to get the MOPP suit back on, then tried to locate the tank! I started walking and suddenly realized I was heading in the wrong direction. I was but a few feet from the tank and I was completely disorientated. Lost! I remember thinking I could wander about in that darkness forever, and no one would ever find me. Do not panic, I said to myself, at least I knew that I was somewhere in the Kuwait desert.

I knew I had to be somewhere near the right rear of the tank when I fell off. I crawled on my hands and knees until I felt the tracks of the tank in the soft desert sands. Patting the ground I could feel the track indentations. I was literally scared out of my mind. What would happen if the orders to start the company in motion arrived and one of the tanks drove over me? It has been known to happen.

Which way do I go to find the stinking tank? As long as I had the track I knew I was not lost and not that far away. I hoped! If I went in one direction for ten or fifteen feet and no tank, then all I had to do was turn around and head in the other direction. I hoped no one was watching all this with a thermal sight. I must have looked like some fool down on my hands and knees.

When I turned to my right I ran directly into the tank, smacking my head on the track. I uttered several wonderful expletives that only Marine tankers know. Former tankers who may read this book will know and understand the love-hate relationship a tanker has with his hog.

I managed to get my hand on the sprocket, pull myself up by my hands, and jump into the open hatch. Of course, I never let on about my exploits to Florence and the rest. Lieutenants never admit to anything that goes wrong, especially getting lost two feet from the tank. So, Florence, now you and the rest of the crew know.

Around 2400, the 1st Platoon Commander, Lieutenant Croteau, known to all as Red One, called to ask if I was listening to the game on the Divisional net?

"No, why?"

"Well, you might want to flip over real quick and give a listen. It's very interesting."

We had ten freqs that we had preset so I just flipped over and listened. There was this urgent, frantic voice calling for help. Help?

"Division under attack. This is General of the Marines, Myatt's forward CP! We are under assault by a tank battalion! We are in need of help! HELP!"

I looked around at the intensity of the darkness and said aloud, "Someone has to be kidding me!" Battalion was not volunteering us to help, and if we couldn't see, how could Division see? Who really was making this call for help; where were they?

We sat and listened to this counter attack coming down, wondering where it was coming from? Suddenly it dawned on us, the attack was coming from the Al-Burqan oil fields from where no attack was supposed to happen, our unprotected flank.

"Our tail is getting shot up. Someone help us," shouted voices.

Fortunately the CP had a company of LAVs (Land Assault Vehicles) and they were able to beat back that frontal assault that was never supposed to happen. LAVs against the heavier tank was not a good situation, but the crews in the lighter LAVs fought valiantly, driving off the Iraqi armored force. The Company CO of the LAVs got one of the two Navy Crosses awarded to Marines in the Gulf. This fact speaks more eloquently than I.

The clever Iraqis used the blowing sand and heavy smoke as cover to make their move against what turned out to be General Myatt's CP. We had been told that the smoke was too dangerous for us to inhale and therefore the Iraqis would also have the same difficulty if they decided to hide there. They did hide there, and they waited for night when it was most difficult, if not impossible, to see. I can quickly attest to that.

As the smoke shifted so did the noise level. What started out as a low noise, like a freight train in the background, soon became a rumbling that sounded like an army on the move. Moving an armored battalion is one of the greatest experiences I can think of. Watching a tank unit move, with main gun tubes pointing in alternating directions is an awesome sight. I never tired of seeing all that might and firepower on the move, even when the dust and fumes were so thick you could cut them with a knife.

To get fifty tanks and other assorted tracked vehicles from one spot to another in an administrative mode is one thing, to do so in a tactical environment that has the potential to become instantly hostile is another. A tank battalion formed into a perimeter like a really big covered wagon circle takes up about four grid squares on the map. For non-navigating types, that's approximately four square kilometers. Tankers speak metric. That's a lot of distance between individual tanks. While it is no problem to look across such distances, to be tactically correct tankers do not move when the sun is in the sky. Tankers clank at night!

This is how you do that. Before gathering the mighty iron steeds from the perimeter and commence racing across country, each participating unit sends out a group for a very special purpose. This group proceeds to the selected grid coordinates of the new bivouac site and marks the left and right limit of each unit. Thus coordination takes place, and a proper perimeter can be formed. This little group is known as the quartering party. The group sets out before dark, sets the limits, marks the individual tank positions with chem lights, then waits until dark and the arrival of the battalion.

It is a strange sensation to be sitting in the dark, in the middle of nowhere, talking quietly with the Marines around you, when the Battalion arrives. First there is a low rumbling sound similar to distant thunder that does not stop. Next the ground begins to tremble and shake, and the sound of large numbers of tracks can be heard. Soon engine noise and sounds from individual tanks can be heard. Then out of the dark the first armored behemoth appears with its main gun tube appearing like the sickle of the Grim Reaper. This sight made me glad I was a tanker who rode the beasts, and not one of the grunts who faced them coming out of the dark! It is no wonder tankers refer to our digging brethren as crunchies!

It was the memory of these quartering parties and the sights and sounds that went with them that I thought of when the oil fires from the nearby oil fields made their eerie presence known. The intelligent, logical mind knows that the rumbling and trembling is from massive energies being set loose by hundreds of gallons of petrochemicals being consumed by the blazing fires. That is rational thinking, but in the middle of the night, when one is on watch with only one's fears and nightmares, the memories of the Grim Reaper appearing out of the dark seem very real.

In the pitch darkness of night, sound can create a horrifying effect, like some strange beast tearing up the desert. Looking through a thermal sight made it worse. The burning wells made hundreds of heat signatures standing off in the distance, altogether a surrealistic scene. I began to wonder why I had taken the job of a tanker. Why hadn't I signed up for any specialty except tanks? It would certainly place me somewhere else other than in a tank where it may be impossible to detect an attacking tank in the blur of thermal signatures. While these thoughts raced about in my frantic mind, the oil fires seemed to burn with increasing ferocity!

Around 0100 the TOW critters started getting restless and began moving about in front of us, not a good sign. The only reason they would get nervous and start moving about would be the presence of the Iraqis! The TOW critters were like sharks anticipating a feeding frenzy.

I contacted the TOW critters and got the word that apparently the Iraqi tankers had bailed out of their tanks and were now running about on foot. Later in the night when the light was a little better a member of 2nd Tank Platoon came on the radio yelling, "Gas! Gas! Gas!" That meant we went through the procedure of buttoning up and doing all the requirements accorded a gas attack.

The gas attack turned out to be a spectacular display of Saint Elmo's fire. A blue-green color slowly began working its way down the radio antennae of the tanks, eventually jumping around the tanks with its eerie glow. It had an unearthly beauty as it slowly engulfed each tank. That incident was the first chemical scare of the night.

Everyone had settled back into the routine of 50% watch, 50% snooze, when the TOW critters again became restless. They had picked up someone on foot out in front of us. They brought in an Iraqi tank company commander who was trying to maneuver himself into a position to surrender his forces.

Eventually all this got pushed back to Battalion for a decision. Battalion or Regiment, maybe even Division, decided to send an interrogation team back with the Iraqi to palaver with his troops. That settled, we once again sat and waited.

The night wore on for us and for the Fox Vehicle, our German-made chemical detection vehicle with its state of the art computers. It could detect chemicals in the air down to a few parts per million, screening out pollutants such as sulfides from the oil well fires that raged all about us. I know that the Fox Vehicle detected chemical warfare gasses on at least two or more occasions.

This was not one of the more memorable nights I remember from the desert; burning oil wells, Iraqi tankers wanting to surrender, and the Fox Vehicle detecting chemicals not wanted in the area!

On the morning of day three, G-plus 2, we eventually had the opportunity to examine the chemical detection tapes that had been placed on each tank. We found traces of activation! We had positive chemical activation on several tapes placed in prominent places on the tanks. At the time we attributed the reactions to the petrochemicals that saturated the air. Later when we had returned to the States, I discovered I was wrong, the oil fires had not altered the chemical detection tapes. Whatever they were, there are many that witnessed them.

During the night, I swapped the watch with the FAC and before you could snap your fingers, I was fast asleep curled up under the main gun on the turret floor. While I slept, three quarters of an Iraqi division moved through as it surrendered to our forces. A great moment to be a Marine, a great moment in history, and I slept through it all.

Business Is Business

Scattered everywhere were hundreds of crates of ordnance, everything one could imagine. Disturbing was their sources: Jordan, Syria, Saudi Arabia, Yemen, Soviet Union, even the U.S.

Photo by C. Freitus

Gun ZSU-23-4

This is the ZSU engaged by Red during our breakout from the orchard onto the seventh ring beltway. Note the entry hole of the Heat round in the left rear of the turret.

Photo by C. Freitus

Chapter 12
G-Plus 2, 26 February 1991

The dawn of G-Plus 2 was not characterized by the persistent fog of the morning before. Units quickly moved to their attack positions for the assault. Reports were coming into division headquarters that the Iraqi III Corps had received orders to withdraw. General Boomer did not want the III Corps to get away, part of I MEF's two-division attack. General Myatt directed Colonel Fulford to begin moving at 0654. Boomer wanted both divisions to attack on line and Fulford's first task was to move his force north 10 kilometers to link up with the 8th Marines and the 2nd Light Armored Infantry Battalion of the 2nd Marine Division on his left.

The battleground that Task Force Ripper traversed was littered with enemy tanks and vehicles. Some showed obvious signs of destruction from air bombardment; other vehicles appeared intact but abandoned. However, some crews remained with their vehicles and waited in ambush. As Task Forces Ripper and Papa Bear advanced, each tank unit commander developed different policies for dealing with this threat. In Task Force Papa Bear, 1st Tank Battalion shot at everything, in Task Force Ripper, 3rd Tank Battalion tested Iraqi vehicles with long-range machine gun fire to see if the enemy responded. If it did, a tank round or TOW missile followed and dispatched the Iraqi vehicle. The infantry battalions led with their scout detachments, which

*used TOW thermal sights to determine whether the enemy
vehicle gave a "hot" or "cold" signature. If the Iraqi vehicle
or tank had its systems turned on and registered "hot" as a
result, they engaged it. The frequent firefights interrupted the
rapid advance with numerous stops and starts.*

*The drive to Kuwait City took place in two phases. In
the first part, General Myatt set the limit of advance for Task
Force Ripper at the "30" east-west gridline (marked by a line
of high tension wires) 10 miles south of the Kuwait International
Airport. Myatt ordered Colonel Fulford to hold Ripper there
while the rest of the division came into position for the final
push.*

*At dawn Task Force Ripper deployed into its standard
wedge formation and began the drive with 3rd Tank Battalion
in the lead. Encountering only scattered resistance which the
task force easily brushed aside, Ripper reached the designated
limit of advance at 1130 and halted.*

It was G-Plus 2, the third day of the ground war in the
Gulf. In military speak this sounds more like the terminology
used to describe the various Israeli wars with Egypt like the
Seven Day War. Given our location and how fast the Iraqi army
was crumbling, at least in front of our lines, it seemed we would
have such a label pinned on us. We were sitting in place right
before the Kuwait International Airport, just outside Kuwait
City.

Some time during the day, an additional Frag Order came
through for us. We discovered that we had been held in place so
that the 2nd Division could play catch up. The morning brought
some relief from the smoke, yet it never did get very light. Smoke
continued to obscure everything; only the thermal sights from
the TOW critters kept us informed of what was ahead of us. I
was reminded of the twilight during the Arctic winter night I
had experienced as a student at the University of Alaska,

Fairbanks. When the ambient sunrise in the desert came with improved visibility, I remember feeling great relief.

Upon orders we cranked up our beasts and moved forward across the line of departure. We utilized the same basic formation of tanks as before, clanking north and looking for a company of Iraqi tanks that was supposed to have defected and wanted to surrender. We passed a few burning hulks of BMPs (Personnel Carriers) and the usual surrendering Iraqis, but we ignored them in our search for the tanks.

We did not find those tanks; instead we closed on a major fortified area unlike those that we had encountered at the first and second barriers. They were major, large-scale fortifications. It looked like these Iraqis were a determined bunch and were going to make a stand. It was a congested mess and we secured only a single opening.

We moved Charlie Company through those large fortifications. At the time I thought that was a very bad area, and so I crouched down in the turret. The FAC must have had the same feeling for he held onto a M-16. With turrets traversing left and right gunners sought to acquire targets of any type. It seemed like one of those places where tanks did not belong. It was more of a bad feeling than thoughts of logic and reason.

There were large bunkers about the size of a typical mobile home, and not one of them appeared to have been affected by ordnance of any type, ground or air. They were completely intact.

Military discipline was excellent, and we cleared the bunker complex completely without a single problem. We were lucky for there was always the possibility that there was a lone Iraqi who had not gotten the word and who might suddenly stand up with an RPG and take out a tank. That possibility, although remote, worried me.

It seemed like an eternity for us to clear those bunkers, but once through we quickly dispersed into our standard running formation. We tanked on to a point about two klicks forward and came to a halt. It was at this point that ingrained training almost betrayed me and overcame my common sense. I was tired and so used to running a check on fluids after a certain running time I was about to execute that program which would have required traversing the turret to the rear. I could have placed our tank and crew in danger. The FAC, a sharp guy, warned me not to continue the check because we would be pointing the main gun at the bunkers we had just passed through. He prevented me from making what could have been a grievous mistake. I could have had guns facing into the murk and haze of the bunker complex with our folks still coming through. We remained at the halt area for about 30 minutes. We heard on the radio; the 2nd Marine Division was in the midst of the heaviest fighting of the war. We had been held up an entire day for those guys, yet they were the only ones being mentioned. And of course we were not! It bruised our collective ego. We had been in the desert since day one for months, and they, the late arrivals, were getting all the credit.

During the short halt we had a visit by the Commanding Officer of the Attack Helicopter Squadron that supported us with their Cobra gun-ships. During the first day of the invasion it was relatively easy for them to maintain contact with us, but as the winds began to shift and redirect the smoke from the burning oil fields, contact became extremely difficult. With high transmission power lines dotting the area, and the thick smoke, it was difficult to determine ground zero and where everyone was on the scorecard.

At this time we maintained two choppers up front with us. When it was time to replace them with fresh crews, the Squadron Leader would guide the two replacement choppers to us and return with the two that had been replaced, the best way to maintain an accident free venture. I liked this Marine who thought about saving other Marines!

At one point the Squadron Leader needed to coordinate with us and the FAC. Making contact, he notified us that they were inbound. Suddenly, in a swirling mass of smoke, the chopper appeared out of the blackness no more than twenty feet off the ground. We waved him in, and he set down just behind us. The FAC ran over and the two had a short conversation. As suddenly as he had arrived he departed, disappearing into he swirling black void of smoke. We had Cobra support during the entire mission, never once being interrupted. For his constant coordination with the advancing armor line and his actions, he was awarded the Navy Cross. He certainly deserved the award!

We continued moving north for the rest of the day, almost due south of Kuwait City. Eventually we arrived at a point just south of some enormous power transmission lines and setup camp. Those power lines and supporting towers were larger than anything I had ever seen in the States. They looked as if they ranged upwards to 300 feet in the air. We had driven to the edge of an old rock quarry when we heard of Iraqi personnel carriers moving about, so we drew back and allowed 1/7 to handle any problems with them.

The power lines had been fixed as one of our phase lines and Regiment decided that we would halt and secure our lines. Our west flank was wide open with a large gap, as were a few other flank sections. The large gap was between the 2nd Marine Division and us. They could not keep up.

With the TOW critters out on our flanks for security, it was a good time to stop and top off our fuel. We moved up to the power lines and began refueling; Top Sergeant Graham conducted the operation.

The smoke had lifted slightly, allowing us to see at ground level. It hung about us like a thick blanket of black fog.

Ahead we made out a large airstrip with several large buildings. Near one of them was a quad mounted ZSU-23-4 anti-aircraft gun system of four 57mm auto-loading cannons aimed directly at us! Everyone tensed as this particular weapon had an excellent rate of fire within a three-klick window, just where we sat.

Gunnery Sergeant Cochran came up on radio and reported that to him the emplacement did not appear occupied, but who knew where the gun crew was? FAC was ready to run some air strikes with the Cobras but at that moment there were no Cobras on station. If no Cobras, then how about some fast movers that were orbiting overhead, looking for work? Airborne controllers were flooding the FAC with requests for work and if they did not receive any they would divert the fast movers to another, deeper target.

Our FAC located and directed fast movers onto the target. Thirty minutes later the fast movers were still on station, and the FAC was pulling out what little hair he had left. He ran the nine-line brief over and over again, but then the ceiling began to drop. The air pattern had changed once again. Fast movers could not descend due to smoke. The FAC had to tell Captain Dunlap to scrub the mission.

Captain Ed ordered the target eliminated. We swung right, zeroed the target and fired. ZAPP, no more worries about that rapid-fire 57mm gun emplacement.

Refuelers finished topping off the tanks. We took on a few missing rounds of ammunition, stretched our legs and nibbled a few goodies when suddenly vehicles appeared in the smoke. They were not ours so we had targets.

Reports started flying in to Captain Ed. Disappointed with the response from the fast movers, our Company Commander ordered the FAC to get Cobras, which were then back on station, to deal with the targets.

FAC got on the radio, lasered the target, and Cobras popped up. A missile was launched and looked like it was headed right for the target some five hundred feet away. Instead it threw up dirt and debris in what appeared to be a miss. They say that practice makes perfect so we did it again, lasered the target, Cobras popped up, launched another missile. Hey, the same thing! What was going on? Do we have to engage with our main tank guns? The Cobras requested another go at the target but Captain Dunlap directed Blue to take out the targets.

Tanks hunkered down. The fire command was given. Whappp, somewhere about five hundred feet in front of us something blew up, propelling fire, smoke, bits and pieces in the air.

Someone, I think from Gunnery Sergeant Schofield's tank, identified the Iraqi vehicles as actually just large wooden wire and rope spools. We had destroyed a pile of junk. That explained why the Cobras with their Hellfire missiles were off target. We had lasered in front of the spools really about 100 yards out from where the missiles were supposed to hit because of the dense smoke and blowing sands. I remembered reports of the Golan Heights battle, classic tank combat at extremely close range in similar conditions.

Our maps revealed that we were near the Middle Eastern metropolis of Kuwait City, a point that I thought we might never actually reach. But there we were! I never imagined the fight would be as easy on us as it had been up that point. After all, we were psyched to expect massive hundreds of dead or wounded Marines and the loss of many tanks blown up from under us. We were briefed to expect carnage on a scale never before seen. The slaughter at Tarawa and Iwo Jima would pale compared to the buzz saw we would run into. Yeah, sure, the only hundreds we had yet encountered were the Iraqis heading south, grinning from ear to ear, munching on our pork MREs.

Our maps did not show the entire city of Kuwait and its streets, and other good stuff. We knew that urban fighting is deadly for tanks, and we would do it, but we expected to pay a terrible price.

Southwest of the airport we moved through a blowing dust storm, definitely not fun and joy, then continued to the next graphic control point. What lay ahead in that miserable blowing sand only the Gods of War knew and they were not telling.

Under the towering transmission lines, we moved onward toward Kuwait City. We herded our tanks through the roiling smoke and ran head-on into a series of scattered berms. There was nothing to tell us why they were there. They were not necessarily fighting berms, no troops hiding behind them, just long tank berms. They reminded me of what the Soviets called a Fire Sack, a system for channeling enemy tanks into a desired killing point where both direct and indirect fire can be more easily concentrated.

To break out of a fire sack a tank must climb the berm, a moment of extreme vulnerability because the tank becomes an easy target. None of that came to my mind, despite my tank schooling. Some very able instructors had taught me, all of us, about that very situation. Somehow these were just good ol' sand berms and we tanked right on.

As we continued tanking north I was aware that our company's frontage was shrinking inward as the berms came closer and closer together. We were being channeled. We reached another phase line, paused and waited for the rest of the Battalion.

We were among another set of towering power lines and their enormous supporting towers, more murky haze and the forever blowing sands. We remained submerged in sounds of battle everywhere, although mostly distant. I was with 3rd Platoon on the right of the Charlie Company, Captain Ed way over on the left. Arty started dropping and after a few crumps (hits) in front of us, we realized that it was too close for friendly fire. We reported Snow Storm to Battalion, and they reported to Regiment. They in turn notified various parties where we were and others who would determine where the fire was originating so that air bubbas could run a mission on it. Within four or five minutes from my initial report, a few more rounds fell, hitting closer to us.

"Battalion, Snow Storm!"

"Roger that," an oh-so-calm voice replied.

A few more rounds crumped in front of us and they appeared to be getting our range. Then the fire was shifting, walking each round closer and closer. "Forget Battalion," I called Captain Ed. "Gold, Snow Storm! It's getting a little cold over here. What's with Battalion?"

"They know; we are supposed to wait here."

The arty fire was then slightly behind us and walking back nearer to us. So then I told Captain Ed, "No Snow Storm! It's a blizzard!"

"O.K., let's get out of here. Move it!"

I cannot believe he ever got clearance from higher authority to move past the phase line, but we moved. I was the last to move, picking up the rear, one might say. For some reason I stuck my head down inside the tank and the medallion I had around my neck got hung up on the optics. It is the medallion my father sent me, one that his father had worn as a tanker during the Battle of the Bulge, WWII. When I again tried to stand up in the turret the medallion got hung up stopping me from sticking my head outside the tank. That was something that had never happened before we spent time in the Gulf, and never happened since.

All of a sudden the world moved, the tank lurched, not the ballet-like movement of the tank going down and then out of a hole, but rather like something had hit us from the side. At first I thought we had run into something. At that point I freed the chain from the optics and looked out. Behind me I could see the effects of the arty strike that almost got us!

After the concussion and initial blast effects, we got the

billowing effects of smoke and sand. We had moved just as
someone zeroed us. They had their arty batteries working and
we had been their target! We had received a glancing blow, a
hit.

When I originally called in the Snow Storm and finally
got the word to move, everyone had pretty much cleared the
area except for me, the Tank Platoon Commander. I was at the
rear of the column. I call it a glancing round by virtue of arty
characteristics, but it was a hit more like 20 feet away, from
something like a 105mm. Our sponson box and the right rear
fender were badly mangled, shrapnel holed and littered the gear
stowed aft of the turret in the basket, and some of the antenna
cables were sliced apart.

Mankind, probably most of us anyway, believe in all kinds
of unearthly spirits, god-like interventions and whatever, but I
could have been standing in that turret like some statue, and
instantly shredded with everything else. All that shrapnel
viciously tearing and bouncing around back there would have
done a real job on me. It was, I believe, the medallion that
perhaps saved my worthless grasshopper's hide. Was it my
grandfather, the Battle of the Bulge tanker who intervened?
One peculiar aspect I remember my father telling me about was
how his father had gotten the medallion hung up in his armored
scout car, and as he was disentangling it from the gun's sight, a
shell went off nearby that would have killed him had he not
been stuck. My medallion saved his life and I believe it saved
my life.

A short time later we had another encounter with arty
trying to do us under. It may have been Iraqi, it may have been
ours, but we were shelled. Despite all that we continued to
move through the channeled berms until we moved into an area
that was some kind of orchard. There were plenty of trees but I
never had the time to study the genus, species or variety. It was
an orchard because my map indicated an orchard. Marine Corps

maps are never wrong.

We stopped at the orchard. It was not a place to hide tanks, other types of military vehicles perhaps, but not multi-ton tanks! A so-called open area, or in tanker lingo a pool table, would be a much better place to hide. An urban jungle is not good tank country. There are better places to play.

We pulled up to the orchard in an echelon right deployment. Captain Ed conferred with the folks at Battalion and informed them where we were. The Colonel confirmed that Battalion would bring up the infantry and then we would start our sweep through the area. We were to go through the orchard, not around it.

I cannot believe that anyone at Battalion really understood how big the Emir's orchard was. On the map it occupied several grid squares. That was a big orchard!

I moved up just to the right of 1st Platoon. Before us was a giant berm that ran left to right. Sergeant Fitzpatrick's tank was to my immediate left front, 2nd Platoon's position was to our extreme left, wrapping around the berm. 3rd Platoon continued to move up to our right, slowly getting into position.

I was watching them make their move when I happened to glance left and saw Sergeant Fitzpatrick backing hard, popping his smoke grenades. Each tank is equipped with sixteen red phosphorous grenades, used as screening grenades. They are designed to provide a smoke screen that guards against both visual and thermal optics, such as those used by anti-tank gunners. With the wind blowing left to right, the grenade smoke was quickly in front of me.

"Sagger! Sagger!" Sergeant Fitzpatrick yelled, the term used by tankers to notify other tankers that we were being shot at by anti-tank missiles. The Sagger is also a specific and very dangerous missile made by the Russians, an AT3. As he was backing I ordered Florence to back as well. We had backed away from the berm and were now about fifty yards into our reversal when the top of the berm was hit with a missile. Perhaps it was the one aimed at Sergeant Fitzpatrick's tank? At first we figured it was a one-time deal, a single shot and it was over.

Logic ruled. Since the Russians trained Saddam's mother of all armies, we knew that the Iraqis would not place just a single round into the fire sack, rather they would concentrate their arty or missiles. So where there was one, there was bound to be many more of the little bugs out there seeking our tanks.

Sure enough we spotted a bright red ball coming in on us, a missile. We could tell that someone was controlling it with a joystick because it bobbed up and down as he adjusted to our violent backing maneuvers, with a very nervous hand of course.

We really could not tell if it was an American TOW missile, a Soviet Sagger, Swatter or something else. It really didn't matter, for here was this speeding red ball of death whose singular purpose was to kill us.

We were then backing like crazy, performing all the swinging movements that we had been taught at good ol' Armor U: Back up, make a sharp turn to the left, back up, make a sharp turn to the right, and so on. That was thought to be the approved method of avoiding being hit by an ATM. It was supposed to be difficult for the operator to correct the course of the missile if we were very busy making rapid, corrective turns. In the end the missile over corrects itself and takes a nosedive into the great Saudi sand box. That is the approved doctrine. With the missile coming at us, Florence, my faithful driver, had us backing and watching Fitzpatrick's movements at the same time, so that we did not do the Sagger Dance into or toward each other. This calls for some very tricky driving. Going against the accepted doctrine, I decided to use the Israeli move and had Florence put the tank into a straight left turn. Florence followed my directions never once questioning why.

I hit those smoke grenades, all sixteen of them in order to blind that stinking missile. The wind just blew the smoke right away, leaving us as naked as a Jay Bird against that missile. However, our smoke did cover 3rd Platoon from visual with the missile operator.

We kept backing and backing until I guessed that a sharp right turn was in order. Florence made that turn, backing us at a complete right angle to the missile. The missile missed, burying itself into the sand instead, blowing off the top of the berm. I could see the missile imbed itself into the berm blowing smoke and pulverized sand into the air.

Out of the smoke and flying debris emerged one of our tanks and the two of us came to a roaring halt, barely avoiding each other. Until this day I believe that no others in 3rd Platoon realized that there was an incoming Sagger missile racing directly into their path. They kept coming directly across the rear of where I was sitting, which was their position. I never heard the word Sagger over the Net; I was too busy with Florence trying to elude the missile. Folks behind us blissfully tanked on, moving into their next position.

We sat for a few minutes allowing all that had happened to sink in. We decided it was best to re-arm the smoke grenades. We carried sixteen and had expended sixteen, and might need more in a similar situation. I hopped out of the tank and went to the rear sponson boxes. That is when I discovered the damage that had been done by the arty round. At that moment I realized the Snow Storm I had broadcast was a lot colder and bigger than I had first thought.

I located the grenades mounted outside each rear sponson box and stuffed them into the launcher on the left side of the tank. When I went to fill the right side launcher, I discovered that one of the grenades had not fired. Normal procedure called for announcing a cease-fire and summoning the EOD lads to do their thing. That is what the procedure called for, but I reached down, popped the grenade from the tube and threw the blasted thing as far as my arm would allow.

CAX rules need not apply!

That done, I went around the backside of the tank and examined the coax cable connecting the radio inside the tank with its antenna, a modification that ran the cable outside the turret. The coax had been severed when the arty round tried unsuccessfully to take us out. I yelled down to Scott to hand me my Marine Corps K-BAR knife and a roll of electrical tape. I quickly married the wiring with tape and it stayed that way until the end of the war! So ended close call number two.

We stayed put for a moment and realigned our forces while Regiment sorted things out. They had to do that from time to time because we tended to move faster than they anticipated. Realignment saves friendly fire incidents. With Captain Dunlap nearer the left of our line, I decided to move closer to the center, giving us better command of the line, facing the orchard.

As we chugged toward the center I got the word from Gunnery Sergeant Cochran that one of his tanks was taking small arms fire from behind. My immediate concern was the grunts. Colonel Diggs, Mr. Battalion, was sending grunts forward in their tracked vehicles and even with our backs lit up by the brightly colored international orange identification panels and with our guns facing into the orchards, they might think that we were Iraqi armor. It easily could happen in the haze of battle.

I informed Battalion that we were taking small arms fire to our rear. Popping out of the turret to have a look around I spotted a line of green tracers between my tank and one of 2nd Platoon's tanks. The line of green tracers went whizzing through without hitting anyone. Our tracers were red and these were green, typical Soviet ammo. Therefore it must be Iraqi. That eliminated the possibility that it was Alpha Company shooting at us. It had to be some poor Iraqi angry at us because all his friends had run off and left him behind to be shot at with missiles, bombed and starved. All he wanted to do now was to get out of there as quickly as possible.

FAC popped his head up and wanted to know what was happening.

"There are mucho rounds being shot at us," I informed him.

"OK," he replied and ducked back inside.

Sagger fire from the front and small arms fire from the rear, not good!

Florence, within the safety of the turret, was sitting in the driver's hatch watching to see where the tracers were coming from and where they were going. The 2nd Platoon pulled a couple of tanks back and made a few machine guns rock and roll. The Iraqi must have figured that discretion was the better part of valor. He got out of there as quickly as his legs would move. We never heard from him again. No more green tracers whizzing between tanks. That was close call number three and hopefully the last.

The grunts in their tracks finally arrived. They got the go from Battalion to move through the Emir's orchard. There was the occasional crack of small arms fire, the occasional whump of a grenade; however, we were not certain they had made contact with the Iraqi infantry who were shooting up everything and anything.

Colonel Diggs, Battalion, commented, "I have set loose the dogs of war on the poor Iraqis."

Meanwhile the tankers were doing what tankers do while they wait. Someone was getting out an MRE, another was attending to bodily needs, usual tanker stuff. We suddenly got the word to move out to the dirt road that ran alongside the orchard. That was not a pleasant thought to a tanker. Foliage of the orchard could give an Iraqi grunt with a small missile such as an RPG, a recoilless rifle, or even a satchel charge, an easy opportunity to take out one or more of our tanks. Along with foliage there were berms alongside the roadway, which meant a hiding place for many grunts determined to do us bodily harm.

Captain Ed came up on the radio and issued the order of march. As the column slowly moved up the road, grunts stopped to engage Iraqi forces and that in turn halted everything on the road.

I was behind 2nd Platoon and on my right was a well-fortified bunker position that no one had given much thought to. One of the tankers, or one of the nearby grunts, caught movement, someone in the bunker. The next thing I knew there were grunts swarming all around the tank, firing into the bunker. A grenade arced through the air, landing with a loud explosion. Grunts started cheering wildly. I remember thinking this is not how I imagined John Wayne fighting the war! It seemed more like a Monty Python skit!

We moved along scanning for possible targets. The FAC was searching for something that might need the use of an air strike. That would really entertain the grunts! We had the main gun at a 90-degree angle, aimed directly into the leafy orchard. Although the main gun is generally used for long-range targets we were there to assist the grunts.

After what seemed like an eternity of traveling through the orchard we broke through the trees and out onto the road, the Seventh Ring Highway. At this point Red was in the lead, with White in the middle and Blue in the rear. Spaced in between Red and White was Gold, me between White and Blue. Bringing up the rear of the column was C-53 and Heavy Metal. Just as the last of Blue's tanks rolled up on the pavement pandemonium broke loose.

Red asked Gold for guidance, which direction to take. Gold's answer was to head north toward Kuwait and Red turned left to head up the highway. We were losing light rapidly because of the shifting clouds of thick oil smoke that had begun blowing across the battlefield. So, as Murphy's Law would have it, we had reached a road where we could pick up a little speed, and we could not see a thing. Thus, the Company had formed into a pretty tightly spaced column when from the front Red's guns opened up. It was an incredible light show with the muzzle flash of main guns firing into the night, and stabs of tracers leaving ghostly paths as they passed through the air.

Captain Ed behind the lead element began yelling, "Red? Red? Red? Acknowledge!"

I had never heard that level of concern in Ed's voice before, not panic, just stress. He could not raise Platoon Commander, 1st Lieutenant Croteau, Red! We had no report of what was going down or if there were any casualties. I tried to raise Red, no luck! I dropped the radio frequency down to the platoon common net and tried again to raise him.

Meanwhile the 1st Platoon was cooking off round after round. Explosions were popping off one after the other lighting the darkened sky. I finally managed to make contact with Red One, the platoon commander of 1st Platoon.

"Hey, Red One, give Gold a call right now and give him a sitrep! The man needs to know what's doing. Acknowledge!"

And so he did. Turns out there were two armored vehicles across the roadway. Our guys were firing point blank range. Rounds began to cook off causing our tanks to hurriedly pull back.

Now we had one of those infamous situations right out in front of us on the paved road; 3rd Platoon was emerging from the orchard; 2nd Platoon was trying to move onto the sides of the road in an effort to provide flanking support; 1st Platoon was trying to get out of the way of the secondary cook-offs! Here was a problem. To our left was the stinking orchard and to our right was a series of wire obstacles that prevented us from moving off the paved road. Usually, if wire like this is encountered there are always plenty of mines, in accordance with Soviet doctrine. That is their standard. For tanks, where there are mines, there is a no-go! It was too dark to see anything, and Battalion was doing its usual thing to find out what was happening.

Captain Ed came on the net and gave me a hasty order; "Get us a breach in that wire. ASAP!"

We had an engineer track with us equipped with a line charge. I figured the engineers would blast off the line charge of high explosives with a rocket attached to the end. A wind was coming up and if that foolish rocket went astray, as they were sometimes inclined to do, it might detonate one of our tanks!

Also, we had mine plows up front with us. The mine plow likely would than take some of the barbed wire with it and possibly detonate some mines. That seemed to be the most effective way to go.

I got hold of Blue, "To our immediate right, punch a hole in the barbed wire with a mine plow. Now!"

Lieutenant Gonzalves and Sergeant Martin acknowledged the order and got on with the show. Gonzalves knew the dangers as well as I did, but he punched the mine plow through, catching the wire and ripping a breach in the wire.

Quickly I radioed, "Gold, we have a hole!"

Captain Dunlap acknowledged and ordered, "Take the Company through and push because the Battalion is going to be right behind us!"

We were going to run the entire Battalion through this small hole in the wire. We had our hole but not necessarily a solution to our traffic problem, so I would play traffic director. The plow tank had not ripped up any stray mines and I considered that a good omen.

I got on the net and announced, "OK, everybody, listen up. The hole will be marked by two chem sticks. Look for the two blue chem sticks. I will lead you through."

I yelled down to Corporal Scott, "Get us through the breach."

I climbed out, took off my helmet, ran over to the hole and started waving the two chem sticks.

One by one I passed everyone through the hole. First, 3rd Platoon passed through, then 2nd and 1st Platoons, followed by the engineer track and what seemed like everyone and his uncle. I would not have been surprised to see Bedouins and their camels, sheep and goats pass through.

It never occurred to me that there might be mines, or more likely, someone watching me wave those blue chem sticks, someone who might want to do me bodily harm. In Marine fashion, everyone had a remark for me as they passed through.

With that accomplished, Charlie Company formed up in a modified wedge, which was more of an arc, the so-called beachhead principle. The Battalion pushed on through the orchard in the dark, a decidedly dangerous operation. It was difficult enough for us driving along the roadway, so we could imagine how difficult it was for the rest of the tanks and grunts finding their way through the tangle of trees in absolute darkness.

Once we formed up, Captain Dunlap gave the order to move forward. Darkness had settled in so all we could see was the nearest tank. The FAC had the TOW sight up and cooking, looking for trouble.

Moving away from the wire obstacle, we found ourselves going up a slight rise. On a desert pool table even a slight wrinkle in the surface gets noted. The lead elements with Captain Ed went up the rise and dropped down the other side into a trench.

"Back! Back! Back! Everybody back! Now!" ordered Captain Ed. "Pull back now!"

We backed!

Captain Dunlap had gone over the berm and landed right in the trench next to a live Iraqi soldier!

About 300 meters from our passage through the wire

obstacle, there was a berm and trench that was occupied by eager Iraqis. Things suddenly took on a whole new meaning for me because I had just been out there like some idiot, waving everyone through the hole in the breach. That hole in the breach took us smack into a bunch of Iraqis.

We pulled back a short distance and holed up while Battalion began pulling in behind us. Immediately Battalion sent one company this way, sent Bravo Company that way, and another company in another direction. As on the first day we decided to hold in place, especially because of the total darkness. Before long we had tracked vehicles running in all directions, confusing the issue, and a battalion of folks in an area normally occupied by a single company. SNAFU!

The FAC, looking through the TOW sights, was the only tanker that had "eyes." We immediately went into the routine of getting something to eat, attend bodily functions, make hurried repairs and keep an eye out for courageous Iraqis. We set standard fifty percent watches in the tanks, figuring we would be there for a while.

It seemed that I had just put my head down when the FAC announced, "Red! Red! You have movement to your front! You have one on foot!"

I hurriedly sat up and smacked my head on the underside of the main gun. As all good Marine tankers do in these circumstances, I muttered secret words heard only by members of the warrior race! That hurt! I finally managed to poke my head out of the turret. "What's up?"

"Red has what looks like someone trying to surrender."

While the FAC spoke to Red, the Iraqi walked up to one of the tanks, and waving his hands in the air, surrendered. He was injured and hungry, all good reasons to surrender when you are a member of Saddam's elite.

After a short discussion we got the Iraqi over to the engineer track to see the Doc and the Kuwaiti interpreter. Doc patched up the soldier and saw to it that he was fed, MREs of course. He was in pathetic shape, malnourished and terribly shabby. Through the interpreter we learned that everyone who was manning that particular Iraqi position had taken off and forgot to tell him, they left him behind.

With the excitement over, I decided to go back and catch up on my interrupted sleep. Then I noticed it was near daylight and I had slept most of the night.

"Hey, how come you guys let me sleep so late?" I asked.

"What are you talking about?" the FAC muttered, "It's about 0200, early morning."

It was the lightest night sky I had seen in days. I could look around and see where all the tracked vehicles were positioned. It looked more like an administrative bivouac than a battle set up.

We had crammed Tracked Vehicles, HUMVEEs, everything into this one area. I hoped that no Iraqi arty decided to send a greeting card! Shrugging off this thought, I swapped the rest of the night with the FAC so he could get some badly needed sleep.

What was left of the night and early morning passed quietly. False spottings of roving phantoms stirred groggy thoughts, but no major problems occurred. Around 0500 word filtered down from Battalion that a cease-fire was to take place at 0800. We waited, held our collective breath. Was the war going to be over? Had the Army made it all the way to their objectives? Was this all there was going to be? George Bush implied that we were not here just to liberate Kuwait, but to kick Saddam's most prominent part!

The question remained, did the Army really make it all the way? The BBC news was reporting that the Army units had gone as far as the Euphrates River. What was going on? We felt like mushrooms again.

The 0800 news came through: Cease fire!

Cautiously folks crawled out of the tanks and tracked vehicles and milled around. We spoke softly with one another, shook hands all around and patted each other on the back. The euphoria was slow in building, but the joy of knowing the war was over could be seen in each face. Like the Iraqis we had sent south, we too were grinning from ear to ear. We felt great and very relieved at the same time. We may not have seen the same elephant as those who fought in WWI, WWII, Korea and Vietnam, but we did see our own elephant.

Oil fields continued to spew roiling black smoke high into the morning sky, casting the shadow of gloom everywhere despite the sun struggling to show itself. It no longer mattered so much; the war was over. Our joy left little concern as to whether or not it was worth the vast endeavor. That line of thinking would come later with a clear head and the time to contemplate the war.

A new order came down and Charlie Company ended up staying just about where we were. We faced the highway with Kuwait City pretty much to our back. I believe that we were on what was known as the 7th ring of the Coastal Highway that skirted Kuwait City. Now we did an about face and set up on the other side of the berm.

We had on our flanks either 1st or 2nd Platoons right on the highway. As we were setting up, moving tanks into position, we were told to expect Arab Coalition Forces to be moving through our positions. They would be either Syrians or Egyptians, with the Kuwaitis out in front. That is exactly what finally happened. The Arab forces moved on through us and occupied Kuwait City.

Of course we were in the best position to move into Kuwait City, but the Arabs had to be seen by CNN when they entered the city. That would be a PR moment for the Arabs because they would be seen by the rest of the world as the liberators of Kuwait.

After the Arab armored units moved through, a mass movement of Kuwaiti citizens followed. Of course they were driving back home in their Mercedes, Caddies, Beamers and four wheelers of all types. We had watched them exit Kuwait in large numbers and now we watched them return in large numbers. Frequently traffic would stop and they would give out Kuwaiti flags and hug and kiss any Marine that was fortunate enough to be in the vicinity.

The Morning After?

L-r: Lance Corporal Coleman, Alpha Command Group Cartographer, and Lieutenant Chris Freitus, Executive Officer, on the morning of G-Plus 3 shortly after the cease fire was announced. Note the MOPPS and high state of in-the-field hygiene.

Photo by C. Freitus

Gun Emplacement

One of three guns positioned at the point Charlie Company emerged from the orchard. Note the ready rounds both in the feed chutes and broken out on the ground.

Photo by C. Freitus

Chapter 13
Kuwait International Airport

From 28 February to 5 March, division units remained at the Kuwait International Airport in positions occupied near those established on 26 February. Beginning in March Major General J. K. Myatt directed the withdrawal of his Task Force Ripper, Papa Bear, and Taro on successive days. The initial stopping point for most units was the port of Ras-Al-Mishab, where they unloaded ammunition and began preparing vehicles for going back on board ship. The 1ˢᵗ and 3ʳᵈ Tank Battalions and their M60Als were transported to Jubayl by ship and completed their preparations there. The remainder of the division moved from Mishab to the division support area at Manifah Bay, where it awaited transportation to home bases in the United States, most to Camp Pendleton, California.

Once the movement back to Manifah Bay ended, Major General Myatt cancelled the task organization of division units on 6 March. Two days later, the advance party for the 7ᵗʰ Marines; 628 Marines from 3ʳᵈ Battalion, 3ʳᵈ Marines; and 588 Marines from 1ˢᵗ Battalion, 5ᵗʰ Marines, departed Saudi Arabia. The 1ˢᵗ Battalion, 1ˢᵗ Marines, conducted a tactical TRA (recovery of aircraft and personnel) mission 10-12 March to find the wreckage of an OV-10 (light, observation aircraft), shot down in mid-January. Other units conducted sweeps of all live-fire ranges in Saudi Arabia. The division's main effort

*during the retrograde period was on recovering equipment from
Kuwait and reconstituting equipment for the Maritime
Prepositioned Force. Whether occupied on those tasks or
engaged in making personal preparations for departure, all
Marines waited impatiently for their flights to the United States.
By the end of March, more than half the division had departed
Saudi Arabia. The division completed pre-deployment on 24
April 1991.*

The next four or five days were a blur of activities. We
maintained our roadside position, settling in until the actual
surrender occurred. We continued to watch the massive influx
of traffic as all those who departed when the Iraqis invaded
Kuwait were now returning. Our roadside position gave us an
excellent view of the Kuwait International Airport, and with all
the surrender activity occurring, we watched a tremendous
increase in air traffic. By day helicopters and cargo aircraft were
moving constantly in and out of the airport.

We sent most of our time going through the usual after
action procedures; ammo counts, resupply of those wondrous
packaged meals, the usual tank maintenance and very quickly,
the mail, which we did not have for several days. Many kudos
to the Marine Corps, for as soon as it was possible, they brought
the mail directly to us. It had been several days since we last
had mail and this was a welcome event. No one, unless they
had been in a combat situation, far from home and loved ones,
can realize the value of mail. It is something I shall never take
for granted again. Opening the mail, there was a wonderful letter
from my niece Hali and her Kindergarten class. Inside was an
American flag. It was wonderful to receive it for we had been
forbidden, as members of the coalition forces, to fly the American
flag! No one wanted to upset our hosts.

Someone took a picture of me holding the letter and
the American flag, and if you look carefully you will see tears

running down my dirty, smoke encrusted face. It was an emotional moment to have that flag, at that time and place, sent by young folks from far away in the States. I felt just great!

That night we hoisted a large American flag on C-51, Captain Ed Dunlap's tank, and I hoisted the Marine Corps Flag, that I had brought along for the occasion. We flew the flags from the large radio antenna on the tanks. They looked beautiful fluttering in the evening desert breeze. If anyone drove by on the nearby highway they saw an American Marine Corps tank company complete with flags. We were proud. I still have that flag, oil stains and all. We were United States Marines and we didn't care what the world thought at that moment.

The next few days were punctuated with sporadic gunfire from the Kuwaitis, apparently dealing with the stray Iraqi soldiers and Iraqi folks left behind. Understand that the Iraqis had brutalized them. We were told to keep an eye out for stray Iraqis but we never saw any. Maybe the Kuwaiti got them first.

We were sitting around the tanks finishing our gourmet MREs when out of the gloom and doom appeared what looked like a herd of the angora goats, or sheep, with a Bedouin shepherd. He led his herd right through the scattered tanks, across the roadway, through the wire and into the desert beyond. I remember listening to the animals complain and I wondered where in the world did they come from? Where did the shepherd manage to hide his flock all this time? A time that had shells, missiles, small arms fire, tanks and assorted tracked vehicles from both sides racing through the smoke-choked desert sands? How did he manage to get them past the starving Iraqi troops? We had picked up the military gossip, and from CNN, that the Iraqis had eaten all the animals in the Kuwait zoo. I thought of some humongous animals that must have been in that zoo, for the Emir could well afford to have the best! I wondered how tiger steaks taste, or lion roasts, or....

We sat munching our MREs, watching this young man

dressed in typical Bedouin garb, prodding his flock along and slowly fading into the oblivion of the desert sand. It was an amazing sight to behold.

Waiting, as we were busy doing, continued as one aspect of our military life. Hurry up and wait. We waited for someone to tell us what to do and where to do it. With little else to attract our concentration we began wandering around studying remnants of various fortifications on either side of the road, also the nearby berms. We were able to observe a direct, fixed anti-aircraft battery, three guns. This was a versatile weapon, one that could be used equally well against aircraft and armored vehicles, with devastating results. A weapon like that can wreak havoc on an unsuspecting tracked vehicle. As it turned out there were several such positions in the area. They were more than likely used for protecting the aircraft that flew, or should I say were supposed to fly, out of the airport. Had they been manned when we came dancing through during the night, it would have produced some murderous results. Located on slightly higher terrain, they could have looked down on us and would have controlled the entire area.

It occurred to me while observing those gun emplacements that my stunt with the chem sticks meant that I probably had a guardian angel looking after me.

I warned the troops that if they were going to be curious, they were not to travel alone and were to keep a constant eye out for booby traps. We knew that the lure of souvenirs would draw them to the nearby bunkers and trenches, which were littered with all sorts of military trash. It was like being turned loose in candy land! We constantly reinforced the prospect of surviving the war only to die by some unseen booby trap. We had been lucky to this point; we had not lost anyone to a booby trap.

It was curious to note the many gun emplacements and bunkers so near us and yet completely untouched by the air bubbas. If we had called in our covering Cobras, they most certainly would have wasted those gun emplacements; but we had listened to all the bull roar about how there would be no ground war as the Air Force fast movers would eliminate all ground opposition. No need to put troops on the ground! Well, standing there looking at all those intact gun emplacements and dugouts, it seemed that someone forgot to tell the flyboys; they had missed a good many sites.

We had been instructed that we could not bring back anything that smacked of ordnance such as guns, hand grenades, RPGs, recoilless rifles, tanks, BMPs and so on. Years later, as an instructor at TBS, I met members of the Marine 2nd Division and they had all types of ordnance as souvenirs, bayonets, handguns, etc. Despite the orders we went right on searching for all sorts of junk to bring back home, a memento of the war. I located many enemy maps, a particular interest of mine, and found them to be of better quality than our issue. There were all types of literature, instructional booklets, map material, and Iraqi black berets with inscriptions on them. Significantly, we found gas masks as well as decontamination kits especially fascinating because the decontamination kits were completely empty. As I stood there I wondered what the Iraqis would have done if Saddam had loosed the really mangy dogs of war and utilized germ warfare? Today I wonder do they suffer from the Gulf War Syndrome, as do countless numbers of our veterans?

Most of the physical gear we found appeared to be Russian issue. A few of the items we collected were of particular interest to us, especially the black Russian tanker's helmets. Determined as I was, I found a Coke bottle with all the Arabic inscriptions on it and filled it with Kuwait sand. Despite the warnings and threats of the Customs Inspectors, I managed to get it past all inspections and check points buried in a bag of dirty clothes. I figure the sand was a fair trade for the RPG sight that I was told I could not bring home because it was an ordnance item. No REMF got the sight either. With a twirl in the air by the carrying case strap, the optics of the once vaunted Iraqi troops became so much scrap on the concrete floor of the inspection station.

In collecting the sand to bring home, I was amazed by the difference in the color of sand. The surface was dark, covered with oily droplets from the many burning oil wells, and underneath was the beautiful, white, shining sands of the Kuwait desert. Today, that small bottle of sand remains for me a connection to the war in the desert. I wondered if anyone had bothered to scoop up some sand at Iwo Jima and brought it home as a connection?

When it came to souvenirs what we collected paled compared to what the higher ups decided on. With all the battlefield junk lying about, they decided to go big time, something large, meaningful and certainly memorable like a T-72, Russian-made tank. Yes, the word was sent forth to hunt for a tank.

The crew brought back a BMP and a T-62 tank. It soon turned into a photo opportunity for everyone; cameras clicking as everyone wanted a shot of themselves, or with their buddies, to show the folks back home. You know what they say about Marines, find a Marine and someone nearby will have a camera.

Listening to CNN and BBC news, we began to develop a degree of uncertainty about the course of the war from this point on. In other words, what was happening in the world of military politics? We listened to the news as often as possible, and heard that the coalition forces disagreed over how the war should be conducted now. Do we push on to Baghdad, hunt down the evil Saddam and his royal palace flunkies? Ahhhh, said the Arab bubbas, if we do that then Saddam will lose face, and in the Arab world that is not good. He lost the stinking war, did he not? Or did he? The question raged on; what to do?

We wondered, do we begin to make ready to go home?

As Marines our mission was at an end. We were not occupation troops. Do we stand around, or what? Like all armies we did stand around, and waited, waited and waited.

Rumors intensify in times like that. Where would we be going? When would it happen? This part of war seemed not to have changed since the Egyptians fought the Nubians in the African desert centuries ago. There really was little to do except explore the area, search for souvenirs and become involved in the many discussions of the latest rumors.

The Corps brought in more mail and food. I opened a package that contained a bundle of valentine cards. With them was a picture of Groton Country Day students from Groton, Massachusetts, and my own hometown! I remember looking at their faces and thinking these were such loving and caring youngsters!

We hear many negative things about our young folks every day, but those were students who took time from their busy days to send all those wonderful cards and notes. That mail was very special, more so because it arrived just after the ground war ended. It truly helped to brighten our days. I shared all those cards and notes with my fellow marines. To those youngsters who may read this book, I say, thanks from one very appreciative Marine.

Eventually word came down for us to retrograde from the lush surroundings of Kuwait City. We organized, groaned and got our act together. Onto the paved road we went, turned south like so many of the Iraqi prisoners had done, followed the ring of roads around Kuwait City itself onto the coastal highway and followed it south. This trip was an experience I will not forget.

As we got onto the highway and started the move south we found the way littered with burned out Iraqi vehicles, from either aerial bombardment, TOW engagements, armored confrontations or whatever. It became evident their assets had run into something and had the living breath blown out of them. There were burned out hulks everywhere. We saw burned bodies occasionally, tankers who did not get away in time and died. As far as our eyes could discern oil wells burned across the desert landscape leaving the sands covered with a thick black grime that stuck to you when you walked on it. Many of the wells had enormous pillars of fire reaching into the sky to form a cloud of roiling black smoke that covered the desert sun.

Evidence of the continual aerial bombing was all around us. Burned out buildings, rubble and tracked vehicles were everywhere. In the air the traffic bordered on the New York rush hour. Large transport aircraft, one directly behind the other, landed with assets while choppers from the Marines and the Army passed directly overhead, sometimes in formation.

As we neared the city we began to see the damage the Iraqis had heaped on the folks of Kuwait; houses blown up, windows shot and smashed out, traffic lights shot out, signs shot up by what looked like automatic weapons, manhole covers taken. Anything not nailed down was looted and taken back to Iraq: lampposts, telephone poles cut off at ground level, fire hydrants, park benches were gone. It seemed hilarious the Saudi folks looked upon us as infidels in Allah's chosen land, then what was Saddam?

As we entered the city, people began to come out from buildings to stand along the streets cheering and waving at us. Riding on top of the tank with women, children and men waving and crying, we were reminded of WWII films where you see the victorious Allies cheered as they moved through the streets of France. This scene amid a background of burning oil wells is one many of us will keep close in our memories. We had been sent to help save a small nation and it was extremely satisfying to be appreciated even as we suspected that our government had sent us for political reasons, to save our consumers their precious oil supply. Lawrence of Arabia had said, long before we came to the Gulf, "War was the breakdown in politics."

Looking on the faces of those children, we knew the smile and wave was genuine and meant for us. The cheers were not for the Ruler of Kuwait, or General Norman Schwarzkopf, or any of the brass, it was for us. We had fought well. Being young and perhaps naive, we all felt that what we had accomplished was good even if future history books might allot us only a single paragraph or a footnote.

One last observation on Kuwait City; it was obvious the place had been sacked by the Iraqi Army. Except for the Mosques and other religious structures that seemed to have been left intact, everything else was looted. There was little of what appeared to be collateral damage from the air bubbas or the arty folks.

The move through Kuwait City with the entire Battalion in single file went very smoothly, with our tank retriever dragging our captured BMP. This was to be our war trophy and would be parked out front of 3rd Tanks back at the Stumps, Twentynine Palms, California.

We had a standing order that coalition forces were not to fly the American flag. However, Captain Ed kept an American flag flying from his radio antenna the entire trip from Kuwait south to Saudi land, and I kept the Marine Corps flag flying as we drove up to or passed crowds of folks. They would recognize it and yell, "Marines! Marines!"

When we reached the outskirts of the city we met an Egyptian unit encamped beside the road. I remembered seeing the films about the PLO and others firing their AK47s and other weapons into the air and I wondered where all those bullets fell. I knew many people were wounded or killed because of these bullets flying off into the unknown. So, what did the Egyptians do? Why, shoot off their AK47s into the air, of course. AK47s and light machine guns blasted away, ripping hot lead into the air above. I kept thinking I was going to die. A coalition bullet, fired by some friendly Arab, in celebration of winning the war and cheering us on, was going to land directly in the middle of my CVC helmeted head!

I am not certain any of our people still out in the desert reported taking small arms fire, but I am willing to bet there were folks out there miffed because they had small arms stuff falling all around them long after the cease fire!

Once through the city, we rolled onto a highway four or five lanes wide. We met other units going south, one of them was a Qatar armored unit, equipped with armored scout cars. Actually this was their mechanized unit in the Gulf, four-wheeled scout cars mounted with 105 howitzers. They looked mean, real Middle East fighter types. It was humorous to learn later that these were not Qatarans but mercenaries wearing Qataran uniforms, driving Qataran armored vehicles and flying the Qatar national flag. Maybe they fought so well for an extra bonus. There is nothing like an incentive package!

We moved south and on toward El Kafgi located just inside the Saudi border. The coastal highway was in good shape except for the last three or four miles which were badly torn up by armored vehicles that had been caught on the road when the Iraqis came across the border to attack Kafgi. We made a good many detours off and then back onto the roadway. For tankers who normally clank across the dirt, driving on a paved road was a novelty.

We passed many blown and destroyed vehicles, wrecks of all types, but little evidence of bodies. That suggested to me that many of those vehicles were not occupied when they were taken out. Many had simply broken down or were abandoned, becoming targets of opportunity for the flyboys.

We could see the obstacle belt off in the distance. When we had rehearsed for it's breaching we had utilized engineering tapes and played a game of pretend. We knew guys on the other side were going to dig really big ditches, plant many mines and try to blow us up. Then beyond the obstacle belt we expected flame trenches; gigantic ditches supplied with oil by pipes from the oil pumping stations. The expectation had been that when the war began, some Iraqi would flip a switch and fill those ditches with oil, highly flammable stuff, then ignite the entire mess. We would face a wall of flame and possibly be barbecued without sauce. There was no way to bulldoze those trenches because the stuff would just splash out all over the place.

Well, the closest thing I saw of fire trenches was at the obstacle belt when we came to El Kafgi. There were a few ditches that ran up to and under the road that looked like they had oil in them at one time. We stared at them and marveled. "So, this is what a flame trench looks like!"

Moving closer to Kafgi, we learned how poor our Intel was. We had been told our reactive armor was unique to us, here in the desert. The Israelis had taught us how to use it, but we still worried about heat rounds used by the Iraqis. The heat round is a chemical energy round designed to punch through armor with a focused, shaped charge and blast the inside compartment of the tank. Tanks normally have sloped surfaces designed to reduce the effect of an explosive charge striking the outside of the armor. The Israelis determined that if the effective shape could be further stood off from the tank body, the shaped round may not work as well. To this end they devised the plates of reactive armor. The U.S. military establishment eventually utilized it on our M60A1 tanks in Saudi Arabia.

Knowing that the Russians had adopted reactive armor and were advising their client states to do likewise, a question remained with us; did the Iraqis utilize reactive armor? We had been briefed that the Iraqis did not go in for reactive armor.

What did we see as Charlie Company was moving south? A T-55, an older version of a Russian made third-world tank, stood off to one side with gun barrel drooping into the Saudi sands. Reactive armor covered the turret. Did the intelligence community know about this?

The word

for there is sometimes little intelligence in the intelligence community. Did they know the truth and yet fed us deceptive Intel for a reason? Later when I visited the U.S. Army's Aberdeen Proving Grounds and asked the same question the answer was, "No, that could not be! The Iraqis never used reactive armor!" When I informed them of what we had seen, I was flatly told I was wrong.

Moving through Kafji we passed through a customs checkpoint, and like all good tourists we paid our respects to the custom officials stationed there. They wanted to know if we had anything to declare and indicated they might want to conduct a search. However, our 105mm main gun seemed persuasive and they hurriedly allowed us to pass through. We drove through customs noting that the station buildings did not appear to have any damage. It reminded me of a saying: "Business is business and after the war we will need this checkpoint in order to inspect vehicles."

Kafji was a ghost town other than for some American Marines and Air Force types, and a few Saudi National Guard. There was nobody standing around cheering or waving; no Bedouins, camels, Arabs, goats or sheep. Everyone seemed to be suspiciously absent that day. The place was shot up and abandoned, appearing to have more damage than Kuwait City.

The passage was quick, and once through we stopped just south of the city for a check. Since it had been one of the longest road marches we had accomplished we changed drivers, checked the fluids, left some of our personal fluids behind, checked the tracks and so on. With the need to feel the power of the tank in his own hands, Colonel Diggs drove for a while. Once a tanker always a tanker!

We tanked on until dusk. Captain Ed Dunlap calculated where we were, pulled us off the road and lined us up in four rows, fender-to-fender. It was the closest we had been throughout the entire war. We were at Manifah Bay.

Just as we were about to shut down all systems, our Polaris System, the famed positioning black box that had died at the beginning of the war, suddenly bleeped back to life. The area director demanded that we identify ourselves. With a laugh I reached over and shut the thing down, accompanied by several unprintable words.

The first order of business was to find a gedunk for snacks and sweets, and a telephone, in that order. In short order we found a PX as well as a telephone center. It was interesting to walk into the huge tent, looking at all the gedunk stuff they had to offer, pringles, cup of soup, junk-food of every description. We wanted everything. After buying some goodies and picking up mail, I sauntered (we had by then developed a strange walk from being too long in the desert sands) over and waited in line to make a telephone call. Waiting in a phone line would take hours, but no one ever lost their temper.

First I tried calling home to my wife Venus; she was at work, teaching. So, I called Mom and Dad collect, and to this day I can hear my father's voice as he called to Mom. "Anne, it's Chris; he's alive and on the telephone!"

All I could get out was, "Hello, I'm alive and well."

I did not know what to say, no pearls of wisdom, no catchy verbiage or shouts of joy, just the fact that I was alive. We had a brief conversation, and Dad agreed to call my wife later on. We discussed happenings in the desert war and how fast everything would occur from that point. I was not the same person after the battle, trying to talk with a lump in my throat and make sense to my father, an older warrior.

The night set in. People who still had a ground cot slept there. If not, the tank fender was no stranger; we had all slept on it many times. It certainly was not the Hilton or the Imperial Hotel, but it was better than sleeping on the ground. There were too many little critters that bit in the dark!

The Marines Have Landed

The crew of C-52 surveying one of the Iraqi gun positions. Far left is the FAC (Forward Air Controller), Captain Jeff "Mumbly" Butler, who replaced Lance Corporal Reedy as our loader. This gun was fully functional with a round in the chamber.

Photo by unknown member of Charlie Company

Chapter 14
Retrograde to the States

The next morning we sallied forth to the ammo dump to off load; no one wants little sand colored monsters running around the more civilized portions of the sand box with live rounds. The ammo turn-in was not what we expected, to say the least. Our operating history at the Stumps had taught us there is a definite system for the issuance and return of ordnance. Uncle Sam's children have a system for just about everything. When the Company returned from the field there were multiple checks by everyone conceivable to make sure all bullets and other ka-boom toys were returned to storage. Everything had better tally up or there would be consequences!

Here in the great litter box there was no such system in place, we simply dropped the tarps off the tanks, unloaded all the bullets, grenades, flares, mines, rockets, and other assorted items of ordnance. Once the Company had off-loaded, and a tank company can off-load a pretty good amount of ammo when it is loaded for combat, we drove off into the sand toward our next stop, Al-Mishab. No paper was produced by any ammo-tech wanting or requiring a signature, so I do not have the foggiest idea of what became of the ammo we off-loaded, or who was the responsible account-keeping adult. As we tanked off to our next destination, I was relieved not to be the one who signed for it; I did not have to worry about the ammo count. As far as I know, that stuff still may be there in the sand, wandered over by camels and goats!

At the mighty port complex of Al-Mishab, we assumed the military mode that has prevailed perhaps before the days of Roman Legions, hurry up and wait! We enjoyed watching the REMFs and others in their clean and neat desert warrior attire; their desert camies, their new desert boots and stylish bush-hats. They wore in the approved, correct manner their ever-present shoulder holster for their 9mm Beretta. The rear effort looked sharp. Anyway, as we set up to wait, the rear types started to drift near us and pretty soon the cameras popped out. Everyone wanted a picture with our tracked behemoths, especially around the Iraqi BMP (Soviet Personnel Carrier) that our retriever was dragging behind it.

While we waited, we had the opportunity to see the damage done by Saddam's great oil spill; by this point it had meandered its way down the Saudi coast. What a good neighbor to those around him. It looked like one of the disasters that CNN used to report before it took up wars; oil tankers bashed onto rocks and dumping thousands of gallons of oil into the adjoining water.

The Company formed up into an administrative bivouac, only the second since departing the port complex some five months before. It felt awkward to be so close to the other tanks and their crews, and, more importantly, not to have the Company set at the 25-50% watch we had maintained as our normal procedure for so long. We set a roving sentry around the perimeter of the Company Lager Compound, but somehow I felt naked, vulnerable. I guess being only hours out of the active war zone of the KTO (Kuwaiti Theater of Operations on the CNN briefs) it really had not sunk in that our fighting days were through, over, complete, finis!

Charlie made the move to the port complex of Al-Mishab, where Navy gray monsters were located. A lonely wharf, really a dock, jutting into the deep, oil slick waters of the Gulf held two U.S. Navy amphibious transports. Looking back, I believe one was a LSD (Landing Ship Drydock) and the other an LST (Landing Ship Tank). My amphib experience was rather limited at that point!

Off to the side was a very large landing craft capable of loading onto or off of an amphibious transport. Tanks, at the time, usually loaded onto LCM's (Landing Craft Medium), and the LST was usually our transport of choice if we needed to board ship. The LCAC (Landing Craft Air Cushion), a hovercraft, was slightly bigger but this landing craft looked like a small ship unto itself. That strange craft belonged not to the Navy but to the U.S. Army. They were branching off into amphib operations—had they their own navy—with a craft capable of carrying an entire company of M1A1s in one lift; the LCM cannot carry even one M1A1 because the tank is much too wide. The next larger craft, the LCAC, can carry only one M1A1 at a time. Consider massing a force and dropping an entire company of tanks at one time!

It was not our turn to move aboard so we ended up staging waterside, and executed the age-old mission, hurry up and wait.

A walk along the shoreline of the Persian Gulf quickly revealed the extent of damage Saddam's scorched earth policy had caused. The eco-damage in Kuwait was so widespread it was mind numbing, but here along the edge of the Gulf the thick black sludge riding gently with the tide surpassed what we had seen before. The crude oil released from offshore wells and pipes, and making its way south, might be better described as eco-terrorism. Why did we not take out Saddam when we had the chance? These sentiments seem only reinforced with time.

Charlie Company settled in and attention shifted to the massive gray hulls looming at the wharf. The Marine Corps is part of the Navy, at times a stormy relationship, but when times are hard the bond is still there, or so we thought. After we had our tanks bedded down attempts were made to board the ships to get a hot shower and use the flush toilets. The short stop we made the night before provided a telephone and PX, but we had as yet received nothing in the way of creature comforts.

The ship people had other plans, however, and pulled the welcome mat off the porch as we uninvited guests walked up the front steps.

I cannot really blame the ship drivers for not granting us access to their splendid palace. We were far from the military model of spit and polish. We looked downright scary. From head to toe we were covered in sooty oil smoke so ground into our skins that repeated scrubbing with our meager means could not erase it. Our clothes were fetid, and to describe us as having a certain air about us would be an understatement. We stank, thus the ship driver's reluctance to allow us on board.

Looking back on this I can understand and sympathize with the swabbies, but at the time I wanted to see how many main gun rounds below the water line those huge ocean-going taxies could take. Basically, the purpose of the Amphibious Fleet of the U.S. Navy is to support Marines; I do not recall whole companies of sailors charging a sandy beach anywhere lately! Here was a big ship with things we wanted most, hot showers, toilets that flush, soda machines, and it was beyond our reach! We had to grovel in the sand beside our steel beasts while the navy basked in the luxury of an over-inflated yacht! A couple of resourceful senior NCO types did gain access to the treasures of the ships, but I was not among them. As the chant goes, shades of "1775 when my Marine Corps came alive!" Thus, an uneventful night was passed in the shadow of the mighty Navy.

In the morning the landing craft returned and the Company boarded in due course. After all the vehicles were dogged, the craft backed out and began the trip south. The ship was so big it had a galley and large berthing spaces for the crew, and was capable of making independent ocean voyages. The duties of the embarked Marines were none, so people began to filter to quiet spaces, sometimes turret tops, to pass the time. By this point, we were highly qualified in the art of killing time. I started the trip atop the turret of my tank C-52, but soon I began exploring. On the bridge, I met the vessel's Captain, an Army Warrant Officer, and then wandered off onto the flying bridge and sat to enjoy the passing view. The tanks of Charlie Company, below me, were no longer the pride and joy of the MPS fleet we had started with, they were panzer tigers that had been rode hard and put away wet and nasty. The turrets and hulls were smeared with oil smoke, and battle damage was evident on many.

As I looked down on my tank I thought of an instructor I had at Fort Knox while attending the Armor Officer's Basic Course. Students were required to complete a technical summary of an armored vehicle and I chose the tank that I would eventually meet as Tank Commander and Platoon Leader, the M60A1! In my summary I asserted that the M60A1 was still a viable weapons platform in Marine involvement of Third World conflicts. My instructor had retorted cynically on my paper and lowered my overall grade. Well, Captain of the U.S. Army, I still graduated as the Distinguished Graduate of AOBC 9-88, and the M60A1 I looked down on stood tall with the victors. Incidentally, Marines were onsite and ready with those M60A1s before the U.S. Army could even start their arrival.

Our voyage was uneventful. Watching dolphins riding the bow wake proved to be the most exciting pastime of the trip. Soon the hazy smudge of land grew larger as the craft turned back toward the Saudi shore. Towering cranes and warehouses of the port became clear, and it was a strange feeling to be coming back to where we started those long months ago at the port complex of Al Jubayl!

Eventually we received our rotation date out, but we had to watch the 24th Mech leave first. Marines had been among the first here to hold the line; but Stormin' Norman's old division got to go home earlier.

The days following our return to Al Jubayl were a let down. We parked and locked the tanks and, with the exception of several limited working parties, just left them parked outside the fence at the back gate to the Al Jubayl port complex. Then came the waiting game to rotate back home. After about a week of nothing to do but stare at the Persian Gulf, I took one of the Hummers to get a change of scenery. No officers are supposed to drive themselves around in military vehicles; we are not even issued military drivers licenses. This did not stop me. I had a new attitude: because I was a combat veteran I could drive that Hummer anywhere I wanted.

My new line of thinking almost got me killed! I set off in my Hummer, much happier away from the port. For a few minutes it was just me, with no one around to ask for anything or answer for anything. I cruised along enjoying my freedom when I spied ahead a SANG (Saudi Arabian National Guard) Check Point. Up to this point the SANG had not stopped or bothered with American traffic. We would slow down, wave and cruise by with smiles from all around. Well, this roadblock was manned by six desert cami-clad MPs; SMG toting SANG troopers who at that moment had no other traffic to check, just me. I slowed down and began to pass through as usual.

My Arabic was not fluent, not even half-good. I could order hands up, get on the ground, or head south, but that was about the extent of my vocabulary. When half a dozen MPs, SMG (sub machine gun)) toting Arabs, started yelling in my face, I started translating real quick. I stopped the Hummer, now! The senior MP made himself known by sticking his head through my open window and began yelling at me in Arabic. loud and loudest. I asked him to speak English and you would have thought I had slapped him. He started yelling about how the infidels have defiled his country, about how we swagger around and pollute Allah's land, how we disregard the SANG's authority by ignoring check points. I told him sorry, but I just came back from Kuwait. He started yelling again, enough to make me a little nervous.

I noticed the other SANG troopers spreading out with their weapons pointed into my vehicle, fingers near triggers, and there was no other traffic; no support or witnesses in sight. Then, the mouth went a wee bit too far. He proceeded to tell me that the mighty SANG did not need my help, that Dictator Bush forced us here.

I surely had no desire to visit this place, be apart from my family for months and live through the terror of the ground war while he was perhaps safe down in old Saudi. The MPs kept me from saying all this, but not thinking it. At that point in this dance I was unsure whether I faced a bluff, or was about to get splattered. Had I lived through the war to get blown away by an ally after the shooting was over?

I have been well versed in the fine art of defensive warfare. Attack! I proceeded to even the odds. While the mouth continued his tirade, I slowly drew my 9mm pistol and cocked it. When he leaned in the window, he got my friendly Beretta up under his chin. I had everybody's attention and for the first time in about five minutes, the mouth shut up.

Pushing my advantage, I asked my now attentive SANG warrior if he would like to meet the Allah he had been speaking of, that I was ready to go with him. His eyes opened wide. I told him to drop the SMGs, and to tell the others to do the same. Then I started moving my vehicle slowly down the road with my safe passage walking alongside me, my 9mm crammed under his chin. When we were far enough away, I eased the pistol and finally took a good look at that senior ally officer. A SANG Captain, he outranked me.

When I returned to the port I reported the incident and expected to hear immediately that I had started an international incident. However, nothing ever came of the matter. It must not have been politically correct to rattle the host nation over one Marine Lieutenant.

We waited. I feel it was a good thing we were not sent directly back to CONUS after the ground war ended. After living in our tanks, an informal world of a tank Company called Charlie, we were probably unprepared to return to the States. At the time you could not have sold that to me for all the tea in China, but a pretty good example comes to mind, one that shows just how far out of touch we were.

After moving back into the warehouses, we began making runs to Camp 13. We did not own it, but the chow hall still fed us, the laundry was still available to us, and the Pakistani-run store had a better selection of stuff than any military PX. One day I caught a ride to the Camp to get a bite to eat. Technically, if a unit did not operate out of the facility, or did not supply mess men, unit personnel were not authorized to eat there. So? After seven months of being rained on, shot at and nearly broiled or frozen in that desert litter box, I intended to eat wherever I pleased. Lead, bleed or get out of the way comes to mind. In the company of several other Charlie Company members I headed over to search for chow among the REMFs.

Who should approach us on our mission but a poster child; an immaculate Marine wearing desert camies, desert boots and shoulder holster. He wore the chevrons of a 1st Sergeant. On active duty I had great respect for Senior NCOs, more than I have for many of the Officer Corps who sometimes have more ego than common sense!

This poster child locked onto us like a Stinger missile to

a jet in after burner. After seven months in the field, our entire company may have been able to put together one decent uniform, but we did not today. Our camies were tattered and badly worn, mended when possible, shredded when not. Our boots were scuffed beyond recognition, and the desert boots were stained a blackish color from all the oil. We were not exactly Evening Parade material. To top that off, we were armed! Within the walls of Camp 13 the REMFs took the bullets out of the bullet thrower and left them in their rooms. As we had no rooms, we carried our issue around with us, in the bullet throwers.

Poster child let fly with his first volley. He thought us a disgrace to his Corps, his Camp and his war. He could not fathom how we could be so slovenly, how we could carry loaded weapons inside the compound, and how I, as an officer, could tolerate this criminal behavior. In short, he disturbed my serenity.

The 1st Sergeant attempted to prevent our departure until he had vented his spleen on us raggedy Marines. I am not certain if it was loud thoughts raging through my brain, or the look that clouded my face, but something caused the startled SNCO (Staff Non Commissioned Officer) to back pedal. He stepped back from us. We continued on our way to the chow hall and I expected the MPs to come charging in through the door after us.

The incident was definitely not one of my best moments. I guess similar occurrences are what cause animosity between line units and the support types. I wasn't trying to cause anyone grief, certainly not SNCOs; all I wanted was to eat a hot meal and maybe buy a can of Pringles. I could not understand how anyone among the REMF, who had everything, could stand there and belittle and scorn those who had practically nothing in the way of creature comforts or amenities.

He was right that we did indeed look bad and that our state of being had fallen a bit below what would be considered satisfactory for Marines. He was right about our loaded weapons. I think our attitude resulted because I, and those I was responsible for, had gone without so much for so long: and had worked so hard to make do with so little. I did the only thing I could. I told the Marines with me to follow me and started to walk away. If I stayed I knew I was going to do something extremely stupid, even if gratifying.

Looking back on that incident, I realize that being a part of Task Force Ripper made me part of something special. I was actually part of the big blue arrow that Stormin' Norman had up on his map, 1st Mar Div. It was my honor to have been at the pointy tip of that spear, briefly. When my children are old enough, I can tell them I helped liberate Kuwait, not that I chewed out hapless field Marines because their camies were torn and their boots scuffed up. Truly, the 1st Sergeant and all SNCOs are the backbone of the Corps, but at that point in Camp 13 he was just another REMF. I am very happy he still has all his teeth!

Do not misunderstand me; the trigger puller today needs a support network of approximately 15:1 to be able to operate in the battlefield. That means fifteen supporters for every trigger puller. It also means that out of 500,000 of us in the Gulf, very few actually pulled a trigger or heard a shot fired in anger. I am glad they were there, and fully appreciate the wonderful job they did. Without the support echelon—the REMFs— my job would have been impossible. That thought went quickly astray, in a blink of my eye at Camp 13 that day.

Finally, it was our turn to go home and we rejoiced mightily. The freedom bird came and winged us westward to home; one could almost hear Beethoven's Ninth Symphony, the famed *Ode to Joy!*

Semper Fi, Marines!

Afterword

The trip back from the great litter box ended as stylishly as it began. We flew home on a chartered airliner complete with chicken meals, some bottles of firewater and long-legged flight attendants in form fitting uniforms to ogle. A quick layover in Egypt (I can say I saw the Pyramids), a short stop at Shannon Airport in Ireland, and we were on to the land of the big PX.

Sometime in the late dark hours of the night, after refueling in Newfoundland, the Captain came on the intercom. He apologized for interrupting our sleep, but he figured we would want to know we had just crossed back into U.S. air space. At first there was silence, then a massive outburst of cheering and clapping. I'll never forget the feeling!

Touchdown on American soil brought us back to where we began months ago, at Long Beach Naval Air Station. It was still dark when we emerged from the plane, and a slow, steady rain fell as we sorted ourselves out. I felt strange when I gave up one of my companions of the last several months, my Berretta 9mm. Several hurried calls to the base revealed that our arrival had not been announced, so we knew that the dependents were going to be surprised at our return.

We climbed onto the Navy's white whales, buses used for everything and everybody, for the journey home to the stumps. The trip was subdued. Months of stress and jet lag were very much present. I kept expecting to be waked up by one of the crew, to find that I was still in the sand box and it was my turn for watch. Although all hands were excited about returning home, I don't think the shock of the situation had worked off yet. The bus trip remains to this day one of the longest rides of my life

It was first light as the convoy topped the Morongo Grade and passed through Yucca Valley. Due to the early hour and our unexpected arrival, no crowds lined the way, but people who were out waved and shouted as we drove past. As we passed through Joshua Tree, I looked out of the bus to the school where my wife taught 3rd grade and thought of all she must have had to endure over the past few months. There's a saying in the Corps that the only thing more difficult than being a Marine is being married to one. There's a lot of truth to that, I think.

When the town of Twentynine Palms came into view, it was very different from the place we left behind almost eight months ago. Although not a major metropolis to begin with, it now appeared to be a ghost town. Still, banners hung everywhere, welcoming home the Marines and Sailors; and folks recognized us with waves, or honked their horns in greeting.

Changes had occurred at the base in our absence. A new gate greeted our arrival; several months old already it stood as a reminder of our absence in the Gulf. As we drove past the commissary and along the edge of Lake Bhandini, everything looked different somehow. It took me several moments to realize that the base had not really changed that much, but that I had changed that much.

The white whales pulled into the parking lot of the base gym located across the street from the Battalion CP; the very spot where I had hugged my wife and child good bye. As the Marines stepped of the bus, the married ones with dependents still on the base look hurriedly around to spot them. In spite of the short notice from Long Beach, a crowd was waiting for us. I scanned the faces, but quickly realized that my wife and son were not present, and with a resigned sigh turned my attention back to the demands of the moment. There were Marines to take care of, and the XO has a very important part in that process. So, I began making the inquiries necessary to ensure that the single Marines had BEQ (Bachelor Enlisted Quarters) space and chow hall facilities.

In the gym, I discovered that the Battalion advance party had done a tremendous job of organizing the return of the main body; and that most of the issues in question were well in hand. At one point a minor administrative matter needed to be discussed with Gonzo (1st Lieutenant Jaime Gonzolves, 3rd Platoon Commander, Blue). While I stood talking with him, he suddenly smiled real big and turned me gently by the arm. Standing there behind me was my loving bride and in a stroller in front of her my two year old son. Gonzo had never met my wife, he had joined us out of Armor school after the Company had already deployed to the Gulf; but he had figured out who they were. After hugging my wife from within inches of her life, I looked down to my son who put up his arms and said that magic word, "Daddy!" There are a lot of moments in life that you will never forget, memories that stay with you for a lifetime. That was one of them. He was barely a year and a half old when we deployed; and only took his first real steps on his own the day before we flew out. How he remembered me I'll never know, but I thank God that he did!

The next several weeks were busy ones, settling the Battalion into garrison after so much time in the field took quite an effort. Soon, all of the personal belongings were out of storage, and the basket leave taken. Although it would not show for several months the phenomenon known as Desert Stork had begun, yours truly adding to the roster.

The return home was complete when the first victory

parade in the United States since WWII, was held outside the base in the town of Twentynine Palms. Marines and sailors from all the units that had deployed, with the equipment they had used, paraded down the main road leading to the base. It was an incredible sight to see that day, and a more incredible thing to be part of. As Lieutenant Colonel Diggs led the Battalion in the march, it struck me that we had gone to war, fought for our country, and come home to a very different reception than those who had fought before us. From start to finish the country had supported us, and was now saying thank you. It was a far cry from the welcoming reception the Korean and Vietnam Vets received on their return home. I still feel a little guilty about it. A lot of people sacrificed more then I, and received a whole lot less.

As all things eventually end, so did my time with Charlie Company. The Hail and Farewell that is the traditional greeting and goodbye to a member of a unit was tough. Charlie Company had been my home for three years, and it was tough to say goodbye. Friendships made during times of great stress, such as in combat units, are close ones; and Charlie Company held many of them for me.

After a tour of duty at The Basic School at the Quantico Base in Virginia, my illustrious career as a leader of Marines was brought to a close. Although I would be deemed worthy to be promoted to the rank of Captain, and was given the responsibility of training and educating newly commissioned Second Lieutenants, I would not be selected for retention in the Corps with a Regular Commission. My Marine Corps career ended as it started, in Quantico, Virginia.

Several years have passed since my transition from military life back to civilian life and many changes have occurred. My wonderful wife has given our family a second son, and, for a time I was fortunate to wear the blue and gray uniform of a Virginia State Police Trooper. Now I am embarked on a new career as Special Agent with the United States State Department. The demands of day to day life are simpler, and most decisions less grand in scope compared to those of a tank company Executive Officer forward deployed to a combat zone. Although my life has held moments of terrifying excitement, they generally pale in comparison to the elephant seen in the Gulf.

When people learn that I was an Officer of Marines, they often ask if I miss the Corps. I tell them I miss the enlisted Marines, and I miss what once was. I miss the young kids, and the excitement and energy they brought with them. I miss the pride that the Marines had in themselves and those around them. I miss traveling across the desert floor with the wind whipping my face, surrounded by tons of steel waiting to unleash the awesome power of the main gun. Yes, I miss wearing the Eagle, Globe and Anchor emblems. I miss being a Marine Corps tanker.

But that is all what once was. As times have changed, so has the Corps. The Marine Corps of today is different than the one yesteryear, just as the one ten years from now will differ from the one today. The very nature of the Corps changes with the times. One thing will always remain the same, however; the fiber of the Corps. The faces may change, but Marines will always be Marines! I'm not of the Old Breed, would never claim to be; but I guess I can now understand a little better what the Old Corps means.

A chest full of colorful ribbons and medals now sit in a brass jewelry box on my dresser. My wife tells me someday she's going to mount them in a display box for me. Before going to the Gulf my Dress Blues were adorned with only my rank insignia and the gold and silver Eagle, Globe and Anchor emblems of the collar. After returning from the gulf that empty patch of blue sported three rows of ribbons, one containing a "V" device for valor. The deployment ribbons, unit commendations, and service medals I am proud to have earned. I am equally proud of the Purple Heart that I did not receive.

Somehow, receiving a heart for shrapnel to the hands seemed demeaning to those who had sacrificed much more then I over more than 200 years of the Corps. Somehow, I never got around to telling Doc Perry, our Company Corpsman who was responsible for recording such injuries, about my little mishap with the arty round. The scars on my fingers and the ache that they feel when the weather changes are the only reminder I need of where I went, and what I once did.

Yet, none of those bits of cloth or medals really matter. It's the experience of having lived through those hectic days that has come to mean the most to me. The deployment during Desert Shield, and the eventual combat of Desert Storm are treasures in themselves. I wouldn't trade them for a million dollars; but I wouldn't pay you five cents for them. It's a hard thing to try to explain. I'm not sure I can.

When all is said and done, and I look back over the years to my experience in the Persian Gulf; it is hard to believe that I once helped to lead Marines into harms way. When asked if it angers me that I fought for oil, I tell people no, because I didn't fight for oil, I fought for the Marines around me; I fought for Charlie Company. Marines do not fight for national policy objectives or diplomatic resolutions, they fight for each other! General John A. Lejeune, the 13th Commandant of the Marine Corps, probably said it better than anyone, and far better than I: "Among all the honors, among all the postings, promotions and medals that have been awarded to me, the one thing in which I take the most pride is to be able to say, I am a Marine."

Semper Fi!

Christopher J. Freitus

Roster
of Charlie Company, 3rd Tank Battalion

Lance Corporal John E **Ackerman Jr**
Corporal Francis S **Anderson Jr**
Corporal Timothy P **Barlow**
Corporal Rick K **Bates**
Sergeant Craig R **Brooks**
Hospitalman4 Lawrence A **Bunch**
Private First Class George W **Burton Jr**
Captain Jeff (Mumbly) **Butler**
Staff Sergeant C C **Cabat**
Lance Corporal S M **Calfa**
Corporal Ishmael P **Castillo**
Lance Corporal G W **Chical Jr**
Gunnery Sergeant Paul S **Cochran**
Gunnery Sergeant Francisco **Codero**
Lance Corporal S A **Couturier**
Gunnery Sergeant Richard J **Cronin**
2nd Lieutenant Christopher J **Croteau**
Sergeant Allen J **Cunningham**
Lance Corporal A G **Davis**
Corporal David A **Decker**
Corporal John R **Dilling**
Corporal Robert C **Dixon Jr**

Captain Edward T **Dunlap**, Company Commander
Lance Corporal Jamusz S **Dusza**
Lance Corporal P E **Estes**
Lance Corporal Luis A **Escobar**
Corporal Cory J **Farmer**
Lance Corporal B E **Fine**
Sergeant Dan P **Fitzpatrick**
Corporal Warren J **Flood Jr**
Lance Corporal James W **Florence**
Corporal Martin H **Flores**
Lance Corporal Nelson **Franco**
1st Lieutenant Christopher J **Freitus**, Company Executive
    Officer
Lance Corporal Sean C **Gardner**
Lance Corporal R J **Gese**
Corporal William J **Gilger**
2nd Lieutenant James D **Gonsalves**
Private First Class Edward C **Gordon**
Lance Corporal R S **Grace**
Master Sergeant Jerry W **Graham**
Corporal Dwayne A **Green**
Sergeant Rigoberto C **Guzman**
Corporal M A **Hartley**
Private First Class Timothy J **Haskell**
Lance Corporal Hermilo **Hernandez**
Lance Corporal Ryan W **Hoover**
Lance Corporal Steven F **Hunnings**
Private Thomas L **Jenkins Jr**
Corporal R J **Jensen**
Corporal A J **Jessee**
Private First Class James P **Johnson**
Lance Corporal Brian P **Jones**
Corporal Jeffery D **Jones**
Sergeant David W **Jones**

Lance Corporal Wesley E **King**
Lance Corporal Gary P **Koger**
Lance Corporal T W **Landon**
Lance Corporal Donald R **Letendre**
Corporal Alvie R **Lucero**
Lance Corporal C P **Martepy**
Sergeant Scott A **Martin**
1st Sergeant Alfonso **Martinez**
Corporal Wilbur **McClendon**
Lance Corporal Wayne J **McMillen Jr**
Corporal Alister W **Millwood**
Lance Corporal M G **Monfelt**
Staff Sergeant Michael E **Mummey**
Lance Corporal Eric D **Newton**
Lance Corporal K E **Niedens**
Corporal Thomas L **Opitz**
Lance Corporal Ganiu U **Oshodi**
Hospitalman2 Charles M **Perry**
Lance Corporal John M **Pirhalla**
Corporal Sean M **Pulliam**
Lance Corporal George L **Reedy III**
Corporal Jose L **Rivera**
Lance Corporal Manuel A **Rodriguez**
Corporal Allan W **Salmon**
Lance Corporal David G **Santiago Jr**
Lance Corporal William J **Schiferl**
Corporal David M **Schmidt**
Gunnery Sergeant Donald E **Schofield**
Sergeant Terry G **Schweniner**
Corporal Clifton J **Scott**
Corporal D A **Selakuku**
Lance Corporal Vincent E **Shambaugh**
Private First Class Beauford W **Shirey Jr**
Lance Corporal James E **Siow**

Lance Corporal Robert D **South**
Lance Corporal Frank W **Spears**
Lance Corporal William T **Spreen**
Hospitalman2 J T **Stanley**
Corporal Thomas J **Stier**
Private First Class Charles W **Stutsman**
1st Lieutenant V J **Sumang**
Lance Corporal Christopher J **Swift**
Corporal William J **Thompson**
Sergeant Evan W **Thompson IV**
Lance Corporal Ward E **Ulery**
Staff Sergeant Nelson **Villegas**
Staff Sergeant David D **Walters**
Lance Corporal J A **Watkins**
Corporal Ronald J **Weatherford**
Sergeant Jeffery M **Welsh**
Corporal Ford F **White II**
Sergeant Edward A **Williams**
Lance Corporal Michael D **Wimp**
Private First Class Cameron T **Zoucha**

Total Company Strength, including attached personnel: **109**

Glossary and Abbreviations

1/7   Shortened version of the unit designation: 1st Battalion of Infantry of the 7th Marine Regiment.

7th MEB   7th Marine Expeditionary Brigade. Primary purpose unit for the Middle East. Combat power with supporting logistical units.

8th & I Marine   The Marines stationed at the barracks at 8th and I Streets in Washington, D.C. These are the Marines seen at the White House, some of the sharpest Marines in the Corps.

24th MECH   24th Mechanized Infantry Division. By doctrine, the type of unit that fights the big armored land battles of U.S. interest. The former command of General H. Norman Schwarzkopf.

.50 Cal MG   The TC's personal weapon onboard the tank. Fires belted, or linked together .50 caliber bullets

AAV Amphibious Assault Vehicle.

AAV Battalion   Parent organization of the LVT-P7A1. Amphibious Assault Battalions attach vehicles to differing infantry units to form mechanized infantry units.

Afrika Korps The German troops of WWII who fought under

Field Marshall Rommel in the deserts of North Africa. Although they did not win, they understood the desert and its terrain.

AK The designation of the Soviet family of assault rifles and light machine guns. Most of the military hardware used by Saddam's forces was of Soviet manufacture. Many of the rifles were the venerable AK-47.

AMX-30 A French made armored scout car.

AOBC Armor Officer Basic Course. This is where Second Lieutenants go to learn about Tankology; namely how to be a leader of armored forces. Located at Fort Knox, Kentucky, the course is run by the Army. Marine officers, usually 10-20 a year, attend this course following their Basic Officer's Training course (TBS).

APC Armored Personnel Carrier. Usually a tracked vehicle that carries a squad across the battlefield, faster than their legs could. The Marine Corps has no true APC, rather employs its amphibious assault vehicle (LVT-P7A1) in this role.

ARAMCO Arabian American Oil Company. Composed of Westerners who produce oil in Saudi, the multinational company provided awesome picnics on the desert.

ARC LIGHT Term used since Vietnam to describe the air strikes conducted by Air Force B-52 Bombers. Such a strike can devastate the area it is dropped upon.

Arty Folks The troops of the artillery battalions.

Arty Tubes Big guns of the field artillery.

A Team Term taken from a reputed comment made by the

Commandant of the Corps, General Al Gray, to the 2nd Marine Division prior to its deployment to the Gulf. Big Al was the former Commanding General of the 2nd Marine Division, obviously not the 1st!

AWACS Airborne Warning and Control System. An Air Force modified Boeing 707 turned into an electronic surveillance and command and control platform with the mission to coordinate use of the air assets operating in a given area. The huge spinning radar antenna on top of the 707 distinguishes this aircraft.

Basket leave Special leave taken after war when a soldier's Leave Request remains in a basket, and only counted if needed.

Battalion Commander Commanding Officer of a battalion-sized unit.

Battalion XO Battalion Executive Officer, second in command of a battalion-sized unit.

BERM Take some dirt and pile it up, you now have a Berm. If you place them in certain patterns, armored opponents can be channeled into lanes for ambush. If a tracked vehicle goes over a berm it exposes its softer under belly.

BFO Black Floating Object. Term used to describe the female Arab floating across the heated desert sands around Saudi Arabia in her head-to-foot black robes.

Boon Dockers The high-topped, thick-soled combat boots that Marines have worn since time immemorial.

BMP The designation given to a family of Soviet manufactured personnel carriers. Over the history of the Soviet military, several versions were exported to client states; usually the older, out dated variety. This is a tracked vehicle that can mount an Anti-tank missile and is armed with a heavy caliber machine gun.

BP Battle Position.

C-4 Plastic Explosive. A stable compound that can be exposed to extremes of temperature, shot and pounded upon without mishap.

C.A.A.T. Combined Anti-Armor Team. A grouping of anti-armor assets into a quick response team capable of bringing coordinated fire to bear upon enemy armor. Mounted in vehicles, usually Hummers, the C.A.A.T. places together FO's (Forward Observers), FAC's (Forward Air Controllers), and possibly Naval Gunfire Spotters with thermal sights and laser designators.

Camies Camouflaged utility uniform worn by most members of the U.S. Armed Forces. The Army calls theirs BDU's, or Battlefield Dress Uniform.

Camo Netting The really annoying equipment that is supposed to provide concealment for an object that is placed under it! It was like trying to hide a cue ball on a pool table under a green cloth. The bump could still be seen!

Camp 13 A walled encampment formerly used by Western oil workers that became the rear area for several 1st Marine Division units during Desert Shield. The facility, containing air-conditioned showers, a mess hall, and storage, was taken over eventually by the 2nd Marine Division.

CAX Combined Arms Exercise. The designation given to the live fire exercises and work up exercises that occur at the Twentynine Palms Marine Corps Air Ground Combat Center in California (Mojave Desert).

CENTCOM Central Command commanded by General H. Norman Schwarzkopf.

Cook-off Usually a secondary-explosion of ammunition or fuel stores. Sometimes used to describe the firing of main guns.

Chem Stick Chemical illumination stick. A plastic tube with separate chemicals contained therein. Activated, the chemicals mix and cause a reaction that glows in the dark for 4-10 hours, depending on the stick. Great for command and control in the dark, only problem, the enemy can see it, too.

CP Command Post. A unit's commander and his support staff lead from a CP. In the case of a mechanized unit, the CP is located in tracked vehicles equipped with additional radios to maintain command and control on the move.

CP1 Mechanized CP in vehicle with additional communications and control equipment to sustain operations on the move.

Chobum armor The composite armor used in the construction of the M1 series of tanks. Made out of layers of steel, ceramic and depleted Uranium.

CNN Cable News Network, sometimes called "Combat News Network" by recent warriors.

Cobra AH-1W Helicopter gun ship of USMC. Capable of launching a variety of weapon systems, including the laser guided Hell Fire missile; and a chin mounted chain gun. The squadron that supported us were called the Snakes.

Company CO Commanding Officer of a company sized unit.

Company XO Company Executive Officer. Second in

command of a company sized unit. In a tank company also the HQ platoon Commander.

Control Point A graphic control measure placed on a map to control the movement of forces on a battle field. Denotes a specific spot on a map, such as a march along a road.

CONUS Continental United States.

Cupola The small turret that sits on top of the big turret. The TC (Tank Commander) is positioned here with a .50 cal machine gun.

CVC Combat Vehicle Crewman. Used as an abbreviation when speaking about the equipment used by armored vehicle crewmen. Can refer to the coveralls made of fire retardant Nomex, or to the earphones and boom mike in the helmets similar to the ones worn by helicopter pilots.

C-51 The designation of Charlie Company CO's (Command Officer's) tank.

C-52 Charlie Company XO's (Executive Officer's) tank.

Desert Rats Nickname given to the British troops of the famed 7th Armored Division of WWII who fought against the German Afrika Corps.

Desert Shield Term given to the movement of forces to protect the Kingdom of Saudi Arabia shortly after the invasion of Kuwait by Iraq in the 1990s.

Desert Storm The offensive operations of the Persian Gulf War of the 1990s to remove the Iraqi invasion forces from Kuwait.

Dragon Wagon Big, multi-wheeled trucks used by the U.S. forces in the gulf to transport ammunition, fuel, and the mobile kitchens that produced the "wolf burgers."

DOC Term of endearment given the Navy Hospital Corpsman assigned to a Marine ground combat unit. Navy Corpsmen are first line medical providers for Marine Units, often the difference between life and death! Wonderful, brave men!

Dog and Pony Show The expression used to describe the act of putting on a show or presentation for VIPs. Usually involves special resources.

DU Depleted Uranium. The substance that makes the current generation of kinetic anti-tank main gun tank rounds so deadly. Punches through tank armor.

Engineer Track An AAV (Amphibious Assault Vehicle), outfitted with the latest in combat engineering devices, designed to place combat engineers where they were needed to remove explosive ordnance.

EOD Explosive Ordnance Disposal.

EPW Enemy Prisoner of War. A replacement for POW (Prisoner of War).

FAC Forward Air Controller. Marine ground combat units always have a Marine Aviator assigned to them who can coordinate and control air assets used in support of the ground unit In the Persian Gulf the Tank Company's XO had a FAC assigned to them. He filled the position of loader, and did double duty controlling air assets and loading the big gun.

Facimes Large bundles of plastic pipes dropped into anti-tank ditches. The bundles fill up the ditch to allow crossing.

Fast Movers Fixed-wing jet aircraft. Usually refers to fighters.

FFBT Federation For Better Tanking, by C. Freitus.

FEBA Forward Edge Battle Area. Marks the forward advance by friendly troops!

Fire Control Line A graphic control measure that is used to keep friendly forces away from friendly indirect fire; namely artillery and air strikes. Once friendly forces advance to a fire control line, indirect fires are moved forward to another line. Usually named with a color or a name.

Fire Sack By constructing a series of berms one can channel an opponent's armored forces to a predetermined location. Anti-tank guns and missiles and arty and air assets provide the greatest effect here. The Soviets frequently employed fire sacks tactically.

First Shirt 1st Sergeant.

FM Field Manual. Military publication covering a specific topic.

FMF Fleet Marine Forces. The command of Marine forces is divided into FMF-Atlantic and FMF-Pacific. Home where the real Marines live!

FMFM Fleet Marine Force Manual. A topic specific manual issued by the Marine Corps.

FO Forward Observer. The FO relays the requests from the ground-maneuvering unit commander to the supporting artillery unit. Through the FO's eyes on the target location he can direct the fires with corrections. In the Gulf War the tank company had a FO assigned to it.

FOX Vehicle Vehicle provided by the German Army for use in detecting chemical and biological agents in the air. The Marine Corps employed several during the Ground Operations. Its responses are controversial to this day.

Frag Order Fragmentary Order used to pass supplements to Operational Orders, usually during a fast-paced operation. Initial mission orders are passed on in detail in an Operations Order. Follow on missions or change orders can be issued as a Frag Order.

G-Day Start of a campaign. G-Day for the beginning of the ground war in Desert Storm was Feb 24, 1991; G-plus 1 (sometimes G+1) was the day after.

Gang Bang The collective radio call sign for Charlie Company during the Gulf Deployment. If the company commander needed to pass on information to all components of the Company, instead of calling sub-units one at a time, he used a collective call sign. All of the units would then call back to acknowledge his transmission.

Gedunk A term dating back to the China Marines; a store or stand that sells trinkets and junk food.

GPS Global Positioning System. A computerized navigation system that utilizes satellites (three or more) to triangulate and locate its position on the Earth within ten meters or so. During the Gulf War, the Tank Commander had one jury-rigged to a radio battery.

Green Cami The usual camouflage uniform worn by Marines is in green forest-colors, theoretically in random patterns.

Marines that deployed early to Saudi, Operation Desert Shield, were issued desert-pattern camies also called chocolate chips. Due to limited supplies, follow on forces were not issued desert pattern camies.

Grunt Term used to refer to the hard-working Marine infantry.

Hellfire A laser-guided smart missile launched from an aircraft, either fast mover or helicopter. The missile homes in on the target on the reflected energy of a laser designator. With a range well outside the average tank main gun, it is a standoff weapon.

HETT Heavy Equipment Tank Transporter. A big trailer used to move a tank on long trips over the road.

HMMWV High mobility multi-purpose wheeled vehicle, also known as the HUMVEE, the Hummer, and other variants. The vehicle that replaced the Jeep of earlier times.

H&S Company Headquarters and Support Company. The logistical supporters usually referred to as the cooks, bakers and candle stick makers.

HQ Headquarters. The operational command element of any given unit. The so-called Head Shed.

HQ Tanks Command and control tanks of an armored or mechanized unit.

I MEF 1ˢᵗ Marine Expeditionary Force; pronounced "eye meff," or "eye em ee eff." This was the parent command of the two Marine Divisions and their supporting units in the Gulf War. Commanded by Lieutenant General Walter E. Boomer, there were more than 92,900 Marines, including reservists, in the KTO (Kuwaiti Theater of Operations). This was the largest deployment of Marines since Vietnam.

Intel Officer Military Intelligence Officer.

IR Beacon To prevent friendly fire incidents, each tank company was issued one Infra-Red Light Beacon to place on a tank to help mark the Forward Edge of friendly forces Any one using NVG's would be able to see the pulse of light given off from the beacon, friend or foe!

JSTARS Joint Surveillance Target Acquisition Radar System. System jointly designed between Army and Air Force. Uses airborne side-looking radar.

K-Bar Knife Traditional fighting knife of the Marine since WWII.

Kick The radio systems used on the tanks in the Gulf utilized encrypted security components. To load the encryption cipher a small device nicknamed a KICK was used to load the cipher into the encryption component.

Klick A Kilometer.

KTO Kuwaiti Theatre of Operations. The area where all of the forces supporting Desert Shield and Desert Storm were located, and where those who wanted to punch their ticket for promotion might visit.

Lager Tankers gather themselves into a protective huddle called a lager, to refuel and re-arm.

LAV Light Armored Vehicle. The Marine Corps armored vehicle used in what would be a cavalry, scouting, or forward reconnaissance role. Carries grunts. Called fast moving Spam-

In-A-Can.

LCAC Landing Craft Air Cushion. A large hovercraft that floats on a cushion of air. Capable of carrying two M60A1 tanks from the water onto the beach.

LCM Landing Craft Medium. The designation the Navy gives to a medium-sized landing craft, that has a big ramp in the front. It can move three M60A1s from a ship to the beach. There are many of these ships in operation.

Lister Bag A canvas bag that allows water to cool through evaporation.

LSD Landing Ship Dry Dock. A type of vessel in the amphibious fleet of the U.S. Navy used to carry Marines. An LSD has a big dry well that can be flooded and pumped dry for amphibious operations!

LST Landing Ship Tank. An amphibious vessel of the U.S. Navy that can off-load tanks. The LST is designed to drive on to a beach.

LVT-C7A1 Command and control variant of the LVT-P7A1. Designed with multiple radio and command features for Battalion Commanders and above.

LVT-P7A1 Armored assault vehicle used by the Marine Corps for infantry transport. A tracked vehicle designed for amphibious operations. Given its amphibious nature it is often referred to as a "Tuna Boat."

M1A1 The main battle tank that replaced the older M-60 series of tanks. With Chobum armor and a bigger main gun, it is the most formidable tank on the battle field today.

M-16 The M-16A2 Assault rifle is the current issued assault rifle. Each M60A1 tank crew was issued two M-16s. One weapon was stored with the driver, the second in the main crew compartment in the turret.

M113 Lightly armored personnel carrier employed by the US Army. Used by the Airborne Forces that were the early fly-in forces, the trip wire.

M60A1 Tank Tank employed by the Marine Corps at the time of the Gulf War. Initial deploying units were equipped with the M60A1; 2nd Marine Division units deployed with the larger M1A1's!

M-60 Blade Tank Version of the M60A1 battle tank that had an after market kit added, the idea being it could dig fighting positions for the unit's tanks. The blade tank was usually assigned to the Company XO.

M198 A 155mm towed artillery tube, mainstay of the artillery units of the Marine Corps. With a variety of shell types and fuse settings, and an awesome range thrown-in, the M198 helps the arty folks maintain their impression that they are the "king of battle."

MEF Marine Expeditionary Force.

MOPPS Mission Oriented Protective Posture Suits. The chemical and biological protective over-garments and equipment that troops wear to counter exposure to nasty things the enemy might throw at you. Sounds good in theory, but in practice left a lot to be desired! Needs vast improvement!

MOPP 4 Mission Oriented Protective Posture 4. When the threat of exposure to chemical or biological, or even radioactive material, is at its greatest, then all MOPP equipment is used. The over-garments, coat and pants, over booties, gloves, gas mask and hood are all worn. Makes one look like a great big space bug!

MOS Military Occupational Specialty. Everyone in the armed forces has a specific job they are trained for. In the Marine Corps everyone (Officers included) are considered to be Infantry first. Once the art of the grunt is mastered, some go on to other MOSs! A tank crewman, for example, is MOS 1811 while an armor officer is MOS1802. The number tells you what the MOS is.

MPS Marine Pre-positioning Squadron. Moth balled equipment placed on transport ships stationed at Diego Garcia, in the Indian Ocean.

MRE Meal Ready to Eat. The gourmet food of today's warrior is contained within a plastic pouch. The Department of Defense invented a dining experience including the main meal, crackers, dessert, cold beverage powder, coco powder, coffee with cream and sugar, and most importantly, toilet paper! To truly appreciate the MRE, one needs to have dined on them for several months.

M.U.L.E. (Sometimes MULE) Modular Universal Laser Equipment. A laser device that can both determine the range to a target and guide a missile to it. The FAC would aim the MULE at a target, instruct the Cobras to launch a missile, splash the target with a laser light to guide the missile.

NATO North Atlantic Treaty Organization. Alliance of countries formed to counter the Soviet threat of years past. Aimed more toward forested hills then deserts!

NBC Stands for Nuclear, Biological, and Chemical. The bugs and gas people are the experts responsible for training in peace time, and identifying and testing for possible threats when the shooting starts.

NCO Non-Commissioned Officer. The backbone of the Marine Corps is composed of Corporals and Sergeants who take orders and make them reality.

NVG Night Vision Goggles. These vision enhancement devices take the ambient night light and magnify it, allowing the wearer of the goggles to see in the dark, not with the clarity of day time viewing, but much better than looking in the pitch dark!

Obstacle Belts A term referring to the placement of barriers that limit or restrict the movement of the enemy's forces. Tankers are slowed down by barriers of wire and mines, so Saddam had his forces construct these belts of obstacles so that his forces could counter attack and wipe us out. He needs new engineers because the old ones failed miserably!

OP Observation Post. When one sets up a perimeter, one becomes static and restricted in what can be seen. To further the view past the defensive position, a commander sends observers to act as the eyes and ears of the commander forward of his position. The observers man an Observation Post.

OPCON PLANS Operational Contingency Plans maintained on file in the event of real world crisis. These are details for commanders and staffs actions and units to use or deploy for any given problem area of the world.

OV-10 A light aircraft used by the Marine Corps for aerial observation. With a pilot trained in the use of calling for and adjusting supporting arms (Arty, Close Air Support, Navy Gunfire, etc.) an OV-10 could observe an enemy and bring coordinated fire to bear on them. Its main defense, flying low to the earth to hide behind terrain features, was not available in the Gulf.

PAO Pubic Affairs Officer. The command representative acts as a go-between for the troops and the media.

PAKI-RUN The stores and service providers in the part of the Gulf the Marines operated were from Pakistan and India.

Papa Bear Designation given to the 1st Marine Regiment, Task Force Papa Bear. Each of the Infantry Regiments of the 1st Marine Division was designated with a task force name. The 7th Marines were designated Task Force Ripper.

PATRIOT The anti-missile that was supposed to knock out the SCUD threat from Iraq.

PHASE LINE A graphic control measure used to control the movement of forces on a battle field. Usually done on a map, the phase line is drawn to allow a unit room to maneuver to attain the line.

POLARIS Position Locating and Reporting System used to network units together to determine location, and to pass secure communications. Akin to the early Internet but used on military vehicles. The Tank Company XOs had the system in the Gulf, but it went out of service as the ground war kicked in. It came back on line after the war ended!

POSTER CHILD The squared away, perfectly groomed, spotless Marine that one can see on a recruiting poster.

PX Post Exchange, where Marines may purchase clothes and merchandise. In the Gulf's outposts the PXs were located in temporarily erected tents.

Rad Count A measure of radiation.

RDF (Rapid Deployment Force) A force that can rapidly respond to a problem area and solve the situation. Dates from the Carter Era. This is a skill in which the Marine Corps excels.

RCT7 Regimental Combat Team. Formed on the 7th Marine Regiment (Infantry), RCT is infantry with supporting units such as artillery, armor, combat service support, and air support.

Recon Short for reconnaissance. Also used to refer to the Marines of the reconnaissance units within the corps.

REMF A term very loosely translated as Rear Area Marine Force. Derogatory! In other words, it refers to those who fight from the relative safety of the rear area.

Retriever The M-88 Tank retriever is the tracked vehicle that holds the holy of holies, the tank mechanic. An armored tow truck that served double duty in the Gulf as an armored ambulance, as the U.S Marine Corps has no armored ambulance assets.

Ripper Radio call sign for the 7th Marines on the Regiment radio net.

ROE's Rules Of Engagement. Namely who can shoot what at whom, and when! The Gulf War had very open-ended ROE's compared to other wars!

RPG Rocket Propelled Grenade. The generic term for a host of light, anti-tank weapons. Usually referes to the Soviet version of the family tree of RPG's.

SAGGER The Soviet AT-3 anti-tank missile that, once launched, requires visual guidance. Also the generic term used by tankers to refer to anti-tank missiles as well as the term used by tanker crews to avoid a Sagger fired at them.

SANG Saudi Arabian National Guard. The Army of the Kingdom of Saudi Arabia was one of the allies during the Gulf War, and host to our deployment. Mother always said, "If you have absolutely nothing good to say about someone, say absolutely nothing."

SAW Squad Automatic Weapon. A light 5.56 caliber machine gun used by the infantry units; one per four-man fire team.

SCUD The terror weapon of the Gulf War. Sadam's missiles were launched at Israel and urban targets in Saudi.

SEMPER FI! Semper Fidelis. Always Faithful. The motto of the Marine Corps. Often abbreviated to Semper Fi!

Shamal The name given to the winds that blow across the desert in the winter. With little to stop or slow them, they gather speed and pick up lots of sand!

Sheridan Tank The M551, the U.S. Army Airborne forces' light tank. Deliverable by either air-lift or dropable by parachute, the M551's 152mm main gun, provides the paratroopers of the U. S. Airborne units with added punch. (a distant relative to the bigger, modern M1A1).

Sitreps Situation Reports. A short report containing information essential for command and control (i.e. enemy contact, observations of enemy movements, friendly unit movement.) Critical for mechanized units that can cover great distances in very short periods of time.

Skivies Military underwear.

SL3 Kit of accessories for the purpose of keeping the tank operational.

SLRP Surveillance Liaison and Reconnaissance Party. Group preceeding the off-load party. Checks facilities for potential problems.

SMG Sub-machinegun. Generally, a small frame, or compact, automatic weapon that fires at a high rate of fire from a magazine type source. Two examples of SMGs are the Uzi and MP5 series of weapons.

SNAFU Situation Normal All Fouled Up.

Snakes Collective call sign of Marine Light Attack Helicopter Squadron 369, who flew in support of ground combat operations in the Gulf. The Cobras of the "Snakes" provided excellent close-air support in the worst of flying conditions. The Squadron Commander received one of two Navy Crosses awarded Marines for actions in the Gulf War!

SNCO Staff non-Commissioned Officer. The real movers and shakers of the Marine Corps.

STINGER Anti-aircraft surface-to-air missile. Uses heat to lock onto and guide itself to the target.

STUMPS The affectionate name Marines give to the Marine Corps Air Ground Combat Center in Twentynine Palms, California. Located in the majestic Mojave Desert.

Spotting Rounds Rounds fired by artillery to adjust the aim of arty tubes. An arty tube is an indirect fire weapon; so the guys launching the rounds down range depend on someone who can see the target. One round is fired, and spotted by the FO, who gives corrections.

T-72 The formidable, top of the line Iraqi main battle tank, usually given to the best troops (Republican Guards). Exported from the former Soviet Union.

TACP Tactical Air Control Party. Those FACs who communicate, control and coordinate air assets used in support of ground operations. May be spread over several vehicles, but together they work magic!

Tap Line Road A service road across Northern Saudi Arabia. Became a major transportation artery for entire divisions of the Marine Corps and the Army during the build up leading to Desert Storm. An impressive sight to see

Task Force Ripper The designation given to RCT-7 during operations in the Persian Gulf.

Task Force Shepherd Designation adopted by the 1st Light Armored Infantry Battalion early in the Persian Gulf build up. The Battalion CO wanted to give his Marines something to identify with, and chose to honor the 7th Commandant of the Corps, General Lemuel C. Shepherd. Soon after, the 7th Marines adopted the Task Force Ripper name

TBS The Basic School. Located at the Marine Corps Base, Quantico, Virginia, TBS is the school where all newly Commissioned Marine Officers (2nd Lieutenants) learn the mechanics of being leaders of Marines.

TC Tank Commander who orders the tank where to go, and issues commands to engage targets.

TEECG Tactical Exercise Evaluation Control Group. The umpires and referees who form the "Control Group" for the live fire, Combined Arms Exercises (CAXs) held at the Twentynine Palms Marine Corps Base. The controllers help to paint the tactical picture and evaluate units and their leaders on the actions taken and the decision-making process employed.

Tiger Three Radio call sign designating Third Tank Battalion on the Regiment radio net; actually denotes the Commander of the unit, Lieutenant Colonel Diggs.

TOW Tube-launched, Optically tracked, Wire-guided missile. Anti-tank missile launched from a wide variety of ground and air platforms. Once sent down range the operator guides the missile to target.

TRA Tactical Recovery of Aircraft and personnel.

Triangle An area of the great litter box that lay south of the Kuwaiti-Saudi border and north of the Al-Jubayl Port Complex. The eastern side was defined by the Coastal highway that ran north-south along the Persian Gulf, with the two remaining sides made by roads that connected to a highway that led into the interior of Saudi Arabia. A huge area; it became the home of 3rd Tanks from approximately. September until the final staging for the ground war in late February.

Umpty Frats Generic name for someone, sometimes.

USCINCCENT United States Commander in Chief Central Command. In the Gulf War this was General H. Norman Schwarzkopf.

VIP Very Important Person. Some one that has political, financial or military privilege or status.

WEENIE   Term used by the gunslingers to describe those who support them.

Zero Term used by the enlisted ranks to describe an officer. Derived from the letter "O" that precedes an officer's pay grade or rank. Example: First Lieutenant is an O-2, Officer grade two.

A Few Good Men
The Commanders and Senior Enlisted

L-r: Battalion Sergeant Major Steven Jensen, Battalion Commander Lieutenant Colonel Alphonso Buster Diggs, Company Commander Captain Ed Dunlap, Company First Sergeant Al Martinez. The background is a burned out T-62 Main Battle Tank.

Photo by C. Freitus

Bunker

Iraqi bunker discovered near the forward limit of Charlie Company's advance. Typically large enough for three to six men, these bunkers dotted the landscape. Note proximity to Kuwait City in background.

Photo by C. Freitus

Bibliography
And Suggested Reading

Cureton, Charles H. *U.S. Marines in the Persion Gulf, 1990-1991: With the 1st Marine Division in Desert Shield and Desert Storm*, History and Museums Division, Headquarters, U.S. Marine Corps ISBN 0-160418-26-7

Friedman, Norman *Desert Victory: The War for Kuwait* the United States Naval Institute ISBN 1-557502-54-4

Summers Jr., Harry G. *Persion Gulf War Almanac* Facts on File, Incorporated ISBN 0-816028-21-4

Burning Oil Wells

The wells of Kuwait as seen from the seventh ring during our retrograde
(back to Saudi Arabia from Kuwait). Is this a preview of hell?

Photo by C. Freitus

Index

Numeric

A

Lieutenant Colonel **Myers** 185

N

O

volunteers 53

W

Wadi Al-Batin xxvi
waiver 119
Staff Sergeant David D. **Walters** 159
War Fighting Doctrine 190
War of the Worlds 187
War was the breakdown in politics 233
warehouse 56, 58, 88
water bull 80, 81, 83, 84
waving and crying 232
John **Wayne** 132, 163, 175, 216
wedge 145, 152
Sergeant Jeffry M. **Welsh** 22, 46, 158, 159, 166
Orson **Welles** 187
wells of Kuwait 284
werewolf concept 74
White 216
white flag 161
Wire barriers 147
wire entanglements 155
WWI 222
WWII xvi, xx, xxviii, xxxi, 54, 71, 77, 79, 99, 130, 154, 162,
        179, 209, 222, 232, 252

X

XO (Executive Officer) xxiii, 124, 223, 251
XO enjoying the view 318
XO's tank cover, ii, viii

Y

Yemen 39, 199
Yucca Valley 250

Z

Lieutenant Chris Freitus

The XO enjoying the view on the way back to Saudi Arabia after the battle during Desert Storm.

Photo by J. Butler

About Chris Freitus

Christopher John Freitus was commissioned an Officer of Marines aboard the U.S.S. Constitution in Boston, Massachusetts after graduating from the University of Alaska at Fairbanks. Upon completion of basic officer training at The Basic School in Quantico, Virginia, he was assigned Military Occupational Specialty of Armor Officer. A Distinguished Graduate from the U. S. Army's Armor Officer Basic Course at the Fort Knox Armor Center, Fort Knox, Kentucky, he was assigned duties as Platoon Commander, Charlie Company, 3rd Tank Battalion, 7th Marine Expeditionary Brigade, stationed at the Marine Corps Air Ground Combat Center in Twentynine Palms, California. Chris served as Company Executive Officer during the Desert Shield deployment and subsequent ground combat operations during Operation Desert Storm. Upon return from overseas deployment, he came back to The Basic School in Quantico, Virginia and served a tour as tactics instructor and staff training officer. Chris is married to the former Venus Robb, and the couple has two children, Kyle Christopher and Sean Joseph. Upon leaving active duty, Chris assumed employment as a Virginia State Trooper until 2002. He is now employed as a Special Agent in the U. S. Department of State.

Joe Freitus

About Joe Freitus

Joseph Philip Freitus, author, educator, military advisor and historian, has spent most of his life along the Atlantic Seaboard except for his U.S. Navy service during the Korean War. He is author of several books on edible plants and military histories, and many magazine and newspaper articles on education.

Joe, in collaboration with wife Anne, today collects data for more war histories in five volumes dealing with personal experiences of those who served in WWII, Korea, Vietnam and Desert Storm. He does this while putting the final touches on three additional books depicting the history of Old James Towne, Virginia, from the point of view of a stowaway mouse in the original voyage from England.

A man of wide-ranging interests, Joe Freitus devotes as much time as possible to his job as the Old Sail Maker in support of replicas of the three ships that brought the colonists to Old James Towne.

Joe spent many hours audio-taping son Chris' stories of ordeal and adventure during Chris' service in the U.S. Marine Corps. Five more years of additional work and research resulted in *Dial 911 Marines*.

The 215th Birthday of the US Marine Corps
10 November 1990

Charlie Company, 3rd Tank Battalion, 7th Regimental Combat Team, 1st Marine Division, I MEF. Lieutenant Chris Freitus, Company Executive Officer, seated far left in front row.

Photo by member of Charlie Company